African Asylum at a Crossroads

# African Asylum at a Crossroads

## Activism, Expert Testimony, and Refugee Rights

Edited by Iris **Berger**

Tricia Redeker **Hepner**

Benjamin N. **Lawrance**

Joanna T. **Tague,** and

Meredith **Terretta**

Foreword by Penelope Andrews

Afterword by Fallou Ngom

OHIO UNIVERSITY PRESS • ATHENS, OHIO

Ohio University Press, Athens, Ohio 45701
ohioswallow.com
© 2015 by Ohio University Press

To obtain permission to quote, reprint, or otherwise reproduce or distribute material
from Ohio University Press publications, please contact our rights and permissions
department at (740) 593-1154 or (740) 593-4536 (fax).

Printed in the United States of America
Ohio University Press books are printed on acid-free paper ⊚ ™

25 24 23 22 21 20 19 18 17 16 15     5 4 3 2 1

*Library of Congress Cataloging-in-Publication Data*
African asylum at a crossroads : activism, expert testimony, and refugee rights / edited
by Iris Berger [and four others] ; foreword by Penelope Andrews ; afterword by Fallou
Ngom.
    pages cm
  Summary: "African Asylum at a Crossroads: Activism, Expert Testimony, and Refugee
Rights examines the emerging trend of requests for expert opinions in asylum
hearings or refugee status determinations. This is the first book to explore the role
of court-based expertise in relation to African asylum cases and the first to establish
a rigorous analytical framework for interpreting the effects of this new reliance on
expert testimony.  Over the past two decades, courts in Western countries and beyond
have begun demanding expert reports tailored to the experience of the individual
claimant. As courts increasingly draw upon such testimony in their deliberations,
expertise in matters of asylum and refugee status is emerging as an academic area with
its own standards, protocols, and guidelines. This deeply thoughtful book explores
these developments and their effects on both asylum seekers and the experts whose
influence may determine their fate.  Contributors: Iris Berger, Carol Bohmer, John
Campbell, Katherine Luongo, E. Ann McDougall, Karen Musalo, Tricia Redeker
Hepner, Amy Shuman, Joanna T. Tague, Meredith Terretta, and Charlotte Walker-
Said"— Provided by publisher.
  Includes bibliographical references and index.
  ISBN 978-0-8214-2138-3 (hardback) — ISBN 978-0-8214-4518-1 (pdf)
  1. Political refugees—Legal status, laws, etc.—Africa. 2. Asylum, Right of—Africa.
3. Expert testimony. 4. Evidence, Expert. I. Berger, Iris, 1941- editor.
  KQC567.A37 2015
  342.608'3—dc23
                                2015004840

# Contents

# Foreword

This important and timely volume explores an emergent development for scholars engaged in African studies, specifically, requests to provide expert testimony for asylum hearings or refugee status determinations. In other words, those who have and are engaged in scholarly research on Africa now find themselves as expert witnesses in an unforeseen arena—courts of law. As the editors observe, this is the first volume to explore the role of court-based expertise as it pertains to Africa. It is also the first volume to focus, in an interdisciplinary fashion, on the legal subjectivities of African immigrants as a means to acquire new knowledge and ideas about historical and contemporary Africa.

A defining feature of late twentieth-century and early twenty-first-century Africa has been the movement of its people across borders. Championed today as an offshoot of contemporary globalization, this movement of people is supposed to signal yet another successful story of human migration. But such migration, as we know, is often involuntary, reinforcing another aspect of late twentieth-century and early twenty-first-century Africa, namely, refugees and asylum seekers.

The desperate situation for refugees and asylum seekers—spawned by the internal conflicts in many parts of Africa, including the Central African Republic, the Congo, Somalia, and other nations—is recorded with regularity by international human rights and humanitarian organizations and popular media. The chapters in this volume give meaning to the experiences of these refugees as they proceed on their way as asylum seekers in the United States, the United Kingdom, Australia, and elsewhere.

The refugee crisis is fundamentally a human crisis, one that generates expectations, hopes, and fears that will ultimately influence the political and legal arenas. This volume takes the readers from that initial experience of political and geographic dislocation and disruption to a courtroom or other institutional setting, where a refugee or asylum hearing will determine the refugee's fate. This process can be lengthy, with refugees languishing in detention facilities or in ghettos on the outskirts of cities in a kind of legal limbo that often takes years or decades to resolve. The situation of refugees has become one of the defining human tragedies of the late twentieth and early twenty-first centuries.

Collectively, these chapters relate a narrative that begins with the migrant's experience in his or her native country, traces the journey that leads to the courtroom and the expert's testimony, and concludes with the decision of the judge or other adjudicator. The human drama unfolds before witnesses, expert and otherwise, through the historical, geographic, political, and other "facts" and evidence that are presented, under the watchful eye of the judge or adjudicator.

The subject matter of this volume—the use and influence of expert testimony provided by scholars of Africa—is a novel category of research in African law, politics, and society. This research is at the intersection of individualized unique narratives and the relevant expertise required to elaborate and emphasize such uniqueness, while at the same time conforming to legal norms, characterizations, and structures. The need to create an influential and "successful" story of persecution has profoundly altered the legal process with respect to refugee and asylum law, and it raises complicated questions for the migrant as refugee or asylum seeker. These questions involve the subject matter, status, and role of the expertise involved in this process. Who qualifies to be an expert? What constitutes expert knowledge? How is "objectivity" guaranteed? What role is there for advocacy on the part of the expert? Is there a litmus test for cultural uncertainties and fluidity or for contested historical or individual memory?

The contributors to this volume explore and expand upon this human drama by advancing legal, historical, sociological, anthropological, and other academic perspectives to probe the many dimensions of the issues confronting African migrants. They investigate the contradictory imperatives generated by African migrants refugees and asylum seekers—explicitly, individuals who are to be rescued but whose history and culture need to be denigrated if they are to benefit from rescue.

Indeed, the African migrant and his or her quest for political asylum stimulate many tropes, from the "ancient" or "exotic" (as reflected in the practices of witchcraft) to traditional cultural norms to ethnic rivalries. The African migrant's claim for political asylum exists at the juncture of law, advocacy, human rights, and expert evidence. It creates a fragile balance between competing realities of identity, agency, victimhood, truth, and sexuality, on the one hand, and the apparent certainty of law and evidence, on the other.

The contributors to this volume, all authorities in their respective disciplines and subject matters, explore the issues in thoughtful, engaging, and provocative ways. They have produced a wonderful anthology that provides insightful perspectives and raises many questions. *That* is the significance of this anthology; in addition to its rich analyses, it invites continued research on this noteworthy and timely subject. The volume will be an invaluable source for a multidisciplinary range of scholars of Africa in law, the social sciences, and the humanities. Most significantly, it will be a vital reference guide for legal scholars interested in migration, particularly those pursuing refugee or asylum claims.

*Penelope Andrews*
*Albany Law School*

# Preface and Acknowledgments

As is always the case, this edited volume is much more than the sum of its parts. The origins of this book reside with a collective effort that emerged organically from within one of our most cherished institutions, the African Studies Association (ASA). At the organization's fifty-second annual meeting in New Orleans in November 2009, several of us participated in a roundtable examining "African Asylum Claims." A number of us later huddled in the hotel lobby and plotted the next steps, including mobilizing the interest of other scholars and the ASA leadership. We convened another academic roundtable at the fifty-third annual meeting in San Francisco the following November, led by Milton Krieger, James Loucky, and others. At the fifty-fourth meeting in Washington, D.C., in November 2011, with the support of the former ASA presidents Judith Byfield and Aili Tripp and ASA board member Catherine Boone as well as Carol Thompson, we organized a panel entitled "African Asylum Petitions and Expert Testimony." The panel featured Lisa Dornell, an administrative judge with the Executive Office for Immigration Review at the Immigration Court in Baltimore, Maryland; Lori Adams, the managing attorney in the New York office of Human Rights First; Heidi Altman, a clinical teaching fellow at Center for Applied Legal Studies, Georgetown University Law Center; Steven J. Kolleeny, pro bono program supervisor and special counsel in the New York City office of Skadden, Arps, Slate, Meagher & Flom LLP; and Mani Sheik, formerly of the Miller Law Group, San Francisco.

Building on this momentum, we decided to make a wider call for a larger international meeting. The editors and authors whose chapters appear in this volume are indebted to the colleagues who shared thoughts and ideas during the second Conable Conference in International Studies at the Rochester Institute of Technology, entitled "Refugees, Asylum Law, and Expert Testimony: The Construction of Africa & the Global South in Comparative Perspective," held in Rochester, New York, in April 2012. As the book developed its current form, we organized another series of roundtables at the ASA meeting in Baltimore in November 2013. These conversations helped us cement our project, and we thank the audience participation for a stimulating discussion.

Benjamin Lawrance would like to thank the several organizations and entities that made the conference possible, namely, the Conable Endowment for International Studies; the Starr Foundation; the Program in International and Global Studies in the Department of Sociology and Anthropology, in the College of Liberal Arts at Rochester Institute of Technology; the Weill Cornell Center for Human Rights; and the Department of History at Cornell University. He would also like to thank his family, especially Wilson Silva.

Meredith Terretta would like to thank the Social Sciences and Humanities Research Council of Canada for funding research and travel related to this project; the Centre for Research in the Arts, Social Sciences and Humanities at the University of Cambridge, where she was a fellow when writing the chapters in this book; and Antoni Lewkowicz, dean of the Faculty of Arts at the University of Ottawa, for supporting her request for research leave in 2011–12.

The five of us who edited the volume thank the various individuals whose contributions ultimately all feature in this final product, including Cassandra Shellman, James Winebrake, Robert Ulin, Christine Kray, Saabirah Lallmohamed, Barbara Harrell-Bond, Andrea McIntosh, Evan Criddle, Karen Musalo, Jeffrey Herbst, Mary Meg McCarthy, Juan Osuna, Sue Long, Taryn Clark, Penny Andrews, Paul Finkelman, Susan Dicklitch, Natasha Fain, Michelle McKinley, Galya Ruffer, Meridith Murray, Lindsay Harris at the Tahirih Justice Center, and the more than one hundred additional participants in the conference.

Particular appreciation goes to Gill Berchowitz, Nancy Basmajian, Rebecca Welch, John Pratt, Sebastian Biot, Joan Sherman, and the excellent staff at Ohio University Press who so smoothly guided this project toward completion. The authors would also like to thank the anonymous reviewers whose insights strengthened the text. Publication of this book was made possible with the generous financial support of the History Department at the University at Albany, the Faculty of the Arts at the University of Ottawa, the Office of the Provost at Denison University, the University of Tennessee Humanities Center and Department of Anthropology, and a Faculty Research Fund Grant and the Conable Endowment in International Studies, in the College of Liberal Arts at the Rochester Institute of Technology.

ALTHOUGH ALL OF us have lived and worked in sub-Saharan Africa for many years, it was only after serving as an expert witness in an asylum claim for the first time that each of us began to grasp the indescribable torments African men and women endured in the twentieth century and continue to endure in the present epoch. Making sense of why people claim asylum is difficult for many, but that difficulty pales in significance when set against the problems encountered as Africans attempt to narrate their experiences in order to obtain protection. In *The Differend* (1988, 5), the great philosopher Jean-François Lyotard described the violent "double bind" as a *dommage* (a *tort* or *wrong*) "accompanied by the loss of means to prove the damage."

Indeed, the predicament of the refugee is that of an extreme embodied form of injustice insofar as the injury suffered by the victim is accompanied by a deprivation of the means to speak or prove. Lyotard wrote,

> This is the case if the victim is deprived of life, or of all liberties, or of the freedom to make his or her ideas or opinions public, or simply of the right to testify to the damage, or even more simply if the testifying phrase is itself deprived of authority. In all of these cases, to the privation constituted by the damage there is added the impossibility of bringing it to the knowledge of others, and in particular to the knowledge of the tribunal. (Lyotard 1988, 5–6)

This book brings us a little closer to understanding the complexity of Lyotard's "ethical tort" (*differend*). But the translation, contextualization, and substantiation of the claims of asylum seekers and refugees remain onerous tasks. We offer this volume to foster debate, stimulate activism, and provoke engaged scholarship. And we hope it will become an instrument with which others may fathom their unrecognized capacities and capabilities.

As this project originated with a collective effort at the African Studies Association annual meeting, the authors of this volume have decided to donate all royalties in perpetuity to the ASA Endowment Fund. This book is dedicated to the countless African refugees and asylum seekers whose inconceivable bravery immeasurably enriches all of our lives.

### Note

All possible effort has been made to protect the identity and confidentiality of the individuals whose life stories form part of this book. The contributors have employed anonymous or pseudonymous monikers consistent with their respective discipline(s) when needed. Details, including but not limited to race, ethnicity, and national origin, have been changed where necessary and appropriate.

## Reference

Lyotard, Jean-François. 1988. *The Differend: Phrases in Dispute.* Translated by Georges van den Abbeele. Minneapolis: University of Minnesota Press.

# INTRODUCTION

## Law, Expertise, and Protean Ideas about African Migrants

Benjamin N. Lawrance, Iris Berger, Tricia Redeker Hepner,
Joanna T. Tague, and Meredith Terretta

THE EXPERIENCE OF the African asylum seeker is at a crossroads. From the 1960s to 1980s, asylum and refugee status was usually arbitrated by referencing government reports and data produced by the United Nations or other international or intergovernmental agencies. Today, many domestic asylum and refugee status determination procedures in the Global North—including those currently in operation in the United States, the United Kingdom, Canada, and Australia—no longer consider the impersonal or nonspecific nature of these data as constituting a solid or secure basis for individual claims. Increasingly, asylum host nations are developing sophisticated, secure data-collection agencies and storage facilities to provide so-called objective evidence (Good 2004a, 2004b) but with a national imprimatur. And as the numbers of African asylum seekers have swelled dramatically, first in Europe and now globally, countries with such diverse legal traditions as Argentina, South Korea, and the Netherlands are increasingly demanding the production of a specific report tailored to the experience of the individual claimant. Expert testimony, variously as a dispassionate assessment of, sometimes in support of, and occasionally in opposition to, asylum petitions and refugee status determinations now features regularly in North American and European courts and in many other jurisdictions. This book examines this transformation from the perspective of the expert witness.

It is well known among the practicing legal community that asylum petitions and refugee status appeals accompanied by expert reports have a significantly greater likelihood of success, but data on the use of expertise in asylum cases are critically absent. And just as adjudicators are more likely than ever to draw upon expert testimony in determining asylum and refugee claims, expertise is emerging as an academic niche industry, with attendant standards, protocols, and guidelines (Good and Kelly 2013) that mirror those of other legal fields with a rich tradition of expertise, such as patent, copyright, and intellectual property law. Moreover, though experts may often postulate from a disciplinary locus, the venues that feature expertise and the authorities that draw upon expertise increasingly expose scholars to the interdisciplinarity of law, activism, and social justice.

*African Asylum at a Crossroads* examines the dimensions of an emerging trend undertaken by specialists in African studies, namely, the request to produce an expert report for consideration as part of an asylum hearing or refugee status determination. This is the first book to explore the role of court-centered expertise as it pertains to African asylum claims, and it is the first multidisciplinary anthology to focus on the legal subjectivities of African refugees as a context for the production of new knowledge and ideas about historical and contemporary Africa. The assembled chapters were selected from papers delivered at a conference held in April 2012 in Rochester, New York, that explored the role and experience of the expert and the employment of expert testimony in refugee status determination venues. Together, the chapters depict, in broad spectrum, the African migrant experience before adjudicators in the Global North; they also provide a compelling and coherent framework in an emerging subfield of research about African society and politics.

The evidentiary bases for the chapters in this book are primarily the African refugee narrative and the expert report. Asylum petitions and refugee status determinations are rich documentary archives tethered to discrete legal contexts—variously, migration ministries, immigration tribunals, courts of appeal, and panels of experts or citizen-subjects, according to jurisdiction—by knowledge and expertise. Embedded within asylum and refugee narratives and in their successive iterations in rulings, judgments, country of origin information (COI) (Good 2015), appeals, and precedents are analytical categories, constructed identities, and personal narratives of fear, trauma, and violence. Each time an expert is

*B. N. Lawrance, I. Berger, T. R. Hepner, J. T. Tague, and M. Terretta*

engaged to produce a report to assist in the determination of a particular asylum or refugee claim, the archive of the contemporary African experience expands. And yet a paradoxical relationship is unfolding, insofar as protean ideas about Africans—that is, ideas that are changeable and unlikely to look exactly as they did when they were initially presented—are giving way to what appears to be new knowledge. Whereas new ideas about African cultures, languages, practices, behaviors, morality, ethics, and attitudes emerge from asylum petitions and the expert reports that accompany them, these percolate in Northern (read: Western) courts and rarely appear to influence dynamics in the Global South. These new ideas are assembled, embodied, and structured through positivist Western legal frameworks, and introspective and intuitional attempts to gain knowledge are often erased.

This volume constitutes the first attempt to establish a rigorous analytical framework for interpreting the transformative effect of this new reliance on expertise. Informed by a rich scholarly literature on the significance of legal forums in African history broadly (e.g., Chanock 1998; Moore 1986) and specifically the role of courts (Mann and Roberts 1991; Roberts 2005) in the construction of African identities, relationships, and subjectivities (Lawrance, Osborn, and Roberts 2006), this collection is a logical extension of the growing interest in the intersection of law and African social and political life (Burrill, Roberts, and Thornberry 2010; Jeppie, Moosa, and Roberts 2010). Individual essays accompanying this introduction, in concert, provide a powerful new avenue for developing theory and method in our respective disciplines. Together, the chapters reflect critically on the implications of using expertise and knowledge in asylum and refugee adjudication; what constitutes expertise; the transformation of the scholarly research agenda in tandem with serving as an expert; the relationship between experts and adjudicators generally (Lawrance and Ruffer 2015a); and our relationships with the communities among which we work.

The chapters contained herein navigate the claims and counterclaims of Africans and explore the ways in which experts and adjudicators contextualize these claims along the path to status determination. The ten substantive chapters examine African claims based variously on a spectrum of persecutory experiences emerging from the individuals' political, ethnic, religious, racial, national, gender, and sexual identities. We examine the reinvigoration of historical paradigms in asylum courts, including slavery in Mauritania, as discussed by E. Ann McDougall, and witchcraft in Nigeria and Tanzania, as discussed by Katherine Luongo. We reveal the role of asylum and refugee status determination venues in the emergence of analytical and social categories, such as female genital cutting, as discussed in the chapters by Karen Musalo and Iris Berger; statelessness, as explored by John Campbell; and fraudulence, as deliberated by Meredith Terretta. Thematically, the chapters encompass a variety of core jurisprudence issues, including the role of precedent; the place of history and memory; the role of customary law; the legal basis of credibility and/ or plausibility; the determination of and granting of standing as an expert; substantiation and proof; historical patterns in the deployment of expertise; and issues pertaining to research with legal subjects, among them confidentiality, consent, discovery, and disclosure.

The focus on individuated experiences of expert testimony offers a strikingly personal entrée into an unfolding crisis that is all too familiar. As the UN Convention Relating to the Status of Refugees marked its sixtieth anniversary in 2011, eight hundred thousand new refugees fled conflicts in Côte d'Ivoire, Libya, Sierra Leone, and Somalia (UNHCR 2011a, 5). Of the ten countries that produced the most refugees that year, four were located in Africa. Somalia ranked third in the world, just behind Afghanistan and Iraq. Sudan followed in fourth place, and the Democratic Republic of Congo ranked fifth. Eritrea was ninth worldwide (UNHCR 2011a, 14), yet it bore the ignominious distinction of generating the highest number of refugees globally when measured as a percentage of the total population (UNHCR 2010). Now, as in past decades, as Joanna T. Tague's chapter demonstrates with respect to Mozambique and Tanzania, the African continent is an epicenter of refugee crises.

Although most Africans fleeing across international borders remain in neighboring countries or regions (UNHCR 2011a), tens of thousands annually attempt to access wealthy, industrialized nations to file individual asylum claims with domestic authorities. Countries of the Global North and former colonial metropoles remain ideal destinations. Yet as securitized migration policies and discourses foreclose access to Europe and North America especially (Squire 2009), precipitous spikes in asylum seekers appear in countries such as South Africa and Israel. Mobility routes, strategies, and destinations shift and change in response to the limits of official migration avenues. Whether due to the inability of the humanitarian framework to cope with the sheer magnitude of displacement or to

*B. N. Lawrance, I. Berger, T. R. Hepner, J. T. Tague, and M. Terretta*

the pervasive hope that safe haven will be guaranteed in nations touting human rights and the rule of law, many Africans have simply evaded the classic refugee regime and its promises of "durable solutions."[1]

Utilizing a range of complex strategies that include both legal and extralegal dimensions, African asylum seekers demand recognition as individual rights-bearing subjects amid the bureaucratic indifference and xenophobic hostility endemic to the nation-state system and the institutions that manage, and increasingly "actively produce as illegal migrants," out-of-place people (Scheel and Squire 2014, 192). Although asylum seekers are a very small percentage of all refugees (approximately 900,000 out of 15.2 million refugees in 2011; UNHCR 2011b, 6), African asylum mobility constitutes deliberate agency and perhaps even political resistance. It is an indictment of the political and economic conditions that necessitate migration as well as the humanitarian schemes that are ostensibly grounded in human rights norms and yet often experienced by migrants as dehumanizing, unaccountable, and callous (Agier 2007; Verdirame and Harrell-Bond 2005).

In order to make sense of expert testimony production within the dynamic field of refugee and migration studies, we offer our readers this introduction to the realm of expertise in the context of asylum and refugee status adjudication. What follows is our collective attempt to harness our common experiences as experts in the most generalizable sense. We five authors are not lawyers, but what we narrate here reflects a long-term dialogue with legal concepts, demands, expectations, and categories. We first examine the task of the expert and address the specific role of serving as an expert in immigration courts in the broadest sense. As we demonstrate, the expert may not be viewed in isolation; rather, the capacity to bring expertise into the courtroom is very much managed by the presence of legal personnel, most important among them judges and adjudicators. We then tackle what we describe as the craft of the expert. Here, we argue that an expert report is not a simple document but one that is produced through the conduits of rigorous training, acquired academic knowledge, and an uncommon preference among African studies scholars for critically engaged collaboration. Although the gold standard for academic output—anonymous peer review—is not (currently) part of the production of an expert report, individual reports nonetheless demonstrate the critical reflexivity and interrogative frameworks of the authors' scholarly and scientific methods.

Building on this discussion, we turn to the specific issues and ideas about Africans that unfold in asylum contexts. Refugee and asylum tribunals, because of their increasing reliance on scholarly expertise, have emerged as a critical site for the production of knowledge about contemporary Africa. A dependence on narrowly political reports on country conditions has given way to complex arguments about the emergence of identities, subjectivities, and practices, such as the prevalence of new sexual identities and sexual minorities, as discussed in Charlotte Walker-Said's chapter. The textuality of the expert report is marked by three common elements: the exigencies of juridical proof, the substantiation of the claimant's credibility, and the humanitarian trope of the deserving refugee (Mamdani 1996, 2010). And we uncover an uncomfortable contradiction embedded in the role of the expert—that in the production of a report that often substantiates and validates the claim of the asylum seeker, the expert reinforces the authority and power of a routinely unjust and unfair refugee claim assessment apparatus (Ramji-Nogales, Schoenholtz, and Schrag 2007). We conclude with some preliminary observations about disciplinarity and the prevalence of specific disciplines in the expert witness capacity.

## The Task of the Expert

In the most general sense, the role of the expert in asylum casework is to testify as to the political, cultural, and social climate in the asylum seeker's home country and to assess the degree to which he or she would be in danger if repatriated. From the perspective of those people who may be unfamiliar with the legal processes involved in asylum seeking, the figure of the expert may seem relatively straightforward and uncomplicated: they may assume that the act of providing testimony in the courtroom is the only—or at least the most important—task the expert performs. Experts, however, do not only provide testimony. Rather, they fulfill a range of tasks, often over several years. In point of fact, experts tend to remain involved in asylum cases for the duration, or life span, of a case.

That many experts devote a considerable amount of time to asylum casework is a direct reflection of the extent to which adjudicators rely on expert knowledge in order to render decisions. Indeed, government bureaucrats and courts need experts for a variety of reasons. For one, adjudicators engage experts to clarify the social and political conditions in the asylum seeker's home country. Adjudicators may be able to access any number of public materials and reports (such as the annual US State Department human rights reports) or private government databases at the outset of an asylum claim, but all too often, such materials are bald summaries, woefully inaccurate, or no longer current (Carver 2003; Good 2007). Consequently, they provide little assistance to judges in their assessment of country conditions.

Adjudicators increasingly rely on experts in lieu of nonspecific country reports, but this often creates an adversarial relationship between the expert and the court. The expert's knowledge may counter the substance or omissions of a country report, prompting the judge to question the expert on this perceived inconsistency and leaving the expert to then defend his or her own statements about country conditions (Good 2015). Of course, the larger issue is that in times of political turmoil and social upheaval, country conditions may change so quickly that the court cannot access reliable information. Country reports may not be a comprehensive source, but at the same time, it is unlikely that an expert would have been in the country under question recently enough—or long enough, given rapidly changing political conditions—to assess its political or social climate (Lawrance 2013).

Judges and immigration lawyers also need experts when the documentary evidence to an asylum seeker's claims of persecution is insufficient, nonexistent, or imperiled by questions of credibility (Cohen 2001; CREDO 2013; Lawrance and Ruffer 2015b; Millbank 2009; Norman 2007; Sweeny 2009; Thomas 2006; UNHCR 2013). Unfortunately, this concern applies to the vast majority of asylum seekers, who typically lack any documentation. They tend to either flee the homeland without any pertinent legal documents or possess documentation that is not indicative of (and thus cannot support their claims of) political persecution. For the asylum seekers, this is particularly problematic because, in order to receive political asylum in the United States, for example, they must prove that they have a well-founded fear of persecution in their homelands (Shuman and Bohmer 2004, 394). Although the legal system may place the burden of proof squarely upon the shoulders of the asylum seeker, the expert also feels this burden, as his or her task is to fill in the (often enormous) lacunae in knowledge and evidentiary bases for both the asylum seeker and court officials.

Adjudicators ultimately need experts to assess the merit of an asylum seeker's claim to a well-founded fear of persecution and consistency with current country conditions. Questions may arise concerning the validity of a given case, especially in an international climate where—as we see in Terretta's chapter—fears, rumors, and representations of African asylum seekers as having forged documents or invented narratives abound. Beyond identifying bogus or fraudulent claims, however, the primary task of the expert is to try to deduce how likely it is that a claimant would be in danger if repatriated. To determine this, experts must assess a wide range of evidentiary materials. In this light, several key questions emerge. Who qualifies as an expert? At what point does someone's particular qualifications, skills, and/or life experiences coalesce to make him or her an expert? Where does the expertise lie—that is, on what, precisely, is this individual an expert?

Putting aside the ethical implications of the term *expert* (and the rich scholarly corpus debating the very idea that one can ever truly know and represent "the other"), we first propose to historicize, albeit briefly, the figure of the expert and expert testimony in the context of international asylum procedures. At least until the 1980s, asylum legal procedures operated within an informal climate of trust, one in which the applicant was presumed to be telling the truth. Expert testimony from scholars or professionals was almost unheard of. Since then, significant global geopolitical changes—including but not limited to the collapse of the Soviet bloc and the end of the Cold War, as well as the birth of the Internet and other globalized transnational technologies—have conspired to turn the asylum experience upside down. The asylum process is now overshadowed by a "climate of suspicion, in which the asylum seeker is seen as someone trying to take advantage of the country's hospitality" (Fassin and D'Halluin 2005, 600). Claims and counterclaims must be anchored by objective data, publicly sourced information, and arguments substantiated by scholarly evidence. This dramatic and rapid transformation in the asylum procedure partly explains why adjudicators the world over have increasingly come to rely on expert knowledge and expert testimony (see Lawrance and Ruffer 2015a).

Courts have relied on expert testimony for centuries in many different contexts (Rosen 1977). But having experts working on and providing testimony for African asylum casework is a far more recent development, as Tague's chapter discusses. Until the era of decolonization, Africans—as colonial subjects—did not have the option of applying for political asylum abroad. Indeed, until the 1980s, political asylum seekers originated

*B. N. Lawrance, I. Berger, T. R. Hepner, J. T. Tague, and M. Terretta*

from all continents, particularly South America, but rarely from Africa. It is perhaps no coincidence that the rise of a "climate of suspicion" in asylum procedures in the Global North parallels the emergence of Africans as political asylum seekers (see Hyndman and Giles 2011). And the emergence of a new population of asylum seekers required the construction of a new community of experts, or the creation of expert knowledge.

From the perspective of adjudicators, academics are eminently qualified to serve as experts in African cases of political asylum. For several reasons, the marriage of academia and asylum casework appears natural. For one, an expert in any asylum case often needs to demonstrate that he or she has spent considerable time in the country from which the asylum seeker originates: this is but one way to demonstrate an extensive knowledge pertaining to the history and sociopolitical climate of a country. It is this ability to ground oneself in a particular culture that enables the expert to glean essential information on the structure of the community, as well as the existence of particular political and/or social groups in the applicant's home country. In this way, the scholar is more expertly qualified than most to assess the relationship between such groups and the applicant.

An expert is ideally fluent in the language or conversant with the cultural idiom of the asylum seeker, as Campbell's chapter demonstrates. And preferably, although by no means definitively, this expert can demonstrate that he or she has recently been in the country or region in question and can provide background information to the adjudicator that is as current as possible. Adjudicators are acutely aware of the fact that such criteria reflect the lifestyles of many academics working in Africa, who have advanced university degrees and doctorates to showcase their qualifications as experts (Lawrance, forthcoming a). Such experiences in a particular country or region are typical of the academic system of research and travel.

Yet experts may do more than testify to the conditions of a specific country; many may also convey an expert assessment of particular issues, themes, and subjects and are thus able to provide testimony regarding those precise issues in asylum cases, irrespective of the asylum seeker's country of origin. We see this most clearly in Berger's chapter narrating her ability to serve on a case not because of her knowledge about the Central African Republic but because of her expert knowledge as a historian of women and women's experiences in Africa. Further, the assumption that only academics who have spent years living in a particular country, learning local languages, and absorbing the social and political norms of that country are qualified to act as expert witnesses is misguided. Human rights workers, health professionals, and international development officers also lead similar lives; their particular expertise is no less grounded or vital than that of academics.

This prompts us to ask in what ways academic knowledge is distinct from other forms of expert knowledge. One possible answer is that academic training instills a theoretical grounding in the historical and cultural nuances of the peoples and communities in the country about which the individual assumes expert status. The mastery of cultural nuance is a much-needed skill in asylum casework. For example, in order to fulfill the requirements of the US Bureau of Citizenship and Immigration Services, the Netherlands Ministry of Security and Justice, or the UK Border Agency, the accounts that asylum seekers provide must meet certain criteria. A version of the events that led to an individual seeking political asylum ought to maintain a clear, consistent chronology. An account should be clear about which individuals or groups in the country were perpetrators and which were victims. And asylum seekers ought to be able to demonstrate that they were victims of political persecution—that is, not of individual discrimination or oppression (Shuman and Bohmer 2004, 402). In each of these capacities, academics as experts possess the ability to translate cultural nuance within asylum narratives and recover the sociological identity embedded or concealed in the narrative (Kam 2015).

Indeed, translation tends to occur on two levels. Asylum seekers often arrive in the country of asylum and frame their persecution as personal trauma: the expert must then translate the case from "a personal trauma into an act of political aggression" (Shuman and Bohmer 2004, 396). The academic as expert also translates cultural nuance on a second level, for immigration officials and judges alike. Given fluency in the asylum seeker's language, an expert may review previous testimonies to clarify issues of translation, extending also to the body language and nonverbal communication characteristics of the asylum seeker—traits that are often deeply embedded in cultural norms and that may easily go unnoticed by someone not familiar with the cultural nuances the asylum seeker embodies, as Fallou Ngom's afterword explains. This type of translation is a complex interchange; Walker-Said's chapter shows, for example, that African sexual minorities must render their sexuality "legible" to courts as well as to experts.

Although experts possess unique capabilities to translate cultural nuance, adjudicators often pose questions that they are unable to answer. For instance, given the academic background of the expert, court officials may ask a particular individual to make certain predictions about a specific case. Lawyers may ask the expert questions that cannot possibly be answered with any certainty, such as, "If such-and-such were to happen, would this claimant be in danger?" For the academic experts, this line of questioning is a catch-22. They can take a stance—say yes or no—knowing that such speculation would be groundless (Wallace and Wylie 2014). Or they can be truthful and admit that they cannot predict the future and do not know the answer to the question, though in so doing they risk losing their own credibility in the eyes of the court, as McDougall's chapter demonstrates.

Experts, whether members of the academic community or not, obviously can only speculate about what might happen if an asylum seeker's application were denied and he or she had to return home. All they can do is determine the likelihood of persecution if a claimant were repatriated. In this capacity, they are, in effect, sharing their professional opinion with the court, and experts can become an "impediment" to asylum representation (Ardalan 2015). It is this sharing of an opinion that differentiates the expert witness per se from witnesses in legal contexts other than asylum and refugee status determination. Whereas ordinary witnesses cannot express their opinions, asylum law allows experts to put forth theirs, provided the opinions are "based on facts or data obtained using reliable methods reliably applied" (Good 2008, S49; Rosen 1977). It is the privilege and power of being able to express their opinions in such a high-stakes scenario that requires all experts—academic or not—to possess irrefutable qualifications that highlight their abilities to serve on particular asylum cases (Dornell 2015; Wallace and Wylie 2014).

Of course, expert testimony is not solely an academic domain. Even though experts are often drawn from the academic community, this is certainly not true in all cases; in the United States, for example, the Federal Rules of Evidence do not require this (Keast 2005, 1238). In some instances, an adjudicator must admit an individual as an expert (Dornell 2015) and define the parameters of expertise; in other contexts, adjudicators rely heavily on the previous findings of their peers (Lawrance, forthcoming a). Indeed, experts may be found in a wide swath of professions; they include human rights, international development, and health professionals (physicians as well as psychologists). The common, unifying element among these practitioners is that each of them possesses a particular expertise within his or her field that lends itself to certain asylum cases. According to US Federal Rule of Evidence 702, if such specialized knowledge will help the court to "understand the evidence or to determine a fact in issue, a witness qualified as an expert by knowledge, skill, expertise, training, or education, may testify thereto in the form of an opinion" (Malphrus 2010, 3). Similar rules operate in the United Kingdom, where expert reports are addressed to the court, not to the asylum claimant, and must supply dispassionate and "objective unbiased opinion," subject to standards established by the 1993 *Ikarian Reefer* ruling (2 Lloyd's Rep 68) and other regulations (Good 2015; Lawrance 2015).

Recognition of this inherent breadth in expert knowledge means that adjudicators increasingly look to experts in the medical profession to examine forms of evidence and provide testimony in asylum cases (Wallace and Wylie 2014). After examining the asylum seekers physically, physicians issue medical certificates that have the potential to become vital forms of evidence attesting to the applicants' previous persecution or torture in their homelands (thus confirming their well-founded fear of repatriation). According to Didier Fassin and Estelle D'Halluin (2005), immigration officials are less and less willing to rely solely on the narratives of asylum seekers as the dominant evidentiary basis; to support their claims, asylum seekers are discovering that courts require ever more proof and additional forms of evidence. Though medical certificates certainly cannot substitute for the narratives of the asylum seekers, such certificates do have the potential to verify points in their accounts that claim torture (Chelidze et al. 2015). In this way, the body of the asylum seeker emerges as the place that "displays the evidence of truth" (Fassin and D'Halluin 2005, 598).

As a form of evidence, the medical certificate is far from a panacea (Kelly 2012). The United Nations embraced the *Manual on Effective Investigation and Documentation of Torture and Other Cruel, Inhuman or Degrading Treatment or Punishment* (also known as the "Istanbul protocol") in 1999, but this set of guidelines for documenting torture has proven more of an obstacle than an asset in assessing asylum seekers' claims to having been tortured (Lawrance and Ruffer 2015b; Wallace and Wylie 2014). Unfortunately, medical certificates often illustrate the degree to which "bodies speak little"—after all, it is in the interest of the torturer "to silence them" (Fassin and D'Halluin 2005, 598). Torture need not leave physical marks on the body, and medical certificates cannot evaluate the possible psychological scars of torture. For this reason, psychologists and psychiatrists constitute yet another source of expertise, and in this realm, courts draw upon expert knowledge that is often part of a therapy (Gangsei and Deutsch 2007; Marton 2014; Smith, Lustig, and Gangsei 2015).

Psychological evaluations have the potential to indicate that a claimant has a viable fear of returning home, a fear that the physical body cannot testify to and that thus has "no physical translation" (Fassin and D'Halluin 2005, 602). It can, of course, be beyond the capacity of the asylum seeker to speak about the trauma stemming from previous persecution, and the psychologist as expert deals with a range of issues that, again, are far beyond the abilities of the social scientist. However, even if anthropologists, sociologists, and historians lack the capacity to discover this form of evidence, nonmedical country conditions experts may still play a vital role in assessing the implications of medical or psychiatric reports (Lawrance 2013, 2015). In an ideal world, where those deemed experts could devote hours of their time to individual appeals, an array of experts might work in coordination to create a comprehensive picture of the asylum seeker's past.

Whatever their professional or disciplinary backgrounds, all experts perform certain common, overarching tasks (Good 2007), sometimes without even realizing the precise import of their conclusions. Experts examine a range of evidence in order to corroborate an asylum seeker's claim—or possibly to assist in its refutation—by evaluating it for consistency with their expert knowledge of the subject matter and the field broadly. In this way, by drawing on their training, the experts enhance adjudicators' capacity to determine if applicants' claims are truthful or whether those applicants are fabricating their claims by framing them within their knowledge of specific country or regional conditions. Experts engage with published government sources regarding country conditions—for example, US State Department reports on human rights practices in a given applicant's homeland. And experts provide, in the broadest possible sense, a cultural or idiomatic navigation of the asylum process. When they first apply, many asylum seekers encounter difficulties in language and translation; their narratives are not chronological; and they cannot articulate how their persecution was politically—rather than individually—motivated. In this way, asylum seekers are often neither able nor ready to present their applications in terms that are "recogniz-able" to adjudicators (Shuman and Bohmer 2004, 400). And yet in each of these missteps, the expert has the capacity to contribute his or her expertise and thus make the process a little more navigable.

Experts, therefore, not only originate from a wide swath of the professions but also interpret a wide-ranging spectrum of evidence. The knowledge bases and skill sets of experts are diffuse and extensive. But the tasks required of them are also sweeping, and thus, what constitutes "adequate qualifications" to testify as an expert "should be broadly de-fined" (Malphrus 2010, 8). It is essential to bear in mind that because the figure of the expert is diffuse, expert knowledge is itself diffuse. Given the extent to which experts assess evidence within their respective fields and render evidence accessible or knowable to immigration judges, their testimony may be "potentially determinative" in the final decision of whether an asylum seeker's claim is successful (Malphrus 2010, 1).

Throughout the life span of an asylum case, the ultimate predicament of the expert is to facilitate a determination by providing the necessary and appropriate perspective while remaining unbiased and impartial. Personally, politically, and professionally, experts ought to engage with the applicant and the case dispassionately. Becoming emotionally invested in a particular claimant or case compromises the authority of the expert in the eyes of the court, for if the expert becomes invested in a case, it may appear as though he or she cannot assess the evidence fairly.

## The Craft of the Expert

Although there is much to critique about domestic asylum procedures (as the contributions in this volume attest), the opportunity to present one's case directly to an adjudicator in a wealthy country with a well-developed system for asylum adjudication is clearly preferable for those who can achieve it. As Terretta's and Tricia Redeker Hepner's chapters demonstrate, the nature of transnational relations among many migrating African populations means that asylum procedures are often well understood in advance, including the role of the expert. Together with legal counsel, the expert can help articulate or even translate culturally and politically specific dynamics of a claimant's case with respect to domestic and international human rights law (Ardalan 2015). Such options are rarely, if ever, available for the masses of refugees awaiting a durable solution overseas—a fact that is by no means lost on African migrants themselves.

As the numbers of asylum seekers grow and anxieties in would-be host countries mount regarding potential terrorists or "bogus" claimants seeking better economic futures or health care (Lawrance 2013, 2015; Scheel and Squire 2014; Stevens 2010), academics with expertise on countries producing such migrants become key players in the asylum process and the outcome of claims. Yet despite the increasing involvement of academics in African asylum claims, a rich body of scholarship reflecting on asylum and the role of expert knowledge has been slow to emerge (exceptions include Good 2004 and 2007; Lawrance and Ruffer 2015a; and Mahmood 1996).

But what constitutes the craft of the expert? And what possibilities and limitations coalesce around it? Given the considerable time investment required for asylum casework—the vast majority of it offered on a pro bono publica basis—and its lack of recognition within university reward systems, what motivates academics to participate? And as we increasingly worry over the implications of our roles, why do we persist? Certainly, many researchers who serve as expert witnesses are motivated by ethical and moral commitments to those among whom they have worked, lived, and studied. Such imperatives have a venerable history and are rooted in solid methodological and theoretical justification, especially in anthropology. Experts are themselves situated within dense networks of contacts formed over years of research and field study, responsive and even accountable to the expectations of claimants who request, poignantly, that we explain to authorities "what it is like in my country."

Lacking regular, meaningful extra-academic outlets for the practical application and dissemination of our (sometimes arcane) knowledge, we look at asylum as a critical arena in which our scholarship truly matters. Our collaborations with counsel and claimants allow us to help shape legal argumentation and perhaps the law itself as we coproduce narratives and arguments in a high-stakes context. Though often behind the scenes rather than at center stage, the expert is nonetheless a major actor in the asylum process, not a peripheral bit player who dips in and out. Many academics entering the world of asylum casework remain there; they are manifestly committed to assisting the people they have studied through the pragmatic application of their knowledge. Many also find that the rewards of helping to secure safety for a deserving person—of achieving a small human rights victory—are inherently more satisfying than the rewards of academia.

This is not to say that the role of experts in asylum procedures is unproblematic. As Hepner's chapter demonstrates, experts are neither naive nor uncritical of their role, and the same is true of attorneys and adjudicators, as McDougall's and Campbell's essays also evidence. As Carol Bohmer and Amy Shuman argue in their chapter, pitfalls, tensions, contradictions, and unintended consequences abound. Expert knowledge may contribute to the reification of fluid and complex social, cultural, and political realities and the decontextualization of the claimant from his or her political subjectivity to make his or her experience legible to the law (Bloomaert 2009; Fassin 2012; Speed 2006). The very nature of the expertise rendered must conform to legal standards and assumptions about an asylum seeker's lack of credibility, therefore participating in the exclusionary logic of securitization (Squire 2009; Smith, Lustig, and Gangsei 2015). And though one of the critical skills of experts is their ability to render, into a language and cultural frame comprehensible to adjudicators, experiences that are highly embedded in specific cultural and politico-economic contexts (Bohmer and Shuman 2007; Shemak 2011), the implications of such elite "voicing" on behalf of African migrants reinscribes hierarchies of power and difference that some might otherwise consider objectionable.

Nonetheless, one of the key argumentative threads running throughout this book is that asylum is not reducible to the legal procedures that comprise it. It is a multidimensional social, cultural, and political process or, more precisely, a constellation of processes that links with and reflects relationships ranging from the macrohistorical dimensions of North-South inequities to the quotidian and intersubjective details of human lives and relationships. Similarly, the craft of the expert encompasses much more than the specific components of participation in casework—consulting with legal counsel and the claimant, developing the expert statement or affidavit, and delivering oral testimony. It entails critical reflection on epistemology and hermeneutics and on the politics of knowledge in legal contexts, as well as navigation of the considerable tensions that emerge as a result of our decision to act. Though we are sought as experts for our culturally specific knowledge, our intellectual orientation and training as academics force us to engage reflexively, generating insights into the nature of the asylum process that may ultimately mitigate, if not completely alleviate, some of the problems identified within.

In approaching the role with the critical reflexivity and an interrogative stance, experts may, in fact, actively resist the tendencies identified in humanitarian and asylum law that perpetuate violence to the subjectivity and agency of those who happen to be asylum seekers. In addition to contributing to the shaping of case law itself, our participation can expand the meanings of asylum by generating greater solidarity and intersubjective dialogue with the communities from which asylum seekers come and the individual claimants themselves. Indeed, the asylum process becomes one in which experts, legal specialists, and claimants enter into a strategic conversation that draws together human rights concepts, asylum legal norms, and the specific dynamics that shape the claimant's experience and his or her understanding (Good 2007; Lawrance 2015). As we assemble these elements into a common frame, transformations within each may occur. As Hepner's chapter argues, asylum seekers may come to view their experiences—and therefore themselves and their social and political environments—in new ways. This may, of course, be painful and even traumatic, yet it can help even those exposed to horrific abuses to discover new sources of strength and meaning, either publicly or privately (Ortiz 2001).

Experts and legal counsel, together and individually, come to reflect on the law and its requirements in a more nuanced manner as a result of engaging with the claimant's case and may take such insights forth to inform practice. Though certainly not without tensions and contradictions, the asylum process may therefore become productive and generative even as it constrains and limits in other ways. Consequently, experts should reframe their understanding of their craft—and asylum seekers themselves—as agentive and purposeful rather than hopelessly compromised and manipulated by the structural, sovereign power of nation-states, migration policies, and the law. The craft of the expert is multidimensional. It is not limited to what takes place within the confines of asylum casework and legal procedure itself, especially when experts draw on their experiences with asylum to generate new critical insights and strategies for practice.

## Identities, Ideas, and Issues Emerging from African Asylum Seeking

In most years, asylum claims from the African continent are less numerous than those from other areas of the world. In 2010, for example, the largest number of asylum seekers worldwide came from Afghanistan, followed by China and Iraq (Gladstone 2012). Yet African refugees tend to attract substantial, often sensationalized, and seemingly disproportionate attention from the press in the United States, United Kingdom, and elsewhere (Lawrance 2015; Stevens 2010). Possibly the most heavily publicized asylum case in the United States was that of Fauziya Kasinga, the young Togolese woman who received asylum in 1996 based on her fear of undergoing genital cutting if she were repatriated.[2] African examples also abound in more general stories about asylum. An article about fabricated asylum claims (Dolnick 2011) recalled that Amadou Diallo, the African immigrant shot forty-one times by the New York police in 1999, had falsely testified that he came from Mauritania, where his parents had been killed in the course of political conflict. And yet, there are no empirical data to sustain the view that African asylum claims are more often bogus, less deserving, or less legitimate than those of other regions. A New York physician interviewed by the *New York Times,* whose clinic evaluates claims of torture, described the majority of his patients as young, educated men from Africa (Bowen 2011); his examinations validated 87 percent of their torture claims. Whatever the reasons for this unwarranted, popular focus on Africa, asylum claims, both real and fraudulent, raise a range of questions about the application of core legal concepts to the diverse African political, cultural, and linguistic landscape.

Contemporary asylum law, defined in the wake of World War II, rests on the 1951 UN refugee convention and the 1967 UN protocol. Only with the 1967 protocol was refugee status expanded to include populations outside Europe and encompass events occurring after January 1, 1951. These documents have been domesticated with varying degrees of success across the globe (Barutciski 2002; Goodwin-Gill 1999; Kagan 2006). Although not a signatory to the 1951 convention, the US Congress, via a 1980 law, adopted an international definition of a refugee as a person with a "well-founded fear of persecution on account of race, religion, nationality, membership in a particular social group, or political opinion" (Immigration and Nationality Act 1980). These guidelines may seem straightforward, but (adding to the challenges of verifying stories of events that occurred thousands of miles away) some aspects of the law also leave room for ambiguity—such as how to define a "well-founded fear of persecution" or "membership in a particular social group" and what constitutes "political opinion." Furthermore, in many cases, as Jacques Derrida (2001, 12) observes,

*B. N. Lawrance, I. Berger, T. R. Hepner, J. T. Tague, and M. Terretta*

the "aporia" (Shemak 2011, 12) or borderline between "political" and "economic" refugees is difficult to determine. As Jean-François Lyotard has explained, the burden resting on individual asylum seekers to prove claims that often cannot be documented is a *dommage* (a "wrong" or "tort") that is "accompanied by the loss of means to prove the damage" (Lyotard 1983, 9; 1988, 5). Thus, the temptation to stretch, embellish, or invent narratives that conform to asylum law is enormous. The added burden of trauma that many refugees have suffered and the difficulties of communicating across both linguistic barriers and cultural dissonance add to the complexity of the process (Einhorn and Berthold 2015; Smith, Lustig, and Gangsei 2015).

Most of the chapters in this volume address North American asylum cases, but these claimants represent only a small proportion of the refugee flow both from African countries and globally, flows that fluctuate annually depending on the dynamics of conflict in particular countries and regions and the politics around immigration in potential host countries. In the United States, for example, the ceiling set for refugees worldwide in 2010 (80,000) was 65 percent lower than in 1980 (Li and Batalova 2011), although this number does not include people who first arrive on valid visas and then apply for asylum. In any given year, the overwhelming majority of displaced people resettle in neighboring countries and do not seek asylum. In 2008, for instance, neighboring developing countries hosted 80 percent of all refugees. In that same year, with the 28 percent increase worldwide in the number of new asylum seekers, the largest number of individual claims, an astonishing total of 207,000, were filed in South Africa, compared with only 49,600 in the United States (Kriger 2011; UNHCR 2009). The rapid fluctuations are apparent when 2012 data are examined. In 2012, only Somalia and Sudan featured in the top five major source countries for refugees globally. Of the top ten countries in which asylum applications were lodged in the offices of the UN High Commissioner for Refugees (UNHCR), Kenya was ranked first with 20,000 and Cameroon and Somalia were eighth and ninth with 3,500 and 3,400 applications, respectively. Significantly, in 2012, Kenya and Ethiopia, following close behind, hosted the second- and third-largest number of refugees in-country, as a comparative measure of gross domestic product (UNHCR 2012). Some periods also saw sharp increases in refugees from particular countries—between 2008 and 2010, for example, the number of people arriving in the United States from the

Democratic Republic of Congo (DRC) increased fourfold and those from Eritrea tenfold (Li and Batalova 2011).

In constructing narratives about their cases and their identities, both claimants and their attorneys rely on a combination of asylum seekers' own histories and on stories that already have proven acceptable before adjudicators and tribunals. As Berger argues, for African women since the 1996 Kasinga case that has often meant including an account of fearing or having experienced female genital cutting (FGC) and offering resistance to the procedure. But other successful asylum narratives are particular to individual countries. In Mauritania, as McDougall demonstrates, where persecution based on slavery provides a basis for many asylum requests, portraying the slave/master divide as one between blacks and whites has helped to make it more legible, particularly in US courts. This metanarrative originally came not from immigration attorneys but from the strategy of the African Liberation Forces of Mauritania (FLAM), which sought support for exiled refugees by portraying them as black slaves being driven from the country by white masters. Such narratives, once established, tend to acquire a life of their own and to set precedents that shape not only the testimony of individual claimants but also the arguments and statements of the attorneys and expert witnesses who assist them.

The issue of narratives and how they are crafted and understood applies to the stories of asylum seekers and also to the understanding of these accounts in potential host countries. At times, a sympathetic reception may have less to do with claimants' objective circumstances than with global political conflicts. When Soviet-era athletes sought to remain in the free-market democratic West (half the Hungarian Olympic team in 1956), they were portrayed sympathetically as legitimate defectors. By contrast, as Terretta narrates, Cameroonian athletes who disappeared during the 2012 Olympic Games in London were suspected of being economic rather than political migrants, despite their government's widely known record of egregious human rights abuses. This issue is particularly germane to parts of Africa, where decades of violence and political instability in some countries have made the division between political and economic grounds for asylum difficult to disentangle. As currently framed, international law discounts the claims of refugees seeking escape from dysfunctional, corruption-ridden political systems where bending or getting around the rules or producing false documents may be necessary for finding work, food, and shelter. When applied to asylum, however, such survival strategies are labeled as fraud. Making a counterargument, Terretta suggests that judging such claims as illegitimate should rest not on whether individuals have falsified documents and stories but on the extent to which a combination of economic and political factors, often difficult to separate, has made survival at home virtually impossible.

Evaluating African cultural practices that underpin asylum cases is equally challenging. In the wake of a vocal international feminist movement critical of female genital cutting, fear of excision emerged as a grounds for claiming asylum by the mid-1990s. As Berger's and Musalo's chapters show, successful cases involving FGC also opened the way for considering other forms of private, domestic violence and coercion as a basis for claims. In turn, this stretched the previously accepted grounds for defining persecution but nonetheless left open for over a decade the question of whether those who had already been excised could claim sanctuary on such grounds (Seelinger 2010; Wasem 2011). As Walker-Said's chapter demonstrates, Western human rights discourse also has shaped judicial perspectives on the rights of sexual minorities. Regardless of their situation, the law recognizes persecution only on the grounds of having a "lesbian" or "gay" sexual orientation, sometimes a "bisexual" identity (Rehaag 2008, 2009), and occasionally a "transgender" identity (Morgan 2006; Neilson 2004); as a result, claimants are required to frame their experience in terms of American concepts of nonnormative sexual behavior (Massaquoi 2013). Even more difficult to assess and categorize are claims based on fears of witchcraft, although increasing numbers of African asylum seekers allege either that they have been accused of practicing witchcraft or that they have been the victims of such practices, as Luongo discusses in her essay. Unlike other asylum requests, such cases confront the difficulty of providing tangible evidence admissible in court to back up such fears, compounded by the problem of having judges who are likely to dismiss the stories as signs of primitive magical thinking.

In all of these instances—excision practices, sexual orientation, and witchcraft fears—the subtleties and complexities of local cultures have to be reduced and homogenized in order to make them legible to adjudicators and Western legal systems. In cases of female genital cutting, even though older women tend to perform the procedure and the rationales are complex and varied, lawyers have had greater success in portraying the practice more unambiguously as a product of rigid and static "traditional" African patriarchy. Similarly, the sexual human rights agenda imposes problematic categories on other cultures; moreover, by failing to understand or conceptualize the wide range of sexual behaviors that may challenge local political, social, or religious practice, this agenda fails to apply to many Africans in need of protection.

Both individual and group identities figure in critical ways in asylum cases, yet the proof of identity is often problematic. In the Global North, individual identity may be rooted in documents assumed to be neutral and readily available.[3] Accordingly, as Bohmer and Shuman argue here, documents are privileged over personal accounts, and those who produce or use fraudulent documents often find their character questioned. This approach disregards the potential need for fabricated identities in corrupt or dangerous societies. Furthermore and especially in conflict situations, individuals may have multiple and changing identities throughout their lives, rather than the fixed identities that asylum officers assume. For Rwandans during and after the genocide, particularly those of mixed heritage, self-identifying as either Hutu or Tutsi according to the circumstances could mean the difference between death and survival. Equally, in countries torn apart for decades by civil war, such as Somalia or Sierra Leone, and remote rural areas throughout the African continent, presumed basic documents, including birth certificates, may not be widely available. And for dissidents everywhere, false passports may be necessary tools for escape.

Identity is at stake in asylum cases because the law requires documentation of personal narratives and also because of the need to prove persecution based on one of five protected grounds, among them membership in a "particular social group." For a person claiming maltreatment in a witchcraft case, this means identifying either as someone accused of belonging to the invented social group of "witches" or as being a "witchcraft target." In societies where witchcraft beliefs flourish, people often see the ability to practice witchcraft as a fundamental aspect of identity, but being a target of a witchcraft accusation is not necessarily stable and fundamental in the same way; in addition, an individual's apparent identity as a witch would not persist in a new social context. Issues of identity are equally challenging in cases of genital cutting and sexual orientation. In the former, the "social group" requirement usually centers on being a member of a particular ethnic group that enforces excision on young women, a requirement that tends to fix and reify local African categories

that are, in fact, fluid and historically contingent. In the case of those persecuted for their sexual behaviors and identities, applicants are forced to tai-
lor their stories and homogenize their personal identities in relation to fixed
Western notions such as gay and lesbian (Massaquoi 2013; Spijkerboer 2013).

The asylum process and the requirements of asylum law reflect difficult and contradictory tendencies. Crafting successful cases that conform
to the domestic legal requirements has enabled African claimants (and
often their families) a chance to find refuge from horrific political conflict and repression, saving them from torture, imprisonment, or possible
extrajudicial killing. At the same time, particularly in the small number
of highly publicized cases, many aspects of these laws inadvertently play
upon and reinforce negative stereotypes of Africa as a continent of patriarchal tribes that continue to perpetuate primitive, sometimes barbaric
practices dictated by static and unchanging customs. While shaping and
perpetuating attitudes among the general public, these legal requirements present a particular dilemma for academic advocates and expert
witnesses, forcing them at times to compress their understandings of
dynamic, fluid social relationships into the appropriate legal categories.
Finally, the asylum process relies on a narrative of victims in need of rescue by well-intentioned, humane host countries. Though this is true of
asylum seekers from around the globe, the negative effects may be most
acute for those from the African continent, a part of the world that has
been less successful than others at escaping the negative images inherited
from centuries of enslavement and colonial occupation.

## The Textual Form of Expert Testimony

In the new millennium, country conditions testimony and the African
asylum seeker's narrative are tailored to fit contemporary asylum protocols, which increasingly conform more to immigration securitization and
managed migration policies than to terms of the 1951 UN convention
and 1967 UN protocol. Since the 1990s, asylum and refugee legislation in
the Global North has imposed a number of restrictive migration policies
upon asylum seekers, including: "visa regimes, carrier sanctions, airport
liaison officers as well as internal measures such as detention, disper-
sal regimes, [and] restrictions on access to welfare and housing" (Gibney
2004, 2). These securitization measures converge to filter out growing
numbers of would-be claimants before they reach host country soil. The
result has been to establish in the United States, the United Kingdom,

the European Union, Australia, and elsewhere what Vicki Squire (2009, 36) terms "an exclusionary politics of asylum" underwritten by narratives of control and regulatory practices that criminalize asylum seekers as "threatening" or "culpable" subjects.[4]

The ability to manage migration through restrictive controls and the securitization of borders has become a crucial articulation of state sovereignty, and the state's ability to exclude noncitizens has come to define citizenship, belonging, and even national identity (Brown 2010, 67–68; Ifekwunigwe 2006, 85). Simultaneously, porous borders allowing for the free circulation of goods, capital, and economically desirable migrants have weakened state sovereignty, rendering it nearly irrelevant in spaces such as the multinational corporation or banking sector (Brown 2010, 8–26). Discursively, legally, and practically, the restrictive regulations of migration that limit the number of refugees have become legitimate state policy, a means of reinforcing state sovereignty and defining who is to be included or excluded. Yet the scope for the political contestation of managed migration policies and asylum protocols is more and more limited.

The role of the expert witness has evolved concurrently with changing legal, political, and cultural attitudes toward asylum seeking and the application of the principle of nonrefoulement. In the 1950s and 1960s, in the wake of the refugee convention's drafting and application, expert testimony on the persecution or statelessness of groups or individuals found voice in the pages of newspapers or in the forum of the UN General Assembly or its various committees.[5] In the twenty-first century, expert testimony describing country conditions and legitimizing refugees' well-grounded (well-founded) fear of persecution takes the shape of article-length affidavits tailor-made to specific individuals seeking asylum in host country courts. Confined as it is to the discrete legal context afforded by individual asylum hearings, expert testimony today has a much narrower reach than at the time of the convention's creation. However, the stricter immigration controls and standards of proof for asylum seekers afford the legal team supporting them the greatest influence on the outcome of asylum cases in history.

Jennifer Holmes and Linda Keith have found that the largest single factor influencing the outcome of asylum cases is whether the claimant has legal counsel. If so, the probability of a grant increases by 33 percent (Holmes and Keith 2010; see also Schoenholtz and Bernstein 2008). Sean

*B. N. Lawrance, I. Berger, T. R. Hepner, J. T. Tague, and M. Terretta*

Rehaag (2011, 73) discerned similar patterns in Canada and noted that "competent counsel is a key factor driving successful outcomes in refugee claims." In contrast, the level of human rights abuse in the claimant's country of origin increases the probability of a grant only by 0.07 percent, and the level of democratization of the claimant's country decreases his or her chance of receiving a grant by only 0.11 percent. Other variables have comparatively minimal statistical effects (Holmes and Keith 2010).

Arguably, in the current climate, expert testimony serves to insert a wedge, however infinitesimal, under the quickly closing door of asylum by substantiating the claims of asylum seekers. Yet despite its crucial importance to the individuals who make use of it, expert testimony largely fails to critically engage the exclusionary asylum protocols of host countries, in part because it conforms to juridical norms established through political, legal, and cultural trends in those host countries. The prevalence of such testimony may also make courts less apt to recognize claimants' testimony without an expert's corroboration, rendering it more difficult for asylum seekers without professional representation to establish credibility.[6]

It seems that expert testimony fails to reverse current norms that have brought the granting of asylum to an all-time low across the Global North. Even as numbers of asylum seekers increase and as an ever greater cadre of experts provide supportive testimony, restrictive immigration legislation and extraterritorial selection processes have sharply curbed the asylum grant rate throughout the host countries of the Global North since the late 1990s. For example, in the United States as of fiscal year (FY) 2009, the real number of successful affirmative asylum claims decreased by 79 percent since FY1997 (falling from 116,877 in FY1996 to 24,550 in FY2009); defensive asylum claims dropped by 53 percent (Holmes and Keith 2010, 433; Wasem 2011, summary).[7]

Given present-day asylum trends, Squire (2009, 34) argues that expert testimony may seek to overcome the exclusionary logic of securitization but instead actually reinforces it by conforming to protocols set by host country courts, politics, and cultural norms. The protocols have established a conventional textual form for expert testimony composed of three essential ingredients: a narrative fitted to the exigencies of juridical proof; the substantiation of the claimant's credibility; and the humanitarian trope of the deserving refugee.

Guided by the asylum seeker's legal team, expert testimony makes juridical proof its primary objective. The burden of proof for refugees and asylum seekers has increased in recent years. For example, the REAL ID Act passed in the United States in 2005 requires "asylum seekers to demonstrate that their race, religion, nationality, membership in a social group, or political opinion represents 'at least one central reason' for the persecution they suffered or fear" (Wasem 2011, 4). Furthermore, it now falls on the asylum seeker to provide corroborative evidence to his or her claims, and expert testimony is one means of legitimizing and reinforcing the claimant's narrative (Conroy 2009; Galloni 2008). Yet the requirement of juridical proof imposed on asylum seekers exists in tension with the testimony provided by experts, particularly as the application of legal procedures limits the form of evidence in asylum cases. In the United Kingdom, courts routinely seek to "constrain the expert's influence, through such means as the 'hearsay rule' . . . and the 'ultimate issue' rule, which prevents witnesses from giving opinions on the main issues at stake" (Good 2008, S48).

Within the constraints imposed by legal processes, expert testimony seeks to render refugees recognizable according to social and political norms configuring the present-day rule of law and thus to lead to the courts' recognition of claimants as worthy of asylum.[8] Although expert testimony frames asylum seekers' narratives as legal evidence, it also decontextualizes the claimant from his or her social and political subjectivity in order to fit him or her into the host country's applicable rules of law.[9] Furthermore, it is unclear to what extent the evidence contained in expert testimony sways judicial opinion, since political and legal factors may wield an equal or greater influence on the final outcome of the case (Ramji-Nogales, Schoenholtz, and Schrag 2007; Rottman, Fariss, and Poe 2009).

Possible irrelevance is the least of the dangers associated with the conventional form of expert testimony. More troublingly, in appearing to assist with any attempt to legitimize a claimant's narrative and present this individual as a deserving refugee, the expert witness articulates his or her own testimony in a discursive and legal space that is skewed against asylum seekers, thus running the risk of accepting mistrust of the refugee as the starting premise. It is essential then, when considering the form of expert testimony, to critically examine the expert witness's role vis-à-vis the refugee's credibility.

*Expert Testimony and Refugee Credibility*

The role of the expert witness is emerging as a pivotal site of challenge to legal, political, and social assumptions that asylum claims are at best illegitimate or frivolous (meaning primarily economic in nature) or at worst criminal or fraudulent. Because the form makes expert testimony seem necessary to prove the veracity of a claimant's testimony, the process shines a spotlight of suspicion on the latter (Fassin 2012, 109–29).

Yet for Derrida (as quoted in Shemak 2011, 29), the confirmation of the veracity of the claimant's story can never be achieved through expert testimony, which is, in effect, testimony about testimony: "There is no testimony which does not structurally imply in itself the possibility of fiction, simulacra, dissimulation, lie, and perjury. . . . If this possibility that it seems to prohibit were effectively excluded, if testimony thereby became proof, information, certainty, or archive, it would lose its function as testimony." Drawing on Derrida, April Shemak (2011, 29) writes that "testimony is . . . always linked to the possibility of perjury, even as a witness swears to its truthfulness. . . . Testimony always holds the potential to trespass, to breach trust and perjure." Because of the "improvability" of testimony, the asylum seeker is most often already perceived as lying and therefore treacherous before the first word is uttered.

The refugee's narrative, undergirded by expert testimony, provides him or her access to legal, political membership in the host country. For this reason, juridical and immigration authorities, as well as the society at large, view misrepresentation or lying as almost equal to an act of treason. The outcry surrounding allegations that Nafissatou Diallo (the accuser of Dominique Strauss-Kahn, former head of the International Monetary Fund) had lied on her asylum application is illustrative. Should evidence of mendacity ever be discovered, it merely confirms widely held assumptions about asylum grantees and often comes with vicious calls for the "exposed liar's" immediate deportation.[10]

Testimonies of the asylum seeker and the supporting legal team (lawyer, interpreter, and expert witnesses) are "scrutinized for credibility" in immigration courts, making these narratives the "sites of surveillance and policing of national boundaries" (Shemak 2011, 24). Yet in working so hard to restore credibility on a claimant's behalf, the expert witness runs the risk of constructing testimony that confirms dominant perceptions of asylum seekers as illegitimate, deceitful, and potentially treacherous.

### Spinning the Yarn, Narrating the Refugee

In constructing a narrative that will make sense to a judge or asylum officer, the asylum seeker fills the role traditionally occupied by a native informant in historical or ethnographic research, spinning his or her tale of persecution in its raw form. Guided by the legal team, the expert witness translates the claimant's narrative into "the idiom of the host nation" (Shemak 2011, 17), framing it to fit a legal and humanitarian trope of deserving refugee and thus rendering it (and therefore its narrator) recognizable to asylum officers and judges.[11]

Expert testimony measures the plausibility of an asylum seeker's experiences of persecution and the extent to which they justify the claimant's well-grounded fear of persecution (Fassin 2012). By framing the claimant's narrative in such a way as to "render individual suffering and psychic interiority the ground of trauma" (Schaffer and Smith 2004, 10), expert testimony forsakes a schema of historical and cultural intelligibility rooted in the refugee's place of origin for a schema of intelligibility derived from a moral economy of humanitarianism prevalent throughout host countries of the Global North (Butler 2009, 7; Fassin 2010, 269–93).

Fassin argues that isolating the individual's experience of suffering while emphasizing his or her traumatic experience is the surest way to ensure that asylum will be granted, given the unreliability of testimony and the ability of physical or psychological scars to attest nondiscursively to a trauma narrative (in which case medical testimony should ideally be included) (Fassin 2012). In transforming the claimant's narrative into something intelligible, knowable, and recognizable to officials presiding over asylum in a given host country, expert testimony recontextualizes the refugee and his or her experience. This volume begins the process of examining in depth the repercussions of decontextualizing, isolating, and reframing individual asylum seekers' narratives of persecution, a process in which the expert witness participates.

Given the increasing importance of expert testimony, the expert witness is one of the only figures who, through their narratives, have the capacity to contest asylum protocols (Good 2015). However, the constraints imposed on expert testimony's textual form corral it into a legal narrative that serves to reinforce, rather than challenge, circumvent, or overturn, the normative portrayal of asylum seekers in host countries. In other words, the textual form of expert testimony, in order to be successful on a case-by-case basis, must be seen to conform to—and therefore all too often uphold—the legal and political status quo when it comes to the regulation of asylum. Accordingly, it seems that by adhering to a narrative form more or less dictated by the politics, laws, and sociocultural leanings of host countries, specialists who serve as expert witnesses have yet to find a way to live up to their full potential, beyond the discrete legal setting of the particular cases for which they provide testimony.

## Conclusion: Expertise and the Disciplines

As the first book to focus on African asylum practices and expert testimony, this collection provides a unique entrée into the personal, lived experience of asylum seekers and refugees. Our hope is that it will gain the attention of the large international refugee and asylum activist community because, by way of anecdotal narratives of real cases, it may enable others to connect their pending cases and concerns with previously unreported experiences. We hope that these chapters will resonate with the immigration professionals and practitioners, who currently have little to draw upon in terms of real case studies with which to develop and enhance relationships with potential experts.

The volume is multidisciplinary and includes perspectives from those trained in history, anthropology, and political science as well as the interdisciplinary fields of legal studies and folklore/literature studies. By way of conclusion, it may be worth pondering the role of disciplinarity in the production of expertise. It would be an overstatement to suggest that all contemporary academic social science and humanistic disciplines are represented among the core group of individuals who offer their services as experts. The conference from which these papers were selected was the final installment of several years of preparative discussions among a group of engaged Africanist scholars. We met at the annual meeting of the US African Studies Association on at least three occasions informally and also formally in roundtables and plenary sessions. As our group grew and coalesced, we observed that certain disciplinary perspectives (most notably, history) appeared overrepresented in the assembly of individuals who regularly served as experts; seven of the authors in this volume were trained as historians. After historians, the second-largest disciplinary constituency comprises anthropologists.

Implicitly, then, the composition of this volume raises questions generally about the overrepresentation of particular disciplines in expert testimony, specifically about the receptiveness of judges and tribunals to certain intellectual frameworks and arguments. In reviewing the structure and format of expert testimony in support of gender-based violence claims from West Africa, Lawrance (forthcoming b) observes that the basis for the legal claim of persecution must often be contextualized with a history of specific forms of persecution in the respective country. In this way, expert reports inherently compare specific claims with objective evidence about legal remedy, real and purported, and in so doing, they provide a hypothesis for estimating the likelihood of future jeopardy. Expert reports appear backward-looking because they historicize particular claims of jeopardy. But expert reports evaluating claims of gender-based violence are also forward-looking insofar as the asylum seekers, whose claims they evaluate, postulate the reemergence of particular dangers by framing claims as conditional and overlapping, incorporating hypothetical risks encumbered by forcible return.

We do not offer this collection expressly as a manual comprising specific personal narratives of best and worst practices in asylum and refugee status determination, a job admirably accomplished by Anthony Good and Tobias Kelly (2013). But if it operates as a guide for those who seek to assist the most vulnerable in our society, it will be a fitting tribute to the real individuals whose identities are masked by the complexity of their circumstances. It is our hope that this volume will stimulate further debate among scholars, practitioners, and activists about the predilection of jurists for particular narrative and disciplinary agendas, together with the impact this may have in fairly and equitably assessing the claims of refugees and asylum seekers.

## Notes

1. UNHCR, "Durable Solutions" (retrieved September 16, 2014), http://www.unhcr.org/pages/49c3646cf8.html.

2. The correct spelling of her last name is Kassindja, which the Immigration and Naturalization Service (INS) misspelled as Kasinga. This error was reflected in all official documents and thus in most of the legal writing about the case.

3. Recent controversies over voter ID laws in the United States show the difficulty of making this claim even in twenty-first-century America.

4. Squire (2009) deals primarily with the United Kingdom. For France, see Fassin, Morice, and Quiminal (1997).

5. The most dynamic expert witness for the African context was certainly Michael Scott, who spent three decades tirelessly testifying in many forums (including the UN General Assembly and Fourth Committee) about the injustices that South African apartheid rule inflicted upon the indigenous populations of South-West Africa (Anderson 2008; Clark 1981). Roger Baldwin, chairman of the International League of the Rights of Man and founder of the American Civil Liberties Union, acted as expert witness and advocate in the case of French Cameroon's violent decolonization from French rule (Terretta 2012).

6. This point was stressed by Mary Meg McCarthy, director of the National Immigrant Justice Center, in Chicago, Illinois, during the Conable Conference Plenary Session, April 14, 2012, at the Rochester Institute of Technology.

7. Statistical manipulation enables state officialdom to claim—as did Juan Osuna, director of the Executive Office for Immigration Review, Department of Justice, during the Conable Conference Plenary Session in 2012—that the US asylum grant rate had climbed to an all-time high. In percentage terms, this is the case: the asylum grant rate (both affirmative and defensive claims) was 12.44 percent in FY1996 when asylum claims peaked, and it steadily climbed to 36.02 percent by FY2008. Yet the skillfully wielded extraterritorial measures preventing would-be asylum seekers from reaching US borders have led to a decrease in real terms.

8. On recognizability as preparing a subject for recognition fitting current social and political conventions, see Butler (2009, 3–5).

9. On decontextualization, see Fassin (2012, 109–29); on the rules of law taking precedence over evidence, see Latour (2010, 208–16).

10. This is true even among those who consider themselves sympathetic to asylum processes. See, for example, the commentary of a self-declared human rights activist (Murray 2011): "In order to maintain public support for the asylum system, it is essential that it has integrity. If Diallo is not now deported, nobody can believe in that integrity."

11. Schaffer and Smith (2004, 22) put it another way when they write that Holocaust stories are the basis for the psychoanalytic model that privileges "stories suffused with traumatic remembering and suffering and silences other kinds of stories that may not unfold through the Western trope of trauma." Here, we are guided by Judith Butler's (2009) discussion of Hegelian recognizability.

## References

Agier, Michel. 2007. *On the Margins of the World: The Refugee Experience Today*. Cambridge: Polity Press.

Anderson, Carol. 2008. "International Conscience, the Cold War, and Apartheid: The N.A.A.C.P.'s Alliance with the Reverend Michael Scott for South West Africa's Liberation, 1946–1951." *Journal of World History* 19 (3): 297–326.

Ardalan, Sabrineh. 2015. "Expert as Aid and Impediment: Navigating Barriers to Effective Asylum Representation." In *Adjudicating Refugee and Asylum Status,* edited by B. N. Lawrance and G. B. Ruffer, 149–65. Cambridge: Cambridge University Press.

Barutciski, M. 2002. "A Critical View on U.N.H.C.R.'s Mandate Dilemmas." *International Journal of Refugee Law* 14 (2–3): 365–81.

Bloomaert, Jan. 2009. "Language, Asylum and the National Order. *Current Anthropology* 54 (4): 415–41.

Bohmer, Carol, and Amy Shuman. 2007. *Rejecting Refugees: Political Asylum in the 21st Century.* London: Routledge.

Bowen, Alison. 2011. "Proving Torture to Win Asylum." *New York Times*, March 6.

Brown, Wendy. 2010. *Walled States, Waning Sovereignty.* Brooklyn, NY: Zone Books.

Burrill, Emily, Richard L. Roberts, and Elizabeth Thornberry. 2010. *Domestic Violence and the Law in Colonial and Postcolonial Africa.* Athens: Ohio University Press.

Butler, Judith. 2009. *Frames of War: When Is Life Grievable?* London: Verso.

Carver, Nick. 2003. *Home Office Country Assessments: An Analysis.* London: Research and Information Unit, Immigration Advisory Service.

Chanock, Martin. 1998. *Law, Custom, and Social Order: The Colonial Experience in Malawi and Zambia.* Portsmouth, NH: Heinemann.

Chelidze, Khatiya, Nicole Sirotin, Margaret Fabiszak, Terri Edersheim, Alexandra Tatum, Taryn Clark, Luis Villegas, Patriss Wais Moradi, and Joanne Ahola. 2015. "Documenting Torture *Sequelae*: The Weill Cornell Model for Forensic Evaluation, Capacity Building, and Medical Education." In *Adjudicating Refugee and Asylum Status,* edited by B. N. Lawrance and G. B. Ruffer, 166–79. Cambridge: Cambridge University Press.

Clark, Roger S. 1981. "The International League for Human Rights and South West Africa, 1947–1957: The Human Rights NGO as Catalyst in the International Legal Process." *Human Rights Quarterly* 3 (4): 101–36.

Cohen, Juliet. 2001. "Questions of Credibility: Omissions, Discrepancies and Errors of Recall in the Testimony of Asylum Seekers." *International Journal of Refugee Law* 13 (3): 293–309.

Conroy, Melanie A. 2009. "Real Bias: How REAL ID's Credibility and Corroboration Requirements Impair Sexual Minority Asylum Applicants." *Berkeley Journal of Gender, Law & Justice* 24 (1): 1–56.

CREDO. 2013. *Hungarian Helsinki Committee, Credibility Assessment in Asylum Procedures—A Multidisciplinary Training Manual.* Vol. 1. Budapest.

Derrida, Jacques. 2001. *On Cosmopolitanism and Forgiveness.* New York: Routledge.

Dolnick, Sam. 2011. "Immigrants May Be Fed False Stories to Bolster Asylum Pleas." *New York Times,* July 11.

Dornell, Lisa. 2015. "Afterword." In *Adjudicating Refugee and Asylum Status,* edited by B. N. Lawrance and G. B. Ruffer, 245–52. Cambridge: Cambridge University Press.

Einhorn, Bruce, and S. Megan Berthold. 2015. "Reconstructing Babel: Bridging Cultural Dissonance between Asylum Seekers and Adjudicators." In *Adjudicating Asylum and Refugee Status,* edited by B. N. Lawrance and G. B. Ruffer, 27–53. Cambridge: Cambridge University Press.

Fassin, Didier. 2010. "Heart of Humaneness: The Moral Economy of Humanitarian Intervention." In *Contemporary States of Emergency: The Politics of Military and Humanitarian Interventions,* edited by Didier Fassin and Mariella Pandolfi, 269–93. New York: Zone Books.

———. 2012. *Humanitarian Reason: A Moral History of the Present*. Berkeley: University of California Press.

Fassin, Didier, and Estelle D'Halluin. 2005. "The Truth from the Body: Medical Certificates as Ultimate Evidence for Asylum Seekers." *American Anthropologist* 107 (4): 597–608.

Fassin, Didier, Allain Morice, and Catherine Quiminal. 1997. *Les lois de l'hospitalité: Les politiques de l'immigration à l'épreuve des sans-papiers*. Paris: La Découverte.

Galloni, Tania. 2008. "Keeping It Real: Judicial Review of Asylum Credibility Determinations in the Eleventh Circuit after the REAL ID Act." *University of Miami Law Review* 62 (4): 1037–62.

Gangsei, David, and Ana Deutsch. 2007. "Psychological Evaluation of Asylum Seekers as a Therapeutic Process." *Torture* 17 (2): 79–87.

Gibney, Matthew J. 2004. *The Ethics and Politics of Asylum: Liberal Democracy and the Response to Refugees*. Cambridge: Cambridge University Press.

Gladstone, Rick. 2012. "Asylum Claims Rose 20 Percent Last Year, UN Refugee Agency Says." *New York Times,* March 21.

Good, Anthony. 2004a. "Expert Evidence in Asylum and Human Rights Appeals: An Expert's View." *International Journal of Refugee Law* 16 (3): 358–80.

———. 2004b. "Undoubtedly an Expert? Anthropologists in British Asylum Courts." *Journal of the Royal Anthropological Institute* 10 (1): 113–33.

———. 2007. *Anthropology and Expertise in the Asylum Courts*. London: Routledge.

———. 2008. "Cultural Evidence in Courts of Law." *Journal of the Royal Anthropological Institute* 14 (April): S47–S60.

———. 2015. "Anthropological Evidence and Country of Origin Information in British Asylum Courts." In *Adjudicating Refugee and Asylum Status*, edited by B. N. Lawrance and G. B. Ruffer, 122–44. Cambridge: Cambridge University Press.

Good, Anthony, and Tobias Kelly. 2013. *Expert Country Evidence in Asylum and Immigration Cases in the United Kingdom*. School of Social and Political Science, University of Edinburgh.

Goodwin-Gill, Guy S. 1999. "Refugee Identity and Protection's Fading Prospect." In *Refugee Rights and Realities: Evolving International Concepts and Regimes,* edited by Frances Nicholson and Patrick Twomey, 220–49. Cambridge: Cambridge University Press.

Holmes, Jennifer S., and Linda Camp Keith. 2010. "Does the Fear of Terrorists Trump the Fear of Persecution in Asylum Outcomes in the Post-September 11 Era?" *PS: Political Science & Politics* 43 (3): 431–46.

Hyndman, Jennifer, and Wenona Giles. 2011. "Waiting for What? The Feminization of Asylum in Protracted Situations." *Gender, Place and Culture* 18 (3): 361–79.

Ifekwunigwe, Jayne O. 2006. "An Inhospitable Port in the Storm: Recent Clandestine West African Migrants and the Quest for Diasporic Recognition." In *The Situated Politics of Belonging,* edited by N. Yuval-Davis, K. Kannibiran, and U. Vieten, 84–99. London: Sage and International Sociological Association.

Immigration and Nationality Act (INA). 1980. 8 U.S.C.

Jeppie, Shamil, Ebrahim Moosa, and Richard L. Roberts. 2010. *Muslim Family Law in Sub-Saharan Africa: Colonial Legacies and Post-colonial Challenges*. Amsterdam: Amsterdam University Press.

Kagan, Michael. 2006. "The Beleaguered Gatekeeper: Protection Challenges Posed by U.N.H.C.R. Refugee Status Determination." *International Journal of Refugee Law* 18 (1): 1–29.

Kam, Noé Mahop. 2015. "Recovering the Sociological Identity of Asylum Seekers: Language Analysis for Determining National Origin in the European Union." In *Adjudicating Refugee and Asylum Status,* edited by B. N. Lawrance and G. B. Ruffer, 54–83. Cambridge: Cambridge University Press.

Keast, Rachel. 2005. "Using Experts for Asylum Cases in Immigration Court." *Interpreter Releases: Report and Analysis of Immigration and Nationality Law* 82 (30) (August 1), 1–6.

Kelly, Tobias. 2011. *This Side of Silence: Human Rights, Torture, and the Recognition of Cruelty.* Philadelphia: University of Pennsylvania Press.

Kriger, Norma. 2011. "Understanding Asylum Outcomes for Zimbabweans: Comparing the United States and South Africa." *African Arguments,* June 27. http://africanarguments.org/2011/06/27/understanding-asylum-outcomes -for-zimbabweans-in-the-united-states-and-south-africa/.

Latour, Bruno. 2010. *The Making of Law: An Ethnography of the Conseil d'État.* Cambridge: Polity Press.

Lawrance, Benjamin N. 2013. "Humanitarian Claims and Expert Testimonies: Contestation over Health Care for Ghanaian Migrants in the United Kingdom." *Ghana Studies* 15–16 (special double issue on "Health and Health Care"): 251–86.

———. 2015. "'Health Tourism' or 'Atrocious Barbarism'? Contextualizing Migrant Agency, Expertise, and Medical Humanitarian Practice." In *Adjudicating Refugee and Asylum Status,* edited by B. N. Lawrance and G. B. Ruffer, 221-244. Cambridge: Cambridge University Press.

———. Forthcoming a. "De Jure? De Facto? Denied, Deported: State-Effected Statelessness." In *Citizenship-in-Question: Evidentiary Encounters with Blood, Birthright, and Bureaucracy,* edited by Benjamin N. Lawrance and Jacqueline Stevens. Philadelphia: University of Pennsylvania Press.

———. Forthcoming b. "Historicizing as a Legal Trope in Asylum Narratives and Expert Testimonies of Gender-Based Violence." In *Transcending Traditional Tropes: Culture and Conflict in Upper Guinea,* edited by Jacqueline Knörr and Christian Kordt Højbjerg. Palgrave.

Lawrance, Benjamin N., Emily L. Osborn, and Richard L. Roberts, eds. 2006. *Intermediaries, Interpreters and Clerks: African Employees and the Making of Colonial Africa.* Madison: University of Wisconsin Press.

Lawrance, Benjamin N., and Galya Ruffer, eds. 2015a. *Adjudicating Refugee and Asylum Status: The Role of Witness, Expertise, and Testimony.* Cambridge: Cambridge University Press.

———. 2015b. "Witness to the Persecution? Deciphering the Dialectic of Expert Testimony and Asylum Adjudication." In *Adjudicating Refugee and Asylum Status,* edited by B. N. Lawrance and G. B. Ruffer, 1–24. Cambridge: Cambridge University Press.

Li, Monica, and Jeanne Batalova. 2011. "Refugees and Asylees in the United States." Migration Information Source. August. Accessed September 16, 2014. www .migrationinformation.org.

Lyotard, Jean-François. 1983. *Le Différend.* Paris: Éditions de Minuit.

———. 1988. *The Differend: Phrases in Dispute.* Translated by Georges Van Den Abbeele. Minneapolis: University of Minnesota Press.

Mahmood, Cynthia K. 1996. "Asylum, Violence, and the Limits of Advocacy." *Human Organization* 55 (4): 493–98

Malphrus, Garry. 2010. "Expert Witnesses in Immigration Proceedings." *Immigration Law Advisor* 4 (5): 1–14.

Mamdani, Mahmood. 1996. *Citizen and Subject: Contemporary Africa and the Legacy of Late Colonialism.* Princeton, NJ: Princeton University Press.

———. 2010. *Saviors and Survivors: Darfur, Politics, and the War on Terror.* New York: Random House.

Mann, Kristin, and Richard Roberts. 1991. *Law in Colonial Africa.* Portsmouth, NH: Heinemann Educational Books.

Marton, Miriam. 2014. "Beyond Expert Witnessing: Interdisciplinary Practice in Representing Rape Survivors in Asylum Cases." In *Adjudicating Refugee and Asylum Status,* edited by B. N. Lawrance and G. B. Ruffer, 102–21. Cambridge: Cambridge University Press.

Massaquoi, Notisha. 2013. "No Place Like Home: African Refugees and the Emergence of a New Queer Frame of Reference." In *Sexual Diversity in Africa: Politics, Theory, and Citizenship*, edited by S. N. Nyeck and Marc Epprecht, 37–53. Montreal, Canada: McGill-Queen's University Press.

Millbank, Jenni. 2009. "'The Ring of Truth': A Case Study of Credibility Assessment in Particular Social Group Refugee Determinations." *International Journal of Refugee Law* 21 (1): 1–30.

Moore, Sally Falk. 1986. *Social Facts and Fabrications: "Customary" Law on Kilimanjaro, 1880–1980.* Cambridge: Cambridge University Press.

Morgan, Deborah A. 2006. "Not Gay Enough for the Government: Racial and Sexual Stereotypes in Sexual Orientation Asylum Cases." *Tulane Journal of Law and Sexuality* 15:135–61.

Murray, Craig. 2011. "Diallo Must Be Deported." August 23. Accessed March 1, 2012. http://www.craigmurray.org.uk/archives/2011/08/diallo-must-be-deported/.

Neilson, Victoria. 2004. "Uncharted Territory: Choosing an Effective Approach in Transgender-Based Asylum Claims." *Fordham Urban Law Journal* 32 (2): 101–24.

Norman, S. 2007. "Assessing the Credibility of Refugee Applicants: A Judicial Perspective." *International Journal of Refugee Law* 19 (2): 273–92.

Ortiz, Sister Dianna. 2001. "The Survivors' Perspective: Voices from the Center." In *The Mental Health Consequences of Torture,* edited by Ellen Gerrity, Terrence M. Keane, and Farris Tuma, 13–35. New York: Kluwer Academic/Plenum Publishers.

Piot, Charles. 2007. "Representing Africa in the Kasinga Asylum Case." In *Transcultural Bodies: Female Genital Cutting in Global Context,* edited by Ylva Hernlund and Bettina Shell-Duncan, 224–33. New Brunswick, NJ: Rutgers University Press.

Ramji-Nogales, Jaya, Andrew Schoenholtz, and Philip G. Schrag. 2007. "Refugee
    Roulette: Disparities in Asylum Adjudication." *Stanford Law Review* 60 (2): 295–412.
Rehaag, Sean. 2008. "Patrolling the Borders of Sexual Orientation: Bisexual Refugee
    Claims in Canada." *McGill Law Journal* 53 (1): 59–102.
———. 2009. "Bisexuals Need Not Apply: A Comparative Appraisal of Refugee Law
    and Policy in Canada, the United States, and Australia." *International Journal of
    Human Rights* 13 (2): 415–36.
———. 2011. "The Role of Counsel in Canada's Refugee Determination System: An
    Empirical Assessment." *Osgoode Hall Law Journal* 49 (1): 71–116.
Roberts, Richard L. 2005. *Litigants and Households: African Disputes and Colonial Courts in
    the French Soudan, 1895–1912*. New York: Praeger.
Rosen, Lawrence. 1977. "The Anthropologist as Expert Witness." *American
    Anthropologist* 79 (3): 555–78.
Rottman, Andy J., Christopher J. Fariss, and Steven C. Poe. 2009. "The Path to
    Asylum in the U.S. and the Determinants for Who Gets In and Why." *International
    Migration Review* 43 (1): 3–34.
Schaffer, Kay, and Sidonie Smith. 2004. *Human Rights and Narrated Lives: The Ethics of
    Recognition*. New York: Palgrave Macmillan.
Scheel, Stephan, and Vicki Squire. 2014. "Forced Migrants as 'Illegal' Migrants." In *The
    Oxford Handbook of Refugee and Forced Migration Studies*, edited by Elena Fiddian-
    Qasmiyeh, Gil Loescher, Kathy Long, and Nando Sigona, 188–99. Oxford:
    Oxford University Press.
Schoenholtz, Andrew I., and Hamutal Bernstein. 2008. "Improving Immigration
    Adjudications through Competent Counsel." *Georgetown Journal of Legal Ethics* 21
    (1): 55–60.
Seelinger, Kim Thuy. 2010. "Forced Marriage and Asylum: Perceiving the Invisible
    Harm." *Columbia Human Rights Law Review* 42 (1): 55–117.
Shemak, April Ann. 2011. *Asylum Speakers: Caribbean Refugees and Testimonial Discourse*.
    New York: Fordham University Press.
Shuman, Amy, and Carol Bohmer. 2004. "Representing Trauma: Political Asylum
    Narrative." *Journal of American Folklore* 117 (466): 394–414.
Smith, Hawthorne, Stuart L. Lustig, and David Gangsei. 2014. "Incredible until
    Proven Credible: Mental Health Expert Testimony and the Systemic and Cultural
    Challenges Facing Asylum Applicants." In *Adjudicating Refugee and Asylum Status*,
    edited by B. N. Lawrance and G. B. Ruffer, 180–201. Cambridge: Cambridge
    University Press.
Speed, Shannon. 2006. "At the Crossroads of Human Rights and Anthropology:
    Towards a Critically-Engaged Activist Research." *American Anthropologist* 108 (1):
    66–76.
Spijkerboer, Thomas, ed. 2013. *Fleeing Homophobia: Sexual Orientation, Gender Identity
    and Asylum*. New York: Routledge.
Squire, Vicki. 2009. *The Exclusionary Politics of Asylum*. Basingstoke: Palgrave Macmillan.
Stevens, Dallal. 2010. "Asylum Seekers and the Right to Access Health Care." *Northern
    Ireland Legal Quarterly* 61 (4): 363–90.

Sweeney, James A. 2009. "Credibility, Proof and Refugee Law." *International Journal of Refugee Law* 21 (4): 700–726.

Terretta, Meredith. 2012. "'We Had Been Fooled into Thinking That the UN Watches over the Entire World': Human Rights UN Trust Territories, and Africa's Decolonization." *Human Rights Quarterly* 34 (2): 329–60.

Thomas, Robert. 2006. "Assessing the Credibility of Asylum Claims: EU and UK Approaches Examined." *European Journal of Migration and Law* 8: 79–96.

UN High Commissioner for Refugees (UNHCR). 2009. Press release. June 16.

———. 2010. *UNHCR Statistical Yearbook 2010,* 10th ed. Accessed August 23, 2012. http://www.unhcr.org/4ef9cc9c9.html.

———. 2011a. "A Year of Crises: 2011 Global Trends." Accessed November 1, 2012. http://www.unhcr.org/4fd6f87f9.pdf.

———. 2011b. "2011 Refugee Statistics: Full Data." *Guardian,* June 20.

———. 2012. "Global Trends." Accessed February 28, 2014. http://unhcr.org/globaltrendsjune2013/UNHCR%20GLOBAL%20TRENDS%202012_V05.pdf.

———. 2013. "Beyond Proof: Credibility Assessment in EU Asylum Systems." May 2013.

Verdirame, Guglielmo, and Barbara Harrell-Bond. 2005. *Rights in Exile: Janus-Faced Humanitarianism.* New York: Berghahn Books.

Wallace, Rebecca M. M., and Karen Wylie. 2014. "The Reception of Expert Medical Evidence in Refugee Status Determination." *International Journal of Refugee Law* 25 (4): 749–67.

Wasem, Ruth Ellen. 2011. "Asylum and 'Credible Fear' Issues in U.S. Immigration Policy." *Congressional Research Services.* June 29.

# ONE

## Before Asylum and the Expert Witness

*Mozambican Refugee Settlement and Rural Development in Southern Tanzania, 1964–75*

Joanna T. Tague

ON A WINTER day in December 1968, Peter Weiss, president of the American Committee on Africa (hereafter referred to as ACOA), sat in his office in New York City opening his mail. In it, he found a letter from George Houser, the organization's executive director, who had been traveling throughout East Africa for the past several weeks. Struck by the magnitude of the refugee problem in the region, as well as the inability of the international community to provide sufficient assistance, Houser emphasized to Weiss the importance of an organization such as theirs:

> We all know well enough technically what it means to be a
> refugee; to have no home and no country, perhaps no passport
> and no travel documents and so no freedom to travel anywhere, to
> have no money and no possessions and to be unable, as a foreigner,
> to get a job; to have a last desperate hope of a scholarship and
> to find that funds have run out; or to lack the qualifications,
> and never even have had the hope. Being in Africa turns these
> depressing facts into life—into people who look to us when other
> hope is gone. . . . The U.N. never has sufficient funds and just now
> it has none at all. . . . They need our help. It is always useful to
> come to Africa and to see again for oneself what our work is all

about. And it is here that one realizes with particular urgency the need for an organization like ours in the United States—not only to help refugees but to tell, back home, as loudly as we can, the story of why they are refugees. (ACOA, file 55)

George Houser wrote this letter while he was in Tanzania, a newly independent African state.[1] Because Tanzania's nationalist government supported African liberation movements in their quests to end colonial rule throughout the continent, a plethora of liberation groups had established their headquarters in the capital of Tanzania, Dar es Salaam. Subsequently, refugees followed their respective liberation groups to the capital en masse. According to Ann McDougall (in this volume), countries that produce refugees also produce metanarratives regarding their particular refugee crises. The same can be said of host countries. At the time of Houser's visit, refugees from Rwanda, Burundi, Uganda, Kenya, Congo, Sudan, South Africa, Southern Rhodesia, and Mozambique were pouring into Tanzania. This influx generated for Tanzania a metanarrative—which soon circulated throughout the African continent—that celebrated the ability of the young nation to host African liberation groups and assist their refugee populations. In many ways, it fell to the Tanzanian state to support these refugees, as Houser's letter testifies to a UN High Commissioner for Refugees (UNHCR) inundated by these soaring refugee populations. But Houser was an activist, and, typical of the spirit characterizing international humanitarianism in the 1960s, he suggested to Weiss that if UNHCR proved incapable of assisting refugees in Tanzania, then perhaps ACOA could draw the attention of the American public to the needs of these refugees and thereby advocate on their behalf.

Unfortunately, in the 1960s the American public did not have a particularly strong knowledge base pertaining to the African continent. According to Houser (1976, 16), American knowledge about—and interest in—Africa was "something of a joke" at that time. Politically, diplomatic relations between Africa and the US State Department were a relatively new endeavor, with the Bureau on African Affairs having just been established in 1958. In terms of business and finance, exceedingly few American companies had any interest on the continent. Even in the realm of education, most American colleges and universities did not provide courses pertaining to Africa. For these reasons, ACOA came into being in 1953 as a group of people who had "virtually no experience on the African scene"

(Houser 1976, 17). Because ACOA originated in a climate where American expertise on and experience in Africa was scant, throughout the 1960s and 1970s the organization would come to fill a critical role in advocating for and assisting in the settlement of African refugees.

In the 1960s, there were two main ways that humanitarian organizations could assist African refugees: by raising visibility through international advocacy or by assisting in the settlement of refugees in host countries. Since then, however, significant changes have emerged in international refugee law and status. Each year, an estimated three hundred thousand people worldwide apply for political asylum, typically to North America or Western Europe (Hatton 2011, 15).[2] Many of these applicants originate from Africa, and yet international refugee law has historically applied to Africans for less time than it has for, say, European refugee populations. Indeed, throughout the 1960s Africans fell outside the definition and jurisdiction of international refugee law.

The hallmark piece of legislation in international refugee law is the 1951 UN Convention Relating to the Status of Refugees. Devised in a post–World War II climate, it originally conferred refugee status to persons displaced prior to January 1951. It also granted signatories of the convention the possibility of allowing only refugees displaced in Europe to enter their countries (see Musalo in this volume). According to Timothy J. Hatton, two issues kept the international community from assisting African refugee populations spawned during colonial wars for independence. First, industrialized nations proved reluctant to aid refugees because the anticolonial wars that led to their displacement involved European powers. Second, refugee populations outside Europe were "not covered by the Convention" (Hatton 2011, 11). The 1967 UN Protocol Relating to the Status of Refugees, however, significantly expanded the parameters of refugee status to include those displaced after 1951, as well as those displaced beyond Europe.[3] This, of course, raises critical concerns regarding the changing historical legal definition of *refugee* (see Musalo in this volume). For all of these reasons, peoples displaced not only in Africa but also throughout Latin America, Asia, and the Middle East prior to the 1967 UN protocol occupy a unique place in the history of international humanitarianism and refugee settlement.

As the first chapter in a volume that examines the role of the expert in African asylum jurisprudence, this essay investigates the ways in which a range of actors assisted African refugees before Africans were able to apply for asylum abroad. It is based on the premise that in order to understand the history and nuances of African asylum jurisprudence, we must first understand the ways in which African refugees navigated their circumstances before asylum was an option. To do so, this chapter relies on the case study of Mozambique, where, during the war for independence from Portugal (1964–75), two groups of Mozambicans fled to Tanzania: members of an educated urban minority, who settled in Dar es Salaam, and the vast majority of all fleeing Mozambicans, who settled in five refugee settlements throughout southern Tanzania. Both groups looked to small, young humanitarian organizations that lacked concrete experience in (and thus expertise on) Africa for advocacy and assistance.

Colonialism itself allowed European powers (especially France and the United Kingdom) to create bodies of knowledge about Africa, but the same cannot be said of the United States, where such expertise on Africa was rare. Many scholars have examined the creation of colonial knowledge on Africa, but what of the origins of such expertise in the United States? Because so many of the chapters in this volume address North American asylum cases, this essay explores the emergence of expert knowledge in the United States in particular. It suggests that small, humanitarian organizations (such as ACOA) would become leading American experts on the African continent. And yet the approaches of humanitarian organizations toward these two groups of Mozambican refugees in Tanzania differed in fundamental and dramatic ways.

I will argue that not all refugee populations share similar opportunities, as the situation in Mozambique illustrated. Despite the inability of Africans to petition for asylum abroad in the 1960s, international humanitarians helped an educated minority of Mozambican refugees leave Africa to secure their education abroad; the vast majority of Mozambican refugees, however, resided in official Tanzanian settlements, where they contributed to national, rural development projects. This chapter reifies a critical theme discussed within the introduction of this volume: that throughout the 1960s and 1970s—as now—there was a clear distinction between the few who were able to leave Africa and the many who could not. As the volume editors write in their introduction, historically, asylum has been possible for "those who can achieve it," whereas "such options are rarely if ever available for the masses."

To demonstrate this overarching argument, I will first examine discourses surrounding the mythology of international humanitarianism. I do this to complicate our understandings of the history of humanitarian intervention in Africa. One myth, for instance, suggests that humanitarian organizations remain unbiased and impartial during their involvement in crises (Barnett 2011). But in the 1960s, humanitarian organizations collaborated with Mozambican liberation leaders as well as the Tanzanian state in order to aid Mozambican refugees. Does the fact that these early humanitarians worked with the nation-state undermine their humanitarian ethos? Next, I will compare the various ways in which humanitarian organizations assisted Mozambican refugees in Tanzania in the 1960s and 1970s. I will examine how ACOA helped those Mozambican refugees living in Dar es Salaam—a population that consisted of an educated minority, many of whom would receive scholarships to study abroad. The experiences of this population stand in stark contrast to those of the vast majority of Mozambican refugees, who resided in official settlements throughout southern Tanzania. There, the Tanzanian government collaborated with another nascent organization, the Tanganyikan Christian Refugee Service (TCRS), to harness Mozambican refugee labor for Tanzanian rural development projects. I will then conclude by discussing the ways in which Mozambican refugees attained "asylum" prior to their legal ability to do so and by asking why some refugee populations contribute to host country development more than others.

## International Humanitarianism, Development, and the Expert

In the era of decolonization, organizations such as ACOA and TCRS filled a critical niche on the African continent. UNHCR had only begun working in sub-Saharan Africa in the early 1960s, and though it was active in some spaces, it was not yet the continent's dominant refugee relief organization. For that reason, the settlement of refugees and the maintenance of refugee settlements fell to small, nascent humanitarian organizations. Today, of course, this is no longer the case. At the head of what has come to be known as the international refugee regime, UNHCR is the world's leading refugee relief agency, facilitating a complex web of relationships between host governments, international relief organizations, nongovernmental organizations, private aid organizations, religious bodies, individual donors, and volunteers in the quest to assist the displaced (Keely 2001; Loescher 1993, 2001).

The international refugee regime, however, is currently in a state of crisis. The crisis stems from the powerful resilience of three myths pertaining to the nature of humanitarianism in general and refugee assistance in particular. According to Michael Barnett, these myths include the notions that humanitarian intervention is impartial, neutral, and independent: impartial in that humanitarianism aims to provide aid to people in need and does not refuse help under any circumstance; neutral in that humanitarian intervention must not favor any one side during conflict; and independent because humanitarians provide assistance to those in conflict zones and therefore must be apolitical or divorced from the agenda of the nation-state (Barnett 2011, 2). In effect, though, and as Barnett argues, no humanitarian aid agencies operate purely along these lines, and so, these myths surrounding the essence of humanitarianism merely serve to confuse our understanding of the motivations behind humanitarian intervention.

Since the 1990s, the central debate in the international humanitarian community has been about whether it is appropriate that relief aid groups no longer simply provide temporary, lifesaving relief. According to David Rieff (2002, 306), more often than not humanitarian agencies now stay long after a conflict to work on postconflict resolution, democracy building, peacekeeping, and rural development—roles that ultimately make humanitarianism a more "holistic" endeavor. Problematically, the expansion of humanitarian groups into these newfound territories requires collaboration with the state, and such collaboration shatters the myth that humanitarianism is fundamentally impartial or apolitical. Thus, the current crisis in the humanitarian community is that humanitarianism is losing its supposedly defining characteristics; in collaborating with the state, it has made a Faustian bargain (Barnett 2011, 5). As both Rieff and Barnett contend, though, we need to question whether these characteristics ever really defined humanitarianism.

Another feature of modern humanitarianism is the long-standing tendency—on the part of both the humanitarian community as well as host states—to label refugees as problems. Peter Gatrell (2011) and Peter Nyers (2006) have sought to understand how and by whom the figure of the refugee has come to be conceptualized solely as a burden. Historically, there has been a tendency, from the perspective of the host country and also of the humanitarian agency, to conceptualize refugees as drains—as populations that absorb food, water, resources, housing, jobs, and land while giving nothing in return. The counterargument to the refugee-as-burden claim, of course, is that refugees arrive in their host countries with a vast arsenal of skills, knowledge, connections, and resources that they can then harness to the benefit, rather than the detriment, of their hosts. This idea has been elaborated by Shelly Dick (2002) and Karen Jacobsen (2002).

The case study of Mozambican refugees in Tanzania in the 1960s and 1970s merges these debates to examine the ways in which the postcolonial African state viewed refugees not as problems to be solved but as development opportunities to be exploited. Specifically, it addresses the ways in which the Tanzanian state worked with small, nascent relief agencies such as ACOA and TCRS to settle the nearly one hundred thousand Mozambican refugees =who entered the country between 1964 and 1975. Because UNHCR was drawn increasingly to the Great Lakes region during this period, it fell largely to ACOA and TCRS to help the Tanzanian state settle incoming refugees. There is no doubting that these were both humanitarian aid agencies, and yet the fact that they were politically involved agencies did not, at the time, detract from their humanitarian essence.

The conceptualization of refugees as participants in development projects forces us to reexamine the history of development in Africa more broadly. The very concept of "development" stems from colonial endeavors to increase African labor and productivity in order to stimulate European economies in a post–World War II world. Colonial powers rushed an array of bureaucrats, development experts, and planning officials to Africa to "refashion the way farmers farmed and workers worked, to restructure health and education" (Cooper 1998, 64). Timothy Mitchell (2002), Monica Van Beusekom (2002), Joanna Lewis (2000), and Arturo Escobar (1995) have similarly examined colonial development projects and the role of the colonial "expert" in formulating development policy. What has received less attention is the nature of the development projects undertaken by independent African nationalist governments in their immediate postcolonial years. We must keep in mind that the sorts of development projects that independent African states tackled were quite different from those of the colonial era. In the case of Tanzania, rural development took precedence, and refugees were active participants.

As noted earlier, two distinct, fundamentally different groups characterized the Mozambican refugees who fled to Tanzania in the 1960s and 1970s. On the one hand, a minority of relatively better-educated refugees settled in Tanzania's capital, Dar es Salaam. On the other hand, the vast majority—tens of thousands—of Mozambican refugees settled in Tanzania's rural south. By comparing the ways in which the postcolonial Tanzanian state looked to organizations such as ACOA and TCRS to settle both urban and rural refugee populations, two points will be made. First, refugee settlement in Africa in the 1960s was anything but impartial, neutral, or independent: refugee relief agencies openly collaborated with either African liberation leaders or the African state to settle and assist refugees in ways that provided a maximum benefit to the host state. Second, there was no international legal process whereby African refugees could apply for asylum abroad, yet some urban-settled Mozambican refugees ultimately left Africa to pursue educational opportunities abroad; therefore, we can conceptualize an alternative mode of asylum during decolonization, one that enabled some Africans to step beyond the bounds of the limited international asylum process. Nonetheless, the priority of the newly independent Tanzanian state was to settle refugees in specifically rural areas, where they would create settlements and contribute to local rural development. In this way, Tanzania, as a host state, conceived of refugees not as problems to be solved but as opportunities to be exploited. Consequently, as participants in rural development, African host states had a motivating interest to keep refugees on the continent.

## Humanitarian Assistance, Education, and Liberation

Mozambique's war for independence began in September 1964, when the Mozambican Liberation Front (FRELIMO) initiated a guerrilla struggle against the Portuguese. Because the Portuguese government had banned FRELIMO from Mozambique prior to the beginning of the war, the liberation movement was unable to organize an effective resistance at home. FRELIMO leaders therefore established their liberation movement's headquarters in Dar es Salaam. Hundreds of Mozambicans followed. The leaders of FRELIMO began corresponding with ACOA, which soon emerged as the main international advocate for Mozambican refugees in Tanzania's capital. To bring visibility to and raise awareness of the liberation struggle, the agency organized speaking tours for Mozambican leaders in the United States. But in Tanzania, ACOA's focus was the education of Mozambican refugees in Dar es Salaam—specifically, securing scholarships for the refugees.

ACOA did not perceive the provision of such scholarships, however, as a way to avoid participation in the liberation struggle. For example, in July 1963, Paul Bayeke, deputy information secretary for FRELIMO, wrote to George Houser, "We have no money in our party . . . help me to get some food and fare from Dar es Salaam to America. Will you please find a scholarship for me?" (ACOA, file 39). ACOA regularly received such requests from Mozambican refugees who believed that the agency could help them secure education abroad. But the fact that the deputy information secretary for Mozambique's liberation movement was already seeking ways to leave the front, to obtain a scholarship so that he could move to the United States, did not bode well for the future of the liberation struggle. Houser waited a full two months before he responded to Bayeke's request: "Our main work is with the refugees. I don't know that we are in a position to do very much to assist you" (ACOA, file 39).

The correspondence between Houser and Bayeke reflects a larger problem that most African liberation movements faced: many liberation soldiers would rather have obtained a scholarship abroad so that they did not have to be a part of the independence struggle. FRELIMO leadership was well aware of this. In January 1964, Eduardo Mondlane, president of FRELIMO, wrote Houser, "Some of our best young men prefer to be students [rather] than political workers" (ACOA, file 40). Mondlane's words point to a crucial dilemma that confronted African liberation leaders during their wars for independence: liberation movements needed to educate the individuals who would soon be citizens. African leaders had to ensure that at independence, there would be people capable of running the government; managing the banks; and fulfilling positions as teachers, engineers, and scientists. A fundamental conflict inherent in this goal, though, meant that during the war for liberation, those people who would be trained as future specialists could not be soldiers. Conversely, liberation soldiers had to be exempt from educational opportunities; from the perspective of the liberation movement, they had a war to fight. Education could not compromise liberation.

The correspondence between Houser and Mondlane also reveals the mutual interests of humanitarian actors and liberation leaders. Both sought to keep refugees on the African continent. If refugees went abroad, it was to pursue an education that would benefit a future, independent Mozambique. Neither humanitarians nor liberation leaders entertained refugee requests for absolute removal from the continent. In this way, the educational opportunities that ACOA offered were soon directed toward those Mozambican refugees living in Dar es Salaam who were not soldiers and who had already had some exposure to formal education prior to their flight. These refugees were typically students who, while living in Portuguese-ruled Mozambique, came from relatively wealthier households and had received some measure of (mainly missionary) schooling. Because only those students who had obtained a significant level of education before arriving in Dar es Salaam could pursue their education as refugees, only the most qualified refugees could become students. With assistance from ACOA, the leaders of FRELIMO established a school for refugees in Dar es Salaam. The students who attended the school, known as the Mozambique Institute, viewed it as a "kind of academic waiting room" where they could pass the time while their liberation leaders worked to secure scholarships for them abroad (Eldridge, FO 317/176933). By the end of 1964, the institute had a total enrollment of 250 students, all eagerly awaiting scholarships that would enable them to leave Africa and study abroad.

From the students' perspective, a significant difficulty that they encountered at the institute was teacher expectations. Teachers and staff expected that the students were pursuing their education so that after Mozambique achieved independence, they would be the ones chosen to fill positions in the new government; they would be the teachers, the lawyers, the engineers, and the bankers. Two American teachers at the institute, Ruth and Bill Minter, recalled students had to be reminded that their academic performance was a "measure of their dedication to the movement for liberation" (Register of the US National Student Association 1966–67). Given the inadequacy of education in Portuguese-ruled Mozambique, many students were overwhelmed by such expectations. They nonetheless recognized that if they could not be soldiers, then academic success was a direct expression of their dedication to the struggle for independence. Did this not mean that receiving a scholarship abroad—especially to the United States—would demonstrate ultimate devotion? In this way, FRELIMO leadership, Mozambican refugees, and ACOA came to see the institute as the educational front for the liberation movement or, as one individual put it, a "front for the Front" (Wright 1975, 1). By the end of 1965, nearly 150 of the most educated Mozambicans were studying abroad. Indeed, throughout the 1960s the future leaders of what would become an independent Mozambique—Arcanjo Faustino, Antonio Palange, Luis Mascoroa, Joao Mungwambe, Joao Ungai, and Joaquim Chissano (future president of Mozambique, 1986–2005)—all left Africa to pursue their education abroad (ACOA, file 44).

While in the "academic waiting room," Mozambican refugee students at the institute participated in a wide range of activities. There were football teams and volleyball competitions, as well as musical groups in which students played guitars, drums, and pennywhistles. Every Saturday evening, the institute screened films. There was an elected student government, which focused on effective leadership training and management of the school and dormitories. As Ruth Minter noted, Mozambican refugee students at the institute were "among the fortunate, with a sense of purpose—and concrete jobs to do, jobs that contribute to a movement" (Register of the US National Student Association 1966–67). The institute was, in effect, making a future elite. The institute had been carefully designed by an architect, and it was run through a board of trustees. The board selected students from among the hundreds of applications that it received—and the successful applicant was almost certain he or she would leave Africa to study abroad. In this way, the education of Mozambican refugees in Tanzania during the 1960s meant that the institute was "the only one of its kind on the African continent" (Gerhart 1964, 4). Educating refugees became a priority of ACOA in Tanzania's urban north; to some degree, its purpose was to privilege the already privileged.

This privileging of refugee students who attended the institute with prior exposure to formal education is thrown into sharp relief by the fact that the vast majority of Mozambican refugees who fled to Tanzania in the 1960s and 1970s neither settled in Dar es Salaam nor affiliated with the institute. Instead, to settle the tens of thousands of incoming refugees, the Tanzanian government collaborated with the Tanganyikan Christian Refugee Service to create five refugee settlements throughout southern Tanzania. In the urban north, the institute focused on the education of an elite minority in the making, but in rural southern Tanzania, refugee relief required and was based on the harnessing of refugee labor. Humanitarian agencies and the Tanzanian state relied on Mozambican labor to transform an otherwise undeveloped rural hinterland into a built environment with roads, bridges, water lines, health clinics, schools, and communal farms—all essential services that the newly independent Tanzania was finding difficult to provide for its own citizenry.

### Refugee Settlement and Rural Development

The fabric of daily refugee life unfolded very differently in the southern refugee settlements. If the institute in Dar es Salaam understood that being a refugee was a temporary state, embodied in the notion of the academic waiting room, the Tanzanian government and TCRS constructed Mozambican refugee settlements in southern Tanzania under the assumption that this particular population of refugees might very well become permanent residents. State rhetoric exemplified this vision. For example, on the afternoon of Wednesday, October 14, 1964, Tanzania's second vice president, Rashidi Kawawa, and the minister of external affairs, Oscar Kambona, addressed a crowd of more than four thousand Mozambican refugees who had recently crossed the Ruvuma River (the boundary between Tanzania and Mozambique) into southern Tanzania. The two leaders inspected the makeshift shelters that the refugees had erected at what would later become Rutamba Refugee Settlement, 80 miles north of the border with Mozambique. Kawawa informed the refugees: "We heartily welcome you to our country where you should feel at home. . . . We shall give you land to till and build your homes until such time when Mozambique is free and you will be at liberty to return to your motherland or remain in this country" (*Nationalist* 1964). Kawawa's words reflected his government's open-door refugee policy at the time. Land was plentiful in Tanzania, yet the population was small and scattered: if refugees could work the land, achieve self-sufficiency, and ultimately contribute to the national economy, they were free to stay and, eventually, become Tanzanian citizens.

As Mozambique's war with Portugal escalated throughout the 1960s, the five settlements built for Mozambican refugees (Rutamba, Muhukuru, Lundo, Mputa, and Matekwe) quickly filled. From the outset, TCRS anticipated that the creation of these settlements would dovetail with the long-term development politics of the Tanzanian state.[4] According to Brian Neldner, director of TCRS in 1964, "Any effort to assist refugees must be closely related to the agricultural, industrial, social, educational, and medical needs of the area in which refugees are located" (TCRS Annual Report 1964, 3). To meet this goal of simultaneously settling refugees while serving local communities, a central tenet of TCRS institutional policy advocated a model whereby refugee settlements would be built on land donated by the Tanzanian government, in "isolated areas with only the most primitive access roads . . . [so that a] whole new agricultural community will be created" (TCRS Annual Report 1964, 9, 12).

Such language reflected a fascinating semantic shift. Throughout their annual reports and official documents, both TCRS and the Tanzanian government no longer referred to the members of these new communities simply as refugees: now they were "settlers" (TCRS Annual Reports 1967, 1971, 1972, 1975).[5] As such, they lived in settlements, not refugee camps. This stands in stark contrast to the spaces created for refugees in the twenty-first century, where convention dictates that the international refugee regime, with UNHCR at the helm, must settle refugees specifically in camps—in temporary spaces that they will ultimately leave. When did the international humanitarian community no longer envision refugees as permanent residents who worked within the settlements they built? When did refugees start being seen as transient, short-term visitors? Future research needs to investigate the nuances behind this transformation.

In the case of Tanzania, part of the answer to these questions may lie at the intersection of history and geography. By the 1950s, southern Tanzania was already a region with a long history of developmental neglect. Whereas the British had invested in Tanzania's relatively more urban north, they did not pursue the same level of economic development in the rural south. This was largely due to the fact that the region was mineral poor and, at the same time, not agriculturally diverse. As a result, at independence in 1961 the region was sparsely populated. There were no major cities, aside from the larger towns of Songea in the west and Mtwara in the east. Between these two cities, along the 400-mile border with Mozambique, Tanzanian citizens lived in scattered homesteads in a vast swath of territory that for the most part lacked roads, bridges, and access to safe and reliable sources of drinking water. It was not uncommon for citizens living in southern Tanzania to walk two or three days in order to visit health clinics or primary schools.

In such sparsely populated, remote spaces, the labor that went into constructing Mozambican refugee settlements significantly altered the Tanzanian landscape.[6] Between 1964 and 1975, Mozambican refugees constructed hundreds of miles of roads throughout southern Tanzania, transforming dirt roads that were impassable during the rainy season to roads that were passable year-round. They also built dozens of concrete bridges to replace wooden or rope bridges (TCRS Annual Report 1972). At the five settlements, refugees dug dozens of wells and erected over twenty water towers. Before TCRS could establish health clinics at each settlement, the agency needed to ensure access to a reliable, clean source of water. For that reason, once refugee labor constructed wells and water towers at each settlement, the construction of health clinics quickly followed. Each of the five settlements also had multiple health clinics; an average of one in four of the patients who sought treatment at these clinics were Tanzanian citizens. Finally, Mozambican refugee labor built dozens of schools throughout the region. Depending on the location of the settlement, anywhere from one in three to one in seven students at these refugee schools were Tanzanian citizens (TCRS Annual Reports 1967, 1971, 1972, 1975).

TCRS managed each of these settlements. Members of the aid agency recognized that refugee settlement could and should foster rural development within the newly independent African state. With regard to Rutamba Settlement, one TCRS staff member celebrated the fact that what was "once an isolated, sparsely populated plateau and seldom visited, is now an established community, made up not only of refugees, but also including a group of farmers . . . and local villagers . . . who have been drawn to the settlement area through the refugee projects" (TCRS Annual Report 1971, 2). Thus, the settlement model of refugee assistance enabled both Mozambican refugees and Tanzanian citizens to access essential services—roads, bridges, primary schools, health clinics, water supplies, and communal farms—many for the first time ever.

In 1975, Mozambique's war for independence from Portugal came to an end. Refugees began returning to an independent homeland. TCRS handed all five Mozambican refugee settlements over to the Tanzanian government, and the settlements became Tanzanian (and subsequently Ujamaa) villages, equipped with all the necessary infrastructure and social services. Moreover, the Tanzanian government emerged as an international advocate for refugee integration, stressing to the world community the symbiotic relationship between refugee settlement and rural development. In 1979, UNHCR convened the Conference on the African Refugee Problem, hosted by Tanzania and attended by a diverse crowd of African dignitaries, UN officials, religious leaders, and members of various humanitarian aid agencies. All told, conference attendees came from thirty-eight African countries, twenty non-African countries, sixteen regional aid organizations, and five African liberation movements. In his inaugural speech, Tanzanian president Julius Nyerere advised those at the conference that

> it is impossible to deal with these refugees as if all that is required is temporary relief from distress. They must as quickly as possible be given a means of producing or earning their own livelihood.

The only practical way of proceeding is to work as if they are likely to be permanent inhabitants of their host state. Investment to meet their needs will never be wasted in the growing African economies. . . . We in Tanzania have been able to develop . . . area settlement schemes which deal with the special needs of the refugees and at the same time uplift the productive capacity and the social provisions for all the people living nearby. (Eriksson, Melander, and Nobel 1981, 68–69)

One interesting consequence emerges out of this tendency for the newly independent Tanzanian state to rely on the settlement model (as opposed to the camp model) of refugee assistance.

Today, as the international refugee regime of the twenty-first century looks to the camp model as the default form of refugee assistance, one prominent issue humanitarian organizations face is the attempted flight of refugees out of camps. But in southern Tanzania in the 1960s, the inverse unfolded: rather than seeing Mozambican refugees trying to break out of the settlements, this historical moment witnessed Tanzanian citizens trying to break into the Lundo, Matekwe, Mputa, Muhukuru, and Rutamba Settlements in order to benefit from the essential services available in these locations (Benue 2009). Ultimately, the model of refugee settlement employed in southern Tanzania in the 1960s and 1970s illustrated a much hoped for, though rarely realized, scenario on the part of the international humanitarian community, proving that integration was possible. Settlements could simultaneously provide for the refugee and benefit the host citizen as well. The small humanitarian aid agency could collaborate with the host state, to mutual advantage.

COMPARING THE URBAN and rural experiences of Mozambican refugees in Tanzania in the 1960s and 1970s highlights several critical points about the history of international humanitarianism and expert knowledge on African refugees in the twentieth century. It clearly shows that the very process of decolonization meant humanitarian assistance could not be apolitical. Because newly independent African states relied on collaboration with small relief agencies such as ACOA and TCRS to settle and assist refugees, such groups could not simply divorce themselves from the larger political context. Rather, in Dar es Salaam and other urban areas, an organization such as ACOA worked with FRELIMO leaders to secure scholarships for refugees who would comprise the future political and professional classes of an independent Mozambique. More important, these refugees were not and could not be characterized as asylum seekers, but they did leave the continent in the midst of their colony's violent war for liberation. Beyond the purview of international refugee law, asylum in this context can be understood as their ability to pursue the educational attainments that were needed in order to build a new nation, at war's end. This, of course, attests to the fact that asylum is never apolitical either, for this form of asylum was facilitated by an anticolonial liberation group in the midst of a protracted war for independence.

Further, in rural spaces such as southern Tanzania, an agency like TCRS could collaborate with the Tanzanian state to ensure that refugee settlements would serve the dual purpose of refugee relief and rural development. Thus, a comparative approach to the study of the methodologies employed by both ACOA and TCRS in Tanzania at the time reaffirms that the principles of impartiality, neutrality, and independence were not part of humanitarianism's "original DNA" (Barnett 2011, 5). Instead, as Michael Barnett (2011) and David Rieff (2002) have argued, these myths of the essence of humanitarianism originated as relief agencies met the multiple, complex crises of the late twentieth century. And yet, rather than conceptualizing relief organizations as timeless, inherently apolitical actors, should we not be asking about the benefits that stem from collaboration with the host state? Can we not see in the history of refugee relief in Africa that as the international humanitarian community has receded from open collaboration with the host state, refugee settlement and maintenance have become increasingly unstable and untenable?

In the study of Mozambican refugees in Tanzania in the 1960s and 1970s, a second critical point can be made about the history of international humanitarianism and expert knowledge on African refugees. This case study challenges the still prevalent notion that refugees are essentially burdens or problems to be solved. Indeed, it reveals that refugees can actually benefit the state (Jacobsen 2002). Moreover, it illustrates that some refugee populations possessed incredible power during the era of decolonization. Decolonization created a unique historical moment in which refugees could simultaneously contribute to the nation-building agendas of two would-be nations. Urban refugees symbolized the nation-in-waiting, the expectation on the part of ACOA and FRELIMO liberation leaders alike being that the professional training refugees received through their educations abroad would be necessary to the building of a future, independent Mozambique. At the same time, rural refugees stood at the forefront of a newly independent nation-in-the-making, with Mozambican refugee labor acting as a surrogate for the Tanzanian host government—a government that desperately needed assistance in providing infrastructure and social services to its own citizenry.

Finally, we are left with one undeniable truth. Refugees are not homogenous populations. This case study illustrates that some refugees benefit host states more than other refugees. Because Mozambican refugees in Dar es Salaam received educational opportunities that enabled them to leave Africa, FRELIMO, ACOA, and the Tanzanian government understood their status as remarkably temporary. Conversely, the Tanzanian government and TCRS relied on the relatively less-educated (or less-connected to the liberation movement) Mozambican refugees to build the rural south. Both TCRS and the Tanzanian government envisioned this particular population of refugees as distinctly permanent. This is significant because in the 1960s and 1970s, before the rise of the expert witness—indeed, prior to the birth of the American expert on Africa (as distinct from European colonial bodies of knowledge and expertise)—ACOA was forging expertise in the realm of African issues. We must historicize and contextualize the origination of the figure of the expert on African refugee settlement, assistance, and asylum in order to understand the issues that experts face in the asylum process. What emerges as most striking, as articulated in the introduction of this volume, is that whereas humanitarian and governmental understandings of refugee crises focused on the refugee-as-group concept throughout the 1960s and 1970s, by the turn of the twenty-first century those involved in governmental asylum and refugee status determination procedures began to expect "the production of a specific report tailored to the experience of the individual claimant" (see introduction in this volume). And we cannot, as this chapter suggests, understand the construction of such reports if we do not have an understanding of the humanitarian world before them.

## Notes

1. Tanganyika achieved independence from the United Kingdom in 1961. It merged with Zanzibar in 1964 to become the United Republic of Tanzania.

2. Hatton claims that the number of asylum applications to "industrialized countries" increased from roughly 100,000 per year in the mid-1980s to a peak of 850,000 in 1992. With the end of the Cold War, there was a rapid decline in

application numbers, until another peak of 600,000 occurred in 2001. Since then, he estimates there are, on average, 300,000 applications worldwide per year.

3. This calls into question the use of the word *refugee* as opposed to the phrase *internally displaced person* (IDP). As mentioned, prior to the 1967 protocol the vast majority of Africans would not have qualified as refugees. I employ that term, however, because throughout the 1960s, all governmental as well as international humanitarian organizations (e.g., UNHCR, ACOA, TCRS, and the World Food Program [WFP]) referred to Mozambican refugees in Tanzania, in their memoranda and annual reports, as refugees and not as IDPs, despite the fact that Africans were denied such status.

4. Though this is beyond the scope of the present volume and chapter, I argue elsewhere that these Mozambican refugee settlements provided a foundation and contributed significantly to Julius Nyerere's planning and implementation of Ujamaa villagization. Indeed, the labeling of these refugee spaces as settlements and not camps was, in part, a reflection of Tanzania's dominant socialist ideology.

5. The term *settlers* is used throughout all TCRS annual reports (from 1967 to 1975 as well as in the report *TCRS after Twenty Years*) when referring to the farming activities of Mozambican refugees in southern Tanzania.

6. The number of refugees resident at each settlement varied considerably. There were an estimated 15,000 refugees at Rutamba; 15,000 at Mputa; 9,000 at Lundo; 6,000 at Muhukuru; and 8,000 at Matekwe. At each of these five settlements, refugees received 2 acres of land, on which they not only built their homes but also established their own gardens for home food consumption. All refugees received WFP rations for the first two years of settlement. Thereafter, TCRS and the Tanzanian government expected Mozambican refugees to grow their own food from their household plots.

## References

American Committee on Africa (ACOA). Box 142, files 39, 40, 44, and 55. Amistad Research Center, New Orleans, LA.

Barnett, Michael. 2011. *Empire of Humanity: A History of Humanitarianism.* Ithaca, NY: Cornell University Press.

Benue, Father. Interview with the author. Ndanda Mission, Tanzania, November 13, 2009.

Black, Richard. 1998a. "Putting Refugees in Camps." *Forced Migration Review* 2:4–7.

————. 1998b. *Refugees, Environment, and Development.* London: Longman Press.

Cooper, Frederick. 1998. "Modernizing Bureaucrats, Backward Africans, and the Development Concept." In *International Development and the Social Sciences: Essays on the History and Politics of Knowledge,* edited by Frederick Cooper and Randall Packard, 64–92. Berkeley: University of California Press.

Crisp, Jeffrey. 2001. "Mind the Gap! UNHCR, Humanitarian Assistance, and the Development Process." *International Migration Review* 35 (1): 168–91.

Dick, Shelly. 2002. "Liberians in Ghana: Living without Humanitarian Assistance." New Issues in Refugee Research Working Paper no. 57. UNHCR. Accessed January 27, 2014. http://www.unhcr.org/3c8398f24.html.

Eldridge, John. "The African-American Institute Report on the Special Scholarships and Training Program, Dar es Salaam (May 1964)." FO 317/176933. The National Archives, Kew, UK.

Eriksson, Lars-Gunnar, Göran Melander, and Peter Nobel. 1981. *An Analyzing Account of the Conference on the African Refugee Problem, Arusha, May 1979*. Uppsala, Sweden: Scandinavian Institute of African Studies.

Escobar, Arturo. 1995. *Encountering Development: The Making and Unmaking of the Third World*. Princeton, NJ: Princeton University Press.

Gatrell, Peter. 2011. *Free World? The Campaign to Save the World's Refugees, 1956–1963*. New York: Cambridge University Press.

Gerhart, John D. 1964. "Dar es Salaam Becomes Center of Refugee Intrigue: Nine Exiled Regimes Have Headquarters in City." *Crimson* (Harvard University), September 25.

Hatton, Timothy J. 2011. "Seeking Asylum: Trends and Policies in the OECD." Center for Economic Policy Research, London. Accessed January 27, 2014. http://www.voxeu.org/sites/default/files/file/Hatton%20Seeking%20Asylum.pdf.

Houser, George M. 1976. "Meeting Africa's Challenge: The Story of the American Committee on Africa." *Issue: A Journal of Opinion* 6 (2–3): 16–26.

Jacobsen, Karen. 2001. "The Forgotten Solution: Local Integration for Refugees in Developing Countries." *UNHCR New Issues in Refugee Research*. Working Paper no. 45. Accessed January 27, 2014. http://www.unhcr.org/cgibin/texis/vtx/home/opendocPDFViewer.html?docid=3b7d24059&query=karen%20jacobsen.

———. 2002. "Can Refugees Benefit the State? Refugee Resources and African Statebuilding." *Journal of Modern African Studies* 40 (4): 577–96.

Keely, Charles B. 2001. "The International Refugee Regime(s): The End of the Cold War Matters." *International Migration Review* 35 (1): 303–14.

Lewis, Joanna. 2000. *Empire State-Building: War and Welfare in Kenya, 1922–1952*. Oxford: James Currey.

Loescher, Gilbert. 1993. *Beyond Charity: International Cooperation and the Global Refugee Crisis*. Oxford: Oxford University Press.

———. 2001. *The UNHCR and World Politics: A Perilous Path*. Oxford: Oxford University Press.

Minter, Bill. 2007. *No Easy Victories: African Liberation and American Activists over a Half Century, 1950–2000*. Trenton, NJ: African World Press.

Mitchell, Timothy. 2002. *Rule of Experts: Egypt, Techno-politics, Modernity*. Berkeley: University of California Press.

*Nationalist* (Tanzanian newspaper). 1964. "Feel at Home—Kawawa." October 15.

Nyers, Peter. 2006. *Rethinking Refugees: Beyond States of Emergency*. New York: Routledge.

Register of the US National Student Association, International Commission Records, 1966–67. Box 283, "The Mozambique Institute" file, Letters from Ruth and Bill Minter. Hoover Archives, Stanford University, Palo Alto, CA.

Rieff, David. 2002. *A Bed for the Night: Humanitarianism in Crisis*. New York: Simon and Schuster.

Tague, Joanna. 2012. "A War to Build the Nation: Mozambican Refugees, Rural Development, and State Sovereignty in Tanzania, 1964–1975." PhD diss., University of California, Davis.

Tanganyika Christian Refugee Service (TCRS). Annual Reports 1964, 1967, 1971, 1972, 1975, and *TCRS after Twenty Years*. Archives in Dar es Salaam, Tanzania.

Van Beusekom, Monica. 2002. *Negotiating Development: African Farmers and the Colonial Experts at the Office du Niger, 1920–1960*. Portsmouth, NH: Heinemann.

Wright, Robin. 1975. "Janet Mondlane of the Mozambique Institute: American 'Godmother' to an African Revolution." *Christian Science Monitor*, May 12.

# TWO

## Fraudulent Asylum Seeking as Transnational Mobilization[1]

*The Case of Cameroon*

Meredith Terretta

> This distinction between the economic and the political
> . . . makes it virtually impossible ever to grant political
> asylum and even, in a sense, to apply the law.
>
> —Jacques Derrida, *On Cosmopolitanism*
> *and Forgiveness*

> The sovereign must continuously exclude and include
> the refugee to maintain its power.
>
> —Giorgio Agamben, *Homo Sacer*

DURING THE 2012 Summer Olympics in London, the story of seven Cameroonian Olympians who "absconded" from the Olympic Village made headlines around the world. In particular, the story was reported in all the major news venues in the United Kingdom (including the *Guardian,* the *Daily Mail,* and the BBC), France (*Le Figaro,* France 24, and RFI), and the United States (NPR, CNN, and Fox News). Initial reports stated that five male boxers, a swimmer, and a female soccer player had "disappeared" (Taylor, Jones, and Hirsch 2012). Within days, media reported that although these athletes were legally allowed to stay in the United Kingdom until November 8, 2012, it was "feared" that the seven planned to request asylum for economic reasons, as Cameroon was one of the poorest countries in the world (Associated Press 2012; Doyle 2012). The *Daily Mail* stated that it was "not the first time" that "Cameroonian athletes have gone missing during international sports competitions" (Goodenough 2012). Another report explained that immigration staff estimated "up to two percent of Olympic visitors from some continents may claim refuge in the UK" and that "investigators" had "identified several countries" . . . in the Middle East and Africa . . . "where they 'expect' asylum claims from athletes and supporters given visas specifically to attend London 2012" (Williams and Eccles 2012).[2]

After describing Cameroon as one of the most stable countries in Africa, the *Daily Mail* commented that "even those from some countries regarded as safe will have to be processed and removed, putting further pressure on the asylum system" (Doyle 2012; also see Williams and Eccles 2012). Among the most striking comments, posted online in response to the news reports, were those of "Steve" and "Dr. Evil," who wrote, "[The athletes] must be found and deported immediately, and told to apply through the correct channels. These people who come here either on false pretences or false documents need to be stopped dead in their tracks. . . . How can they now say that if they return their lives will be at risk? . . . Economic reasons are not valid for claiming political asylum" (see comments to Goodenough 2012). Other commentators expressed surprise that North Korean athletes, who, living under a repressive political regime, "had legitimate cause to defect, had not done so" (Wallechinsky 2012).

Among those familiar with asylum trends, the 2012 case of the disappearing athletes fit easily into a general perception of Cameroonians—who hailed from what Transparency International has marked since 1998 as one of the most corrupt countries in the world—as particularly adept at filing faked asylum claims. Amid questions of whether the police were involved in the disappeared athletes' retrieval, suggestions that their trainers should have kept their passports, and the vain solicitation of commentary from the British Home Office, officials from the UK Border Agency stated that "the majority of asylum applicants from Cameroon are refused and deported" (Associated Press 2012). Follow-up stories soon explained that the Cameroonian Olympians were not legitimate asylum seekers but merely athletes seeking a better financial deal (Williams and Eccles 2012). Offering some perspective on the situation, Cameroonian economist Flaubert Mbiekop commented: "The bottom line is to look at the economic conditions in Cameroon and see how hard the system is for many people, especially the athletes who don't receive any support from the government. London presented an opportunity; I'm not at all surprised that they took it" (as quoted in Taylor, Jones, and Hirsch 2012).

The media hype about the seven missing Cameroonian Olympians illustrates fears, prevalent throughout the Global North in recent years, that economic migrants abuse and therefore threaten the asylum system. When compared and contrasted with the stories of Soviet era athletes who stayed in the West (including, in 1956, half the Hungarian Olympic team) and were sympathetically portrayed as "defectors" and widely welcomed, the story of the London 2012 Olympian "absconders" pushes us to ask how asylum protocols have changed since the creation of the 1951 Convention relating to the Status of Refugees. It also requires those of us who offer legal assistance or expert testimony to asylum seekers to: (1) consider how claims are presented as legitimate or illegitimate as a way of discerning who deserves refuge in the globalized world, (2) assess who should decide which refugees are deserving of help, and (3) determine what criteria should be used in making such decisions. Finally, it pushes us to think about the agency of asylum seekers themselves, particularly what recourse they have whenever stricter asylum protocols make it more and more difficult to reach host country borders, as well as the ways in which they—and we, as expert witnesses who lend credence to their narratives of persecution—might challenge those norms.

### Asylum Seekers from the "Most Corrupt" Country in the World: The Case of Cameroon

In 1998 and 1999, Cameroon was ranked the most corrupt country in the world on Transparency International's Corruption Perceptions Index (CPI). Over the course of the next five years, Cameroon remained in the top twenty most corrupt countries, ranging from sixth to eighteenth. Since 2005, its ranking has improved somewhat, but its CPI score has remained in the range of 2.2 to 2.6 (on a scale of 1 to 10, with 10 being the least corrupt).[3]

In fiscal year (FY) 2003, Cameroon was ranked seventh among source countries of asylum seekers in the United States. It was ranked first among African source countries and was the only one of these in the top ten countries of origin for asylum seekers in the United States. It was also the country with the highest rate of approval of affirmative asylum cases (50 percent) (Wasem 2005, 14). Furthermore, it was not among the top ten source countries for asylum cases submitted to the Executive Office for Immigration Review (EOIR) (Wasem 2005, 15). Cameroon had an additional 186 defensive asylum cases approved in FY2003, bringing the total approval rate to 1,000 out of 1,601, or about 62 percent. The statistical data reveal that in FY2003, asylum officers in airports, the port of entry for those from Cameroon, had comparatively few questions regarding the legitimacy of Cameroonian claims and approved cases without sending them on to be adjudicated in the courts. In FY2006, however, Cameroon had 359 asylum grants approved as EOIR cases, which outnumbered the 224 direct approvals for affirmative cases; this indicates that US officials subjected a growing number of asylum seekers from Cameroon to the scrutiny of the immigration review process. The total approvals for asylum-seeking Cameroonians fell to 583 in FY2006 (Wasem 2011, 34, 35) and to 501 in FY2007, and they remained below 450 yearly from FY2008 through FY2012 (US Department of Homeland Security 2013, 44–53).

Evidence from a cable sent in November 2004 (FY2005) from the American embassy in Yaoundé to the secretary of state, the Department of Homeland Security (DHS), the Immigration and Customs Enforcement (ICE) headquarters, and American embassies in Berlin, London, and Paris sheds light on possible reasons for the sudden change.[4] The cable began by stating, "Post believes that most of these original asylum claims [from Cameroon] are frivolous or fraudulent. Post advises DHS to view such Cameroonian asylum requests with skepticism and use all tools available to adjudicate follow-to-join derivative applications." The cable then explained that Cameroon was "the asylum leader among all African countries" as of FY2003 and that the number of its approved asylum claims put it "in the top five source countries worldwide (keeping company with China, Haiti, and Colombia)."[5]

According to "Post," Cameroon's current political situation did not justify the statistics because it had "not degenerated materially since 1991" when no asylum claims were filed. Of course, the political situation had deteriorated enormously since 1991, particularly as 1992 was the year in which internal and external observers alike concurred that John Fru Ndi of the Social Democratic Front was the winner of the presidential elections, not Paul Biya, who has been president since 1982 and is still in power despite Cameroon's official multiparty transition in 1990. The literature providing accounts of the rapid decline of the political situation in the early 1990s, compounded by widespread economic insecurity, is exhaustive (Boulaga 1997; Konings 2002; Mehler, 1997; Ngayap 1999; Pommerolle 2008; Priso 1994; Takougang and Krieger 1998). But for "Post," Cameroon's political and economic situation was not dire enough to warrant the high numbers of asylum seekers: he pointed out that Cameroon had not experienced civil war "as have many other African countries, including Ethiopia and Congo-DRC." Instead, the worsening economy (which was, according to the post agent, completely independent of the political sphere) was the push factor that explained why so many "economic migrants" were making "frivolous or fraudulent" asylum claims.

The report explained that most of the claims were made by "mala fide Cameroonian nonimmigrant visa applicants" who, upon arrival in the United States, made use of photographs and "fake medical reports attesting to abuse and letters from political parties or local human rights N.G.O.s attesting to an asylee [sic] applicant's activities." Furthermore, the report stated, these applicants made their claims with the aid of "rings of facilitators," both in Cameroon and in the United States, who "charge[d] Cameroonians high fees" for their services: the "consular section's fraud investigator has investigated scores of such documents at the request of Immigration Judges and D.H.S. prosecutors, and all (yes, all) of them have turned out to be false."

The reporting consular official suggested a series of measures to cut down on the number of fraudulent applications and thus reduce the "consular's workload." First, beginning with a sort of mea culpa, the post agent stipulated that the number of nonimmigrant visas issued had to be reduced. Second, he called for a greater degree of corroboration, including checking issuance records in the Consular Consolidated Database and requiring DNA testing for those filing follow-to-join (I-730) petitions and Visas 92 applications on the basis of being relatives of asylum grantees. These measures constitute the preemptive extraterritorial "selective processes" that the US government began to put in effect in the mid-1900s. Finally, he asked for greater transatlantic collaboration between "Post" and the US government agencies regulating asylum. The report ended by indicating that the high proportion of Cameroonian claims approved was "enormously disproportionate to the actual political situation here, especially when compared with the number of approved claims from other countries in Africa and worldwide." "Post" urged the Department of Homeland Security "to view Cameroonian asylum requests" with "skepticism," and he expressed a desire to have the "fraud issue" brought "to the attention of DHS asylum adjudicators and Immigration Judges."

In 2007, another cable from the US embassy in Cameroon summarized the asylum situation in 2006. Similar in tone to the November 2004 communication, this cable referred to "canned claims of persecution" and added that,

> [as] one of the world's most corrupt countries . . . almost everything is for sale [in Cameroon], including membership cards in "outlawed" organizations, newspaper articles, letters from non-licensed individuals claiming to be medical authorities attesting to medical treatment as a result of political persecution, fraudulent documents concerning the "arrest" of a political prisoner signed by actual police officials, photographs of supposed political prisoners in jail cells with actual police officers present, and attorneys and bailiffs writing affidavits claiming events that have never taken place such as the burning of houses by alleged government agents. The Embassy has seen direct evidence of all these self-serving activities and believes that the vast majority of asylum claims by Cameroonians are fraudulent.[6]

The reporting post agent suggested prescriptive measures, including revocation of status and removal for those who had been granted asylum using fraudulent methods.[7]

### Fraudulent Economic Migrants or Transnational Protestors?

Reports generated by the American embassy in Cameroon make for an unlikely juxtaposition with the US Department of State's portrayal of the country since the early 2000s. From 2002 through 2006, the State Department rated Cameroon a four out of a possible five on the political terror scale. A rating of four means that "civil and political rights violations have expanded to large numbers of the population. Murders, disappearances, and torture are a common part of life. In spite of its generality, on this level terror affects those who interest themselves in politics or ideas" (Gibney et al. 2002–6). Given the US government's conflicting portrayals of Cameroon's political situation, it is easy to read the US consulate's presentation of the nonimmigrant visa applicant−*cum*−criminal illegal immigrant as part of a broader initiative to reduce the number of asylum claims and grants.

However, portions of the reports from "Post" ring true. Certainly, a proportion of Cameroonian asylum cases are based, in part or in whole, on fake documents and false claims. But cases of torture and brutalization or harassment of political oppositionists and people deemed subversive in Cameroon do occur, with spikes during election years and at other times when the Biya regime feels it is on the defensive. It must be assumed that "Post" was vastly overstating the issue while minimizing the desperation of the political situation in Cameroon in order to comply with a general desire to reduce the number of asylum applications and grants—a trend common to the United States, the United Kingdom, and the European Union since the early 2000s (Fassin 2012; Gibney 2004; Squire 2009).

Given the prevalence of fake documents and invented narratives among Cameroonians applying for asylum, some humanitarians and lawyers stigmatize the fraudulent asylum seekers who ruin this essential protective system for the world's legitimate victims of persecution (see, e.g., Murray 2011). Following this school of thought, those faking claims make the burden of proof more arduous and decrease overall opportunities for asylum for the innocent, truthful victims who are most deserving of refuge.

But there is another way to understand the convergence of fraud, corruption, the US embassy's overstated accusations thereof, and Cameroon's dangerously dysfunctional political economy. Cameroonian asylum seekers, whether fraudulent or not and with varying degrees of intentionality, demonstrate how asylum protocols have failed to keep pace with changing global political and economic realities. The Cameroon case prompts us to rethink asylum norms that legally and morally categorize economic migrants as illegitimate asylum seekers to whom the UN convention of 1951 does not apply. In the context of current anti-immigrant social and political conditions that frame the asylum process in host countries, "illegitimate" asylum seekers include those seeking escape from a dysfunctional political economy that denies access to "food, shelter, work, medical care, education, rights of mobility and expression, [and] protection against injury and oppression" (Butler 2009, 22).[8] State officialdom in host countries, as well as many human rights advocates involved in asylum and refugee processes and media reports, portray economic migrants as "bogus" (Neumayer 2005). They are to be unfavorably contrasted with "legitimate" asylum seekers, defined as those who face political, religious, or social persecution or a denial of their human rights (narrowly conceived as negative protections for individuals, a safeguard against physical pain and trauma).[9]

Symptoms of the rigid polarization between legitimate and illegitimate refugees are readily apparent in the cables from Cameroon in which the US vice consul defined rampant corruption as economic rather than political. Yet the arena of corruption to which the vice consul referred is precisely the sort of interstice between political and economic that calls into question any effort to delineate a rigid boundary between these two spheres. In Cameroon, corruption does more than facilitate the route to asylum for a handful of emigrants. Though engaging in corruption may offer a way out of a dangerously dysfunctional political economy to a few, the excesses of a corrupt authoritarian regime in power since 1982 render life precarious for Cameroonians.[10] Here, widespread corruption becomes a part of a larger question of the legitimacy of the claims of politico-economic migrants.

In the asylum cases I have worked on for Cameroonian claimants and their lawyers, the feature that resurfaces most commonly is corruption. Corruption is a reality of daily life in Cameroon that acts upon every citizen, blocking both economic opportunity (making the start-up costs of a legitimate small business unaffordable due to the amount of graft, for example), social status (the "pot of wine"—a euphemism for a bribe—is a condition of hiring or promotion, particularly in the government sector and civil service), and access to education (Nyamnjoh 1999). It is also the most salient feature of daily political processes, permeating the politics of the Cameroonian Peoples' Democratic Movement (CPDM) (President Biya's party) and orchestrating the way the Biya regime has co-opted much of the opposition (Terretta and Pouhe 2012). Finally, Cameroonians consistently perceive employees of the public sector as being the most corrupt, starting with the police and followed by members of the judiciary, customs and tax officials, and public educators (Transparency International 2004, 18; 2007, 22; 2009; 2013).

Corruption is the mode through which the Cameroonian state both preys on the population and maintains itself in power by ensuring Biya's perpetual reelection; it trickles down into the most subaltern echelons of society. For instance, when I lived in Cameroon from 2001 to 2003 and traveled regularly from the Littoral to the West Region, I personally observed that buses and vans carrying passengers from Nkongsamba to Bafang (a distance of about 30 miles) were routinely stopped at each of the twelve roadblocks maintained by state officialdom (police, gendarme, mixed mobile brigade, road security, and so forth), with chauffeurs made to pay 500 CFA francs (the equivalent of about 1 US dollar) as a bribe at each one. The total cost of bribes for the journey was thus 6,000 CFA francs, and the cost per passenger of the journey itself varied from 800 to 1,200 CFA francs, depending on the season and which bus service was used. As a result, passenger fares increased and more people were loaded into a vehicle than legally allowed—making the journey not only unnecessarily long and uncomfortable but also extremely hazardous. Passengers routinely sat between the driver and the driver-side door or on top of the gearbox, for example, limiting the driver's visibility and control of the vehicle, yet I never observed such passengers being required to move or descend from the vehicle at any checkpoint.

Corruption does not merely *act upon* the inhabitants of Cameroon. It also provides ordinary people an avenue through which *to act*. In 2007, some 79 percent of Cameroonians surveyed reported paying a bribe in the prior year to obtain services (Transparency International 2007, 21). In 2013, when Transparency International categorized the data on bribery according to service rendered, the organization found that 69 percent of Cameroonians paid a bribe to the police, 55 percent to the judiciary, 36 percent to education services, 33 percent to medical and health services, and so on (Transparency International 2013). It costs so little to "buy" the exception to the rule of law from state officialdom that doing so is well within the reach of a majority of urban residents and more than a few rural ones. Here, too, examples abound of the ways in which a corrupt public service contributes to the precariousness of life in Cameroon. Thus, to cite just a few examples, it is possible to get a vehicle safety inspection without presenting one's vehicle; a driver's license may be "purchased" without taking an exam or even presenting oneself at the proper office; and one can pay for another person's arrest, imprisonment, and beating at the local jail.[11]

Corruption's dual function as a prohibitive factor as well as an enabling factor resurfaces in the politics of emigration from Cameroon and immigration, via asylum, to northern host countries. Corruption permits individual and collective agency to flourish in an otherwise politically and economically oppressive environment by nurturing *débrouillardise* (the art of daily subsistence by resourcefully engaging the informal economy)—another common feature of daily life in Cameroon. As political scientist

Jean-François Bayart (1999a, 116) suggests, "informal and illicit trade, financial fraud, the systematic evasion of rules and international agreements could turn out to be a means, among others, by which certain Africans manage to survive and to stake their place in the maelstrom of globalization." For Bayart, "only the vision of the jurist" labels as criminal many of the débrouillardise activities (and here, fraud in asylum claims must be included); those performing them view these activities as part of an "ethos of personal savoir-faire and initiative" (Bayart 1999b, 39).

Bayart would categorize débrouillardise, generally, as one of the "ruses of political intelligence" (Bayart 1999b, 32) employed by those seeking to improve their social standing, but I would go a step further when it comes to the relationship between corruption and the disproportionate number of political asylum claims filed by Cameroonians. Those who use fraud in asylum claims have adopted corruption as a necessary mode of transnational civil disobedience.[12] In filing false claims (or in providing services to aid those who do), Cameroonians have mobilized to protest international and national laws that stipulate corruption is not a mode of political persecution. With asylum "advisers" (the US institutions have labeled them "fixers") in Cameroon and in host countries throughout the Global North, Cameroonians have created a transnational network that manages to penetrate, albeit to a limited degree, the territorial sovereignty of host nations in order to benefit from an international convention established in 1951. The Cameroonian asylum seekers who use this approach invent narratives and rely on fake documents for corroborative evidence because their legitimate reasons for seeking asylum are viewed as illegitimate. However, I contend that the legitimacy or illegitimacy of Cameroonian asylum seekers' claims should rest not on their use of fake documents and claims (which, after all, is a moral issue) but on the degree to which economic and political factors in their home country combine to make life unlivable and even precarious.

## Transnational Mobilization to Reform Asylum Legislation

Distinguishing between political and economic refugees has become increasingly difficult in recent years. *Economic migrant* is the phrase used in public and political discourse to designate as illegitimate and even criminal those asylum seekers who come from countries that are both impoverished and politically unstable (Cameroon but also other countries in Africa, the Caribbean, and Central and Latin America). April

Shemak (2011, 20) asserts that by filing a number of claims deemed "disproportionate" by American embassy personnel in Yaoundé and by blatantly using fake documents and fabricated narratives to make their claims, Cameroonians challenge "U.N., U.S. and state, and other institutional definitions that exclude economic circumstances as a basis for asylum." Furthermore, as Shemak (2011, 10) argues in her discussion of Haitian refugees to the United States, their actions demonstrate that "for many refugees the links between politics and economics are inextricable." Jayne O. Ifekwunigwe (2006, 91) observes that "if we examine the root causes of global migratory flows from South to North such as (post)colonial underdevelopment, environmental decay, and globalization, then not only are European nation-states culpable but their international responsibilities transcend the limited definition of a refugee outlined by the U.N. Convention." Although the UN Convention on the Status of Refugees, which passed in 1951, was focused on liberal civil and political rights to the exclusion of socioeconomic factors when defining refugees, the liberal perspective, particularly as represented by the protocol on refugees the United States established as precedent in the 1960s, made "a distinction between 'natural' nonpolitical market activity and the collectivized command economies of the communist nations [which are seen as unnatural—indeed as political—arrangements]" (Nyers 2005, 50).

Yet Cameroon's national economy, confronting the juggernaut of an unofficial state policy of corruption, could hardly be argued to constitute "natural nonpolitical market activity." Every US granting agency and global financial institution has quantitatively documented the degree of corruption permeating Cameroon's political economy. If the officially collectivized economies of the Eastern bloc were categorized as political, then so too should be the corrupt economic policies of a president-for-life political regime.

By shining a spotlight on the practice of corruption, Cameroonian asylum seekers are, in fact, politicizing it on a transnational stage. In so doing, they urge an examination of the correlation between Cameroon's corrupt political economy that pushes inhabitants to emigrate and the "unchecked globalization of capital, postcolonial political deformations, and superpower imperialism" (Brown 2004, 461–62) as the factors that motivate increased international migration. More simply put, they force an acknowledgment of the present-day overlap between economic and political push factors motivating emigration from a number of countries throughout the Global South. The actions of the US-based lobbyists and public relations firms the Biya regime has hired to clean up Cameroon's image for investors and the American Congress—in hopes of being awarded a Millennium Corporation development grant—present just one avenue for examining the ways in which forces of globalization reinforce Cameroon's corrupt political economy (see, e.g., Silverstein 2007).

IN THE TWENTY-FIRST century, it appears that the 1951 UN convention has been narrowly reinterpreted to such an extent that the citizens of host nations are the greatest beneficiaries of current asylum protocols. As Ruth Wasem (2011, 33), a specialist in immigration policy at the Congressional Research Service, observes:

> Overall, asylee adjustments comprised only four percent (41,972) of the 10.3 million L.P.R.s [long-term permanent residents] admitted or adjusted from FY2000 through FY2009. Unlike other facets of U.S. immigration policy, asylum issues are less about the number of foreign nationals involved and more about the qualities of the policies and the efficacy of the procedures. Asylum is an adjudication of a person based upon facts, evidence, beliefs, and circumstances that might be clear at some times yet nebulous at other times.

Although the notion of asylum was conceived in 1951 to offer legal protection to refugees and others in need of it, in today's Global North the order of governance and belonging is, at least in part, "constructed against asylum-cum-illegal-immigration" (Squire 2009, 52).

In appropriating corruption as an escape route, everyday Cameroonians display their knowledge that politics are corrupt and corruption is political. Corruption serves as both obstacle and escape route. Abroad, a transnational Cameroonian network manufacturing narrative testimony and supporting documents as "proof" fitting the host country's rule of law becomes the means for penetrating the tightened immigration controls of the Global North. In turn, this hastens "the process of the dissolution of the nation-state and its sovereignty" (Agamben 1995, 114). Through this process, Cameroonians who employ fraud in migration can reclaim agency and subjectivity at the very sites where these capacities have been denied to them—within Cameroon itself and as liminal citizens (Laguerre 1998) of the border zones of their would-be host countries.

Fraudulent Asylum Seeking as Transnational Mobilization

Through the channel of asylum, Cameroonians have refashioned migration into a process of débrouillardise, or improvisation. How fitting that this route has been claimed primarily through corruption—the very thing that débrouillardise both rises above (when it is a matter of state corruption) and profits from (in the case of entrepreneurs profiting from their knowledge of immigration procedures and the fabrication of documents). The frequency and effrontery with which asylum seekers—such as the Olympic "absconders" who agreed to be interviewed following their defection (Williams and Eccles 2012)—make their claims urge a repositioning of the political designation *refugee* in current global economic conditions.

A November 2013 ruling by the US Board of Immigration Appeals (BIA) suggests that Cameroonian asylum seekers may have begun to prompt reforms to asylum norms and legal precedents. The BIA ruled in favor of a Cameroonian asylum seeker who provided a fake photo as proof that he had been imprisoned and tortured by authorities in his home country. For the BIA, the fake photo was not enough to undermine the asylee's credibility, as the presiding immigration judge had argued: other evidence of record, including expert testimony on country conditions and a medical affidavit from an American doctor, should have been taken into account. The BIA noted that adjudicators must consider the evidence in its ensemble, stating that the "submitted evidence cumulatively may be sufficient to rehabilitate the respondent's credibility or establish independently past persecution or a well-rounded fear of persecution" (Fahamu Refugee Legal Aid Newsletter 2014).

Viewing fraudulent asylum seekers as transnational reformers of asylum protocols—rather than as "liars and cheats who open the way for the malicious to attack the entire system, and cast unfair doubt on the whole principle of providing help to the genuine needy" (Murray 2011)—prompts expert witnesses to rethink their task. If they recognize a correlation between global economic injustice and local persecution and refuse to stigmatize economic migrants seeking a route out of precarious lives, might expert witnesses join with asylum seekers in critically testifying to the ways in which current asylum norms occlude the root causes of global migration from south to north? Several chapters in this volume, most notably that of Tricia Redeker Hepner, help to envision new strategies for experts as activists.

# Notes

1. The phrase *transnational mobilization* is used by Hourya Bentouhami (2007, 1), who asks whether civil disobedience can be used by transnational social movements "which confront new kinds of power distribution that surpass the traditional State."

2. The total number of athletes reported to have disappeared during the 2012 games in London was twenty-four, all of them from Africa: seven Cameroonians, two Sudanese, one Ethiopian, four Congolese, three Guineans, three Ivoirians, and four Eritreans. No other disappearances were reported.

3. All statistics are from the Transparency International website, http://www.transparency.org/cpi2013/results.

4. American Embassy, Yaoundé, cable to Secretary of State, Washington, DC; Homeland Security Center, Washington, DC; American Embassy, Abuja; American Embassy, Kinshasa; American Consul, Frankfurt; and Headquarters ICE, Washington, DC, November 2004, Subject: Asylum remains a popular way for Cameroonians to stay in America—Fraudulently. Quotations in the next two paragraphs are taken from this document.

5. These numbers are inconsistent with DHS statistics for the years in question, one of many instances in which "Post" fails to get the facts straight.

6. American Embassy, Yaoundé, cable to Secretary of State, Washington, DC; Homeland Security Center, Washington, DC; American Embassy, Berlin; American Embassy, London; American Embassy, Paris, April 2007, Subject: Cameroon—Asylum adjudication challenges.

7. Cases from Somalia and Ethiopia have come under the same general scrutiny, with similar correlative drops in the number of approvals (Dzubow 2012a, 2012b).

8. In her discussion of precarious life, Judith Butler (2009, 21) notes that "the one who decides or asserts rights of protection does so in the context of social and political norms that frame the decision-making process. . . . Decisions are social practices, and the assertion of rights emerges precisely where conditions of interlocution can be presupposed or, minimally, invoked and incited when they are not yet institutionalized."

9. On this twenty-first-century definition of human rights, see, for example, the work of Michael Ignatieff (2001, 56–57, 149, 173).

10. On precariousness in this sense, see Butler (2009, 1–32).

11. I personally observed each of these phenomena at least once in Cameroon from 1999 to 2010.

12. Michael Allen (2011, 135) defines transnational civil disobedience as "a form of nonviolent, symbolic, and illegal protest that specifically engages the concepts of global citizens and a global public. It is a model of civil disobedience that takes global citizens to be the agents of civilly disobedient protest who address a global public with a global sense of justice."

# References

Agamben, Giorgio. 1995. "We Refugees." *Symposium* 49 (2): 114–19.

———. 1998. *Homo Sacer: Sovereign Power and Bare Life.* Translated by Daniel Heller-Roazen. Stanford, CA: Stanford University Press.

Allen, Michael. 2011. "Civil Disobedience, Transnational." In *Encyclopedia of Global Justice,* edited by Deen K. Chatterjee. New York: Springer.

Associated Press. 2012. "Missing Cameroonian Olympians Seeking Asylum?" *NewsOne for Black America.* August 8. Accessed January 30, 2014. http://newsone.com /2029650/cameroon-olympic-team-missing/.

Bayart, Jean-François. 1999a. "Conclusion." In *The Criminalization of the State in Africa,* edited by Jean-François Bayart, Stephen Ellis, and Béatrice Hibou, 114–16. Oxford: James Currey.

————. 1999b. "The 'Social Capital' of the Felonious State or the Ruses of Political Intelligence." In *The Criminalization of the State in Africa,* edited by Jean-François Bayart, Stephen Ellis, and Béatrice Hibou, 32–48. Oxford: James Currey.

Bentouhami, Hourya. 2007. "Civil Disobedience from Thoreau to Transnational Mobilizations: The Global Challenge." *Essays in Philosophy: A Biannual Journal* 8 (2), art. 3. Accessed March 7, 2014. http://commons.pacificu.edu/.

Boulaga, Fabien Eboussi. 1997. *La démocratie de transit au Cameroun.* Paris: L'Harmattan.

Brown, Wendy. 2004. "'The Most We Can Hope For . . .': Human Rights and the Politics of Fatalism." *South Atlantic Quarterly* 103 (2–3): 451–63.

Butler, Judith. 2009. *Frames of War: When Is Life Grievable?* London: Verso.

Derrida, Jacques. 2001. *On Cosmopolitanism and Forgiveness.* New York: Routledge.

Doyle, Jack. 2012. "Fears over Asylum Claims as Six More Olympic Athletes Go Missing When They Are Meant to Go Home." *Mail Online,* August 14. Accessed January 29, 2014. http://www.dailymail.co.uk/news/article-2188496/Fears -asylum-claims-Olympic-athletes-missing-meant-home.html.

Dzubow, Jason. 2012a. "Fraud and Asylum." The Asylumist blog, June 2, 2010. Accessed March 1, 2012. http://www.asylumist.com.

————. 2012b. "U.S. Consulate Attempts to Block Asylum Seekers." The Asylumist blog, March 1, 2012. Accessed March 1, 2012. http://www.asylumist.com.

Fahamu Refugee Legal Aid Newsletter. 2014. "U.S. Ruling Establishes 'Cumulative' Credibility Possibility in Establishing Past Persecution." January 1. Accessed March 7, 2014. http://frlan.tumblr.com/post/71890452135/us-ruling -establishes-cumulative credibility.

Fassin, Didier. 2012. *Humanitarian Reason: A Moral History of the Present.* Berkeley: University of California Press.

Gibney, Matthew J. 2004. *The Ethics and Politics of Asylum: Liberal Democracy and the Response to Refugees.* Cambridge: Cambridge University Press.

Gibney, M., L. Cornett, R. Wood, and P. Haschke. 2002–6. *Political Terror Scale 1976– 2012.* Accessed January 27, 2013. http://politicalterrorscale.org.

Goodenough, Tom. 2012. "Seven Cameroon Athletes Including Five Boxers Knocked Out of Competition Disappear from Olympic Village." *Mail Online,* August 7. Accessed January 29, 2014. http://www.dailymail.co.uk/news/article-2184943 /Cameroon-athletes-missing-Olympic-Village-London.html.

Ifekwunigwe, Jayne O. 2006. "An Inhospitable Port in the Storm: Recent Clandestine West African Migrants and the Quest for Diasporic Recognition." In *The Situated*

*Politics of Belonging,* edited by Nira Yuval-Davis, Kalpana Kannabiran, and Ulrike Vieten, 84–99. London: Sage Publications.

Ignatieff, Michael. 2001. *Human Rights as Politics and Idolatry.* Princeton: Princeton University Press.

Konings, Piet. 2002. "University Students' Revolt, Ethnic Militia, and Violence during Political Liberalization in Cameroon." *African Studies Review* 45 (2): 179–204.

Laguerre, Michel S. 1998. *Diasporic Citizenship: Haitian Americans in Transnational America.* New York: Palgrave Macmillan.

Mehler, Andreas. 1997. "Cameroun: Une transition qui n'a pas eu lieu." In *Transitions démocratiques africaines,* edited by Jean-Pascal Daloz and Patrick Quantin, 95–138. Paris: Karthala.

Meister, Robert. 2011. *After Evil: A Politics of Human Rights.* New York: Columbia University Press.

Murray, Craig. 2011. "Diallo Must Be Deported." August 23. Accessed March 1, 2012. http://www.craigmurray.org.uk/archives/2011/08/diallo-must-be-deported/.

Neumayer, Eric. 2005. "Bogus Refugees? The Determinants of Asylum Migration to Western Europe." *International Studies Quarterly* 49 (3): 389–409.

Ngayap, P. F. 1999. *L'opposition au Cameroun: Les années de braise.* Paris: L'Harmattan.

Nyamnjoh, Francis. 1999. "Cameroon: A Country United by Ethnic Ambition and Difference." *African Affairs* 98:101–18.

Nyers, Peter. 2005. *Rethinking Refugees beyond States of Emergency.* New York: Routledge.

Pommerolle, Marie-Emmanuelle. 2008. "La démobilisation collective au Cameroun: Entre régime postautoritaire et militantisme extraverti." *Critique international* 40:73–94.

Priso, Moukoko. 1994. *Cameroun/Kamerun: La transition dans l'impasse.* Paris: L'Harmattan.

Shemak, April. 2011. *Asylum Speakers: Caribbean Refugees and Testimonial Discourse.* New York: Fordham University Press.

Silverstein, Ken. 2007. "Their Men in Washington: Undercover with D.C.'s Lobbyists for Hire." *Harper's Magazine,* July.

Squire, Vicki. 2009. *The Exclusionary Politics of Asylum.* New York: Palgrave Macmillan.

Takougang, Joseph, and Milton Krieger. 1998. *African State and Society in the 1990s: Cameroon's Political Crossroads.* Boulder, CO: Westview Press.

Taylor, Matthew, Sam Jones, and Afua Hirsch. 2012. "London 2012: Seven Cameroonian Athletes Go Missing from Olympics." *Guardian,* August 7. Accessed January 30, 2014. http://www.theguardian.com/sport/2012/aug/07/london-2012-seven-cameroonian-athletes.

Terretta, Meredith, and Dieudonné Pouhe Pouhe. 2012. "Emeutes de la faim et apprentis sorciers: Eléments d'une tradition politique camerounaise après 50 ans d'indépendance et vingt ans d'opposition." *Afroscopie: Revue savante et pluridisciplinaire sur l'Afrique et les communautés noires* 2:13–38.

Transparency International. 2004. "Report on the Transparency International Global Corruption Barometer." Accessed January 28, 2014. http://www.transparency.org/policy_research/surveys_indices/cpi.

Fraudulent Asylum Seeking as Transnational Mobilization

————. 2007. "Report on the Transparency International Global Corruption Barometer." Accessed January 28, 2014. http://www.transparency.org/policy _research/surveys_indices/cpi.

————. 2009. "Global Corruption Barometer." Accessed January 28, 2014. http:// www.transparency.org/policy_research/surveys_indices/cpi.

————. 2013. "Global Corruption Barometer: Cameroon." Accessed January 28, 2014. http://www.transparency.org/gcb2013/country/?country=cameroon.

US Department of Homeland Security. 2013. *Yearbook of Immigration Statistics: 2012*. Washington, DC: US Department of Homeland Security, Office of Immigration Statistics.

Wallechinsky, David. 2012. "Missing Athletes Join Long List of Olympic Defectors: Interview with David Wallechinsky." Interviewed by Melissa Block. National Public Radio, August 8.

Wasem, Ruth E. 2005. *U.S. Immigration Policy on Asylum Seekers*. CRS Report for Congress. CRS RL 32621. Washington, DC: Congressional Research Service.

————. 2011. *Asylum and "Credible Fear" Issues in U.S. Immigration Policy*. CRS Report for Congress. CRS R41753. Washington, DC: Congressional Research Service.

Williams, David, and Louise Eccles. 2012. "And Now the Race to Be First to Claim Asylum: Four Members of Congo's Olympic Team Go Missing as Five Cameroon Boxers Plead to Stay in Britain." *Mail Online*, August 13. Accessed January 28, 2014. http://www.dailymail.co.uk/news/article-2187663/And-race-to-claim-asylum -Four-members-Congos-Olympic-team-missing-Cameroon-boxers-plead-stay -Britain.html.

# THREE

## The Evolving Refugee Definition

*How Shifting Elements of Eligibility Affect the Nature and Focus of Expert Testimony in Asylum Proceedings*

Karen Musalo

THIS CHAPTER FOCUSES on jurisprudence in the United States and the manner in which the evolving requirements for establishing eligibility as a refugee have influenced the use of experts. In the 1980 Refugee Act, Congress adopted the international definition of a refugee as an individual with a "well-founded fear of persecution on account of race, religion, nationality, membership in a particular social group, or political opinion" (Immigration and Nationality Act [INA] 1980, sec. 1101(a)(42)(A)). This definition has its origins in the 1951 UN Convention Relating to the Status of Refugees (art. 1A(2)) and its 1967 Protocol (UN Protocol Relating to the Status of Refugees 1967, art. 1(2)), which came into existence in the wake of World War II and the international community's failure to respond to the plight of Jews and other persecuted groups fleeing the Holocaust.[1]

Individuals arriving in the United States and seeking protection under the Refugee Act's provisions bear the burden of proof of establishing their eligibility. In practical terms, this means they must bring forth evidence adequate to meet each element of the refugee definition—that they fear persecution; that the fear is well founded (that is, reasonable); and that the feared persecution will befall them because of their race, religion, nationality, membership in a particular social group, or political opinion.

The evidentiary requirements for asylum are more daunting than they appear because of factors intrinsic to the asylum process. The events at issue in asylum claims often take place hundreds or, in most cases, thousands of miles outside the United States, and there are unlikely to be witnesses familiar with the facts of the case who can be called to testify or documents easily available to corroborate a claim. Linguistic and cultural differences can cause barriers to communication, and frequently, asylum seekers are suffering from psychological trauma that affects their ability to credibly recount their stories. The challenges inherent to the process have been compounded by the evolving jurisprudence, which has modified the legal requirements for establishing credibility, as well as substantive eligibility, in ways both large and small.

In the context of these challenges, the testimony of experts has become increasingly critical to asylum seekers attempting to meet their burden of proof.[2] Beginning with the Refugee Act's passage in the 1980s, experts have addressed issues pertaining to each element of the refugee definition. They have also provided opinions that shed light on cultural and psychological issues, which can be key to credibility determinations. More recently, the focus of expert testimony has shifted to meet the particular evidentiary requirements of claims based on gender, sexual orientation or gender identity, and status as a child.

As the law has evolved and as the use of expert witnesses in asylum claims has become more common, so has the need for a sharper understanding of an expert's value within the context of the particular case. The most successful advocate will have a clear understanding of the nuanced—albeit shifting—legal requirements and ensure that the witness's expertise allows him or her to address them.[3] This chapter contributes to that understanding by providing a historical and contemporary perspective on how the evolving legal definition has affected the need for particular kinds of experts.

## US Procedures for Seeking Refugee Protection

Countries that ratified the Convention and/or its Protocol committed themselves to *not* return refugees to persecution (the principle of non-refoulement). The 1980 Refugee Act provides two distinct routes for individuals fleeing persecution to secure protection. Through the Overseas Refugee Program (ORP), individuals enter the United States as refugees; their selection and the adjudication of their claims occur outside the

United States, prior to their arrival (INA 1980, sec. 1157, 1101(a)(42) (A), 1159). Not every individual fleeing persecution can take advantage of this route; it is open only to persons living in regions that the US president, in consultation with Congress, has designated (INA 1980, sec. 1157(a)(3)). In addition to the regional designation, the Presidential Determinations identify certain "priority" categories.[4]

Individuals who enter through the ORP do not go through a formal adjudication process in the United States, and this chapter does not discuss barriers particular to their claims for protection. Instead, the focus here is on those who come in under the 1980 Refugee Act, whereby individuals who arrive at or cross the US border may apply for asylum (INA 1980, sec. 1158(b)). Individuals who pursue this route must meet the "well-founded fear" refugee definition set forth earlier and demonstrate that they are worthy of protection.[5] Depending on the person's particular situation, his or her claim may be decided in a nonadversarial interview with an asylum officer or in a contested, adversarial hearing in immigration court. It is in these two venues that evidentiary challenges and the need for experts arise.[6]

A threshold issue in every asylum claim is whether the facts asserted are true; put another way, is the asylum seeker credible? If this question cannot be answered in the affirmative, then an adjudicator need not advance to the legal analysis necessary to determine if the individual merits asylum. The following section examines the collaboration with experts relevant to the asylum seeker's credibility.

### Is the Asylum Seeker to Be Believed?

A number of factors inherent to the refugee experience make issues of proof difficult: the geographic distance between the country of origin and the country of asylum, the potential differences in social and cultural norms between the two countries, and the prevalence of trauma in the population of asylum seekers. The events at the heart of refugee claims take place far away from the country of adjudication. Often, the most egregious acts of persecution occurred out of public view, making it unlikely that there were eyewitnesses. However, even if there were eyewitnesses, these individuals are frequently still in the country of origin, and it is extremely unlikely that they will be available to appear at an asylum office or immigration court to testify. Although clichéd, it is true that asylum seekers often flee with little more than the shirts on their backs, and they frequently do not have time to gather documents that might verify the facts of their claims. Without eyewitnesses or documentation, they must often rely on their testimony alone to prove their claims.

In order for testimony to be accepted as credible, the adjudicator must consider the asylum seeker's account to be plausible (INA 208(b)(1)(B) (iii)). When an applicant is from a country with social norms significantly different from those of the country adjudicating the claim, the adjudicator may simply find the asylum seeker's account to be implausible. The highly publicized case of the Togolese asylum seeker Fauziya Kassindja (often improperly spelled as Kasinga), discussed later in this section, illustrates the problems that arise when an adjudicator does not consider that other societies have different norms (*Matter of Kasinga* 1996).

However, these issues of presumed implausibility arose in the early 1980s, shortly after the passage of the Refugee Act, when tens of thousands of Guatemalans and Salvadorans sought refuge in the United States. Their claims for asylum often did not fare well compared to those advanced by individuals of other nationalities. Though an analysis of the underlying reasons is beyond the purview of this chapter, there were many occasions when adjudicators simply did not find the asylum seeker's account to be plausible.[7] They expressed disbelief that an indigenous Guatemalan would not be able to recall the date on which the military attacked and destroyed his village, for example, or pointed to errors in the date of birth provided for the applicant's child (*Damaize-Job v. I.N.S.* 1986, 1337).

In addition, the stories recounted by asylum seekers often did not "make sense" to the adjudicators. Yet as one of the earliest scholars to write on cross-cultural misunderstandings in the asylum context observed, "Common sense [is] culturally determined and thus not universal" (Kälin 1986, 236). Thus, one immigration judge rejected the credibility of a young Salvadoran male because it made no sense that the applicant "stayed at home to avoid forcible conscription" (FMCARP 1988, 11). The judge assumed that if the military were searching for him, it "could easily find him at his house, so it made no sense for him to hide there" (FMCARP 1988, 11). What the judge failed to consider was that "in El Salvador forcible conscription most frequently occurs in public places where young men are rounded up in military sweeps [and they are] not generally sought out specifically from lists by name or at home" (FMCARP 1988, 11). Within that context, "staying at home, or at least avoiding public meeting places [was] a common sense way of avoiding forcible military service" (FMCARP 1988, 11).

In the 1996 Fauziya Kassindja case, the applicant was fleeing a forced marriage as well as the female genital cutting (FGC) required as part of the marriage arrangement. She testified that her father had protected her from FGC, which was the norm among her ethnic group, the Tchamba Kunsuntu, but that when he died, his family banished Kassindja's mother and took over her life, including selling her into marriage. Kassindja also stated that once her mother was sent away, she had no way to ascertain her whereabouts, and she was subject to the control and decisions of her father's family. The immigration judge found this recounting of events to be implausible. He refused to believe that her father could have protected her against FGC if the practice was as pervasive as claimed; he also found it not credible that her paternal relatives could have forced her mother to leave the family home (Musalo 1996, 855).

On appeal to the Board of Immigration Appeals (BIA), Kassindja's new legal team submitted the affidavit of Merrick Posnansky, professor emeritus of history and anthropology at the University of California, Los Angeles, to address the bases the immigration judge relied upon to find her not credible.[8] Although the BIA was not technically required to accept and consider new evidence on appeal, the substance of the affidavit, which informed national press coverage on the case, was influential on the board's decision.

Posnansky had carried out extensive research in Togo, visiting the country sixteen times between 1979 and 1996. His work put him into contact with a broad section of Togolese society. In his affidavit, he stated that Togo is a patriarchal society and that, within that context, Kassindja's father could, indeed, have protected her from FGC notwithstanding its pervasiveness. He also confirmed that within the context of these patriarchal norms, her father's family could have ordered her mother to leave and made the decision for Kassindja to marry and be subjected to FGC. The BIA was persuaded that these and other aspects of Kassindja's story were true, finding her to be credible in all respects, and it granted her asylum in an important landmark decision.

Cultural norms may also affect credibility in another way as well if the asylum seeker's demeanor does not comport with the adjudicator's concept of truth telling (INA 1980, sec. 1158(b)(1)(B)(iii)). For instance, the belief that an honest individual will make direct eye contact when testifying may undermine the credibility of an individual who comes from a society where direct eye contact is considered aggressive or impolite.

The belief that demeanor is a valid gauge of credibility persists despite empirical evidence to the contrary (DePaulo 1985, 339; Rempell 2011, 379). It continues to be a measure even though the "participants in immigration proceedings have distinctive cultural, ethnic, and linguistic backgrounds that may make generalizations about the significance of demeanor attributes from an American vantage point much harder to extend to those coming from other countries" (Rempell 2011, 403, citing Cianciarulo 2006, 130–31, and Durst 2000, 152–56).

When attorneys began to encounter these potential "cross-cultural misunderstandings" in the 1980s, they sought ways to minimize the likelihood of judicial misperceptions. If adjudicators were making assumptions based on a lack of familiarity with the culture of the asylum seekers in their courtrooms, then providing them with information about these cultures could avoid such misunderstandings. One of the first publications that attempted to address these issues presented the sworn declarations of four experts—two on Guatemala and two on El Salvador (FMCARP 1988, 11). The Guatemalan experts—James P. Curtin, a Maryknoll priest, and James Loucky, an anthropologist—and the Salvadoran experts—Terry Karl, a political scientist, and William Durham, an anthropologist—explained the social and cultural norms as well as the historical context within which contemporary events were unfolding. In their declarations, these experts took special pains to address recurrent issues that led adjudicators to question credibility.[9] Loucky's declaration discussed the comportment of young Guatemalan women who had been the victims of rape, beatings, or kidnapping. He described one "young Indian woman" who "expressed her nervousness in court by frequent smiles or giggles, even at inappropriate times, as when describing the kidnapping of family members" (FMCARP 1988, 29). Although such behavior could be the result of confusion or nervousness, this type of dissonance between content of testimony and emotional affect is now recognized as a symptom of psychological trauma.

In addition to cross-cultural misunderstandings, refugee attorneys in the 1980s also quickly became aware of the evidentiary difficulties posed by psychological trauma. The case of Berta Lidia Iraheta, a young Salvadoran woman who entered the United States in 1980, illustrates this well. The young woman testified that she and her fiancé were activists with several "popular" organizations that worked nonviolently in opposition to the government in their country.[10] Iraheta described how four of her fiancé's six brothers were abducted, noting that "all four of them were killed, and two of the bodies were dismembered and showed signs of torture." Several of her friends who were activists were also "tortured, murdered and dismembered," and her fiancé was subsequently disappeared, never to be found alive again. She herself stayed in hiding for a number of months, and then she fled to the United States, where she sought asylum (*In re Berta Lidia Iraheta* 1990, reproduced in Musalo, Moore, and Boswell 2009, 1026–27).

Although Iraheta testified consistently and although what she described was fully plausible given conditions prevailing in El Salvador at the time, the immigration judge found her to be not credible. His denial was based on a combination of factors, but he seemed most troubled by Iraheta's inability to recount events with a level of detail that met his expectations and by her "hesitant, unemotional and vague" demeanor and testimony (*In re Berta Lidia Iraheta* 1990, reproduced in Musalo, Moore, and Boswell 2009, 1028). In the judge's estimation, she should have been able to provide details about the political agenda of the popular organizations with which she participated (as a teenager), and she had failed to show the emotions he expected of someone describing the death and disappearance of loved ones. As he saw it, Iraheta's overall demeanor and tone were more appropriate to someone who was reading a banal litany of inconsequential occurrences, rather than testifying about unspeakable personal losses.

It is now fairly well recognized that individuals who have experienced trauma may suffer from psychological disorders such as post-traumatic stress disorder (PTSD), which could impact, among other things, their emotional affect and ability to recall detail (American Psychiatric Association 1994). However, this was not common knowledge among asylum adjudicators in the early 1980s. Refugee advocates had not begun to reach out to mental health experts as a means of educating judges and explaining why asylum seekers might display an emotional demeanor inconsistent with the experiences recounted. But other possible means of "proving" truthfulness, such as polygraph tests and the use of scopolamine, or "truth serum," were not considered reliable (*Goel v. Gonzales* 2007, 739;

Bergman 2010, sec. 13:45; Culligan 1989, sec. 1037), which ultimately led lawyers to explore partnering with medical professionals.

Psychological evaluations have now become common practice in refugee advocacy, and a number of publications provide guidance to medical professionals who administer such evaluations (HealthRight International Human Rights Clinic 2009; Physicians for Human Rights 2001; Stadtmauer, Singer, and Metalios 2010, 41–45). A relatively recent study indicated a positive correlation between favorable outcomes in asylum cases and those in which medical evaluations had been submitted (Lustig et al. 2008, 9).

Mental health professionals can provide critical evidence in two broad, interrelated areas having to do with credibility. First, they can diagnose a psychological condition and render their expert opinion as to whether the alleged facts of persecution are consistent with the development of such a condition. Second, and equally important, the mental health professional can help to preempt a finding of noncredibility based on failed memory, inconsistencies, or lack of emotional affect, to the extent that such behavior is consistent with the diagnosis. What a mental health professional cannot do is assert that he or she can attest to the client's veracity. However, the professional can give an expert opinion as to the likelihood of "malingering" or "the intentional production of false or grossly exaggerated physical or psychological symptoms motivated by external incentives" (Rogers 1997, 131).

When refugee lawyers first sought out mental health professionals, it was—as described earlier—principally for the purpose of avoiding adverse credibility determinations. The role and importance of partnering with mental health professionals changed in 1996 with the enactment of the Illegal Immigration Reform and Immigration Responsibility Act (IIRIRA), which imposed a one-year filing deadline on asylum seekers and other restrictive measures (IIRIRA 1996, sec. 1158(a)(2)(B)). Any asylum seeker who fails to apply within a year of arrival in the United States is barred from asylum (though not withholding of removal or protection under the Convention against Torture, or CAT) unless he or she can demonstrate the existence of "changed" or "extraordinary" circumstances (INA 2009, sec. 1158(a)(2)(D). Regulations provide examples of changed or extraordinary circumstances; among the latter is mental or physical disability, "including any effects of persecution or violent harm suffered in the past" (Procedures for Asylum and Withholding of Removal 2009, 8 C.F.R. sec. 208.4(a)(5)).

Since the 1996 enactment of IIRIRA, it has become increasingly common for attorneys to seek out psychological evaluations of their clients in cases where the one-year deadline has not been met. A diagnosis of PTSD, for example, can explain the individual's inability to file within a year of arriving. Individuals suffering from PTSD will "go to great lengths to avoid triggering any sort of reminder" and "often avoid even talking about the traumatic experience because of the unpleasant memories and feelings evoked" (Lustig 2008, 726). In addition, PTSD sufferers often experience what mental health professionals refer to as "foreshortening," meaning that they "often have difficulty anticipating being alive for long, or planning very far ahead beyond their immediate survival needs" (Lustig 2008, 726). These reactions and perceptions can explain the failure to file for asylum in a timely manner; the individual is hampered from planning for the future, and even if he or she could contemplate the benefits of securing the protection of refugee status, having to talk about traumatic events and trigger horrific memories becomes an insurmountable barrier. Within this context, a mental health professional's diagnosis and explanation can often serve as the basis for a successful argument that the failure to meet the one-year bar should be excused.

The preceding discussion highlights the unique evidentiary challenges that asylum seekers face, which gave rise to interdisciplinary collaborations with experts. In light of these difficulties, the UN High Commissioner for Refugees (UNHCR) and other international scholars have made recommendations to ease the asylum seeker's burden by affording him or her the "benefit of the doubt" (UNHCR 1979, ¶¶ 203–5; Grahl-Madsen 1966, 145–46). Paradoxically, not only have these recommendations been ignored but evidentiary requirements in the United States have been tightened as well. Pursuant to the REAL ID Act of 2005, a decision maker can rely on questionable criteria to find an asylum seeker not credible; for instance, any inconsistencies—whether they go to relevant matters or not—can be the basis for disbelieving an applicant (INA 2009, sec. 1158(b)(1)(B)(iii)). In addition, even if an applicant is found to be believable, the decision maker can require corroborating evidence, unless the applicant can show that he or she could not "reasonably obtain" it (INA 2009, sec. 1158(b)(1)(B)(ii)). The question of what documents can be reasonably obtained in a foreign country is best addressed by an expert or another country-specific source of information; it should not be left to the adjudicator's "common sense" judgment (Kälin 1986, 236).

A number of federal court decisions have reversed assumptions by adjudicators that corroboration should have been produced because it was reasonably available. The assessment of a qualified expert on this issue can often be determinative.

## Meeting the Evolving Requirements of the Refugee Definition

The refugee definition—an "individual with a well-founded fear of persecution on account of race, religion, nationality, political opinion or membership in a particular social group"—appears to be relatively straightforward. However, the plethora of cases and commentary analyzing the definition and disagreeing about the proper interpretation of its every word give the lie to any assumption regarding its simplicity. From the questions of what type of harm constitutes "persecution" and what makes a fear "well-founded" to the issue of the proper meaning of "on account of" or the matter of what qualifies as a political opinion and what must be proven to establish a "social group," there have been conflicting federal court opinions—often necessitating resolution at the level of the US Supreme Court.

Court decisions analyzing many of the key terms in the definition have often made it significantly more difficult for asylum seekers to establish eligibility. For instance, some courts have interpreted the term *persecution* to exclude harms that are psychological, as opposed to physical (*Mashiri v. Ashcroft* 2004; *Niang v. Gonzales* 2007), and others have ruled that beatings and death threats during a "legitimate" interrogation are not persecution (*Dinu v. Ashcroft* 2004). Still other decisions have limited the meaning of *political opinion,* rejecting arguments that a deeply held belief in opposition to criminality or gang activity qualifies.

Among the many relevant examples of how evolving definitions heighten proof requirements and make the partnership with an expert all the more crucial, perhaps none are as illustrative as those related to the interpretations of the phrases *on account of* and *particular social group.* The first of these terms addresses the necessary relationship between the persecution feared and one of the five grounds (i.e., well-founded fear of persecution *on account of* race, religion, and so forth). The second is itself one of the enumerated grounds. The interpretations of both can sharply and indisputably limit the scope of refugee protection. The evolving definitions of these terms, their relationship to the asylum seeker's burden of proof, and the resulting heightened need for experts are discussed in the following sections.

There is broad consensus that the phrase *on account of* requires that there be some connection, or "nexus," between persecution and one or more of the enumerated grounds. Although it may not be readily apparent, significant differences in outcomes depend on the particular interpretation of this statutory phrase.

The case of a religiously motivated conscientious objector provides one of the clearest examples. Assume that the conscientious objector in this hypothetical is a devout male adherent of a religion that forbids military service under all circumstances. Further assume that he is from a country that does not allow an exemption from service for reasons of conscience and that the government of his country will impose a prison sentence on him for failure to serve. Can the imprisonment be considered persecution "on account of" religion? Under a number of interpretations, the answer would be yes; under others—including that now prevailing in the United States—it would be no.

Religious persecution would be found if "on account of" simply required a "but for" showing—*but for* his religion, the devout adherent would not be imprisoned. Religious persecution would also be found if "on account of" was determined by the *effect* on the individual, such that the question would be whether the imprisonment for failure to serve had the effect of persecuting him because of his religion. Both of these interpretations are accepted by the tribunals of other countries that are parties to the refugee convention and protocol.

However, in US law, neither a "but for" nor an "effects" analysis is accepted. Instead, an "intents" analysis prevails, wherein proof of the persecutor's intent to persecute because of the protected ground is required. Thus, in the conscientious objector scenario, the asylum seeker would have to demonstrate that the persecutor (in this case, the government) was not simply applying a universally applicable sentence for draft resistance but was *motivated* to imprison him *because* of his religion. This intents test, requiring proof of the persecutor's motivation, was established by the US Supreme Court in its decision in *I.N.S. v. Elias-Zacarias* (1992) and was applied in the conscientious objector context in *Canas-Segovia v. I.N.S.* (1992).

The rule in *Zacarias,* requiring proof of intent, limits protection by precluding cases where persecution is not intended but is nonetheless the result—such as the conscientious objector scenario just discussed. It also limits protection because of the difficulty inherent in proving intent. The case in which the rule was announced illustrates this. It arose during the period of Guatemala's internal armed conflict. Two armed guerrilla members came to Jairo Elias-Zacarias's home, requesting that he join. When he refused, they told him to "think it over" because they would be back. He fled, fearing that the guerrillas would return and take him by force (*I.N.S. v. Elias-Zacarias* 1992, 479–80).

Zacarias was granted asylum by the Ninth Circuit Court of Appeals, which ruled that he had a well-founded fear of persecution on account of his political opinion (*I.N.S. v. Elias-Zacarias* 1992, 480). The Supreme Court reversed, ruling that there was no evidence that the guerrillas were *motivated* to harm him for his political opinion, rather than simply retaliating against him for his refusal to join their efforts (*I.N.S. v. Elias-Zacarias* 1992, 483–84).

Proving the guerrillas' intent would not have been an easy matter. As one federal court observed, persecutors are not likely to sign affidavits attesting to their acts of persecution (*Bolanos-Hernandez v. I.N.S.* 1984); neither are they likely to trumpet their motivations in persecuting.

The rule in *Zacarias,* requiring asylum seekers to prove motivation through either circumstantial or direct evidence, greatly increases the challenges in presenting a winning claim. Only in the rarest of asylum claims will persecutors have revealed their motivation by making statements that leave no doubt. In such a case, the persecutor's beatings or other abuse may be accompanied by derogatory remarks regarding the victim's religion, sexual orientation, or other protected ground attribute.

However, in the majority of cases, the persecutor makes no clear statements revealing motive, and often, the victim "may not be aware of the reasons for the persecution feared" (UNHCR 1979, ¶66). In cases where there is no explicit statement by the persecutor, the motive must be inferred from the circumstances, and it is in these situations that an expert's opinion may be particularly significant.

Experts with a deep understanding of historical and social factors are often able to place the persecution within context, demonstrating that it is motivated by one of the five protected grounds. The testimony of Frank Howard, an expert on human rights, persuaded the court in *Osorio v. I.N.S.* (1994) that the targeting of union leaders during the armed conflict in Guatemala was politically motivated. The testimony of Terry

Karl in *Ramirez-Rivas v. I.N.S.* (1990), a case arising out of El Salvador's civil war, was key to establishing that any future persecution of a woman whose family members were involved with the Farabundo Marti National Liberation Front (FMLN) rebel group would be politically motivated. Likewise, the testimony of Jacques de Lisle, a professor of Chinese law, in *Zhou v. Gonzales* (2006, 1397) helped support the court's finding that the petitioner's persecution by the Chinese government was motivated by a perceived "anti-governmental political opinion."

### The Increasing Importance of the "Particular Social Group" Ground and the Role of Experts

From the Refugee Act's passage in 1980 through the mid-1990s, the majority of published opinions were in cases premised upon the political opinion ground of the refugee definition; *Osorio* and *Ramirez-Rivas* fall within that trend. Although the facts and context of persecution in these cases and others like them were quite different from that of the World War II experience, the asylum seekers in *Osorio* and *Ramirez-Rivas* still fit within the traditional concept of the refugee as a victim of political persecution.

However, beginning in the late 1980s, the paradigmatic image of the refugee as a political dissident began to be challenged by the appearance of a different kind of claim. These claims were brought by individuals whose fear was not necessarily linked to their political opinion but due to their very identity or status. The gay man fleeing persecution at the hands of his government and the general populace (*Matter of Toboso-Alfonso* 1990) or the young women fleeing the cultural practice of female genital cutting (*Matter of Kasinga* 1996) or repressive social norms (*Fatin v. I.N.S.* 1993) exemplified these new asylum seekers.

Their claims met resistance because they did not fit the existing paradigm. Some who opposed their recognition as refugees argued that neither sexual orientation nor gender was among the five enumerated grounds of the refugee definition and that the refugee convention's drafters did not intend to protect people from persecution on such bases. It is beyond the scope of this chapter to detail the legal developments that led to slowly expanded acceptance of these claims (see Meister 1995; Musalo 2010), but it is important to recognize that the majority of such claims— and others that followed in their wake—relied upon the "particular social group" ground. As will be detailed, the evolving definition of this term has been controversial, and experts have been essential to the successful adjudication of claims based on the particular social group ground. The

The Evolving Refugee Definition

drafters of the 1951 refugee convention who added this as the fifth protected ground (after race, religion, nationality, and political opinion) did not provide guidance as to its meaning. The first US decision to interpret the term was *Matter of Acosta* (1985). In light of scant international and domestic guidance, the BIA reasoned that the meaning of *particular social group* should be "construed in a manner consistent" with the other four terms (*Matter of Acosta* 1985, 233). This interpretive approach is known as *ejusdem generis*—which literally means "of the same kind."[11] The board reasoned that the other four terms describe a trait or characteristic that "is either beyond the power of an individual to change or is so fundamental to individual identity or conscience that it ought not be required to change" and that a particular social group should therefore be marked by either immutable or fundamental characteristics (*Matter of Acosta* 1985, 233–34).[12]

The immutable or fundamental approach resulted in grants of protection to groups that had previously been outside the scope of protection. In *Matter of Toboso-Alfonso* (1990), the Board of Immigration Appeals granted protection to a gay Cuban man, recognizing a social group defined by sexual orientation. Six years later, in an equally significant precedential decision, the BIA granted asylum to Fauziya Kassindja, holding that a social group could be defined by gender in combination with other immutable or fundamental traits (*Matter of Kasinga* 1996).

For almost fifteen years, groups that met the immutable or fundamental criteria of *Acosta* were found to be cognizable (legally recognizable) (*Matter of Fuentes* 1988; *Matter of Toboso-Alfonso* 1990; *In re H* 1996; *Matter of Kasinga* 1996; *In re V-T-S-* 1997). However, in 1999, the BIA started to hint at additional requirements in its controversial decision *Matter of R-A-* (*In re R-A-* 1999). In *Matter of R-A-,* the BIA characterized its immutable and fundamental criteria as simply threshold determinations, stating that a proposed group also had to show that it was "recognized and understood to be a societal faction." The BIA did not begin to formalize or actually apply those requirements until 2006, with a series of decisions ruling that the demonstration of immutable and fundamental characteristics was not enough. Social groups also had to meet the requirements of "social visibility" and "particularity."

The imposition of these additional criteria has been controversial, and the meaning of these terms has confounded courts and commentators alike. In some decisions, the BIA has implied that social visibility requires that the group members actually be visible and identifiable as such to society at large (sometimes referred to as the literal or "naked eye" interpretation) (*Matter of C-A-* 2006). In other cases, the implication has been social visibility requires that individuals with the defining characteristics be perceived by society as a particular social group. Particularity, to the degree that it has been described, appears to require that the group members not constitute a "large and diffuse segment of society" or be "too broad and inchoate" (*Valdiviezo-Galdamez v. Attorney General* 2011, 616).

Ultimately, these new requirements may be ruled inconsistent with the refugee statute. In the interim, an asylum seeker whose case relies upon the social group ground must show his or her proposed group can meet criteria that require an assessment of the societal attitudes toward it and that relate to the size and scope of the group. In many of these cases, such proof will not be possible without the participation of experts, who understand the societal roles, dynamics, and attitudes necessary for establishing social visibility and particularity. In *Matter of Kasinga* (1996), the BIA had applied *Acosta*'s (1985) approach to rule that a social group defined by gender in combination with other equally immutable or fundamental characteristics (ethnicity, not having been subjected to FGC, and opposition to it) was legally cognizable. However, as the BIA modified its position, it brought into question the cognizability of other gender-defined social groups. The asylum claim of Rody Alvarado (*Matter of R-A-*), which involved the abuse of domestic violence and took more than a decade to resolve, was emblematic of the ambiguities posed by these new requirements. In 2009, in an attempt to provide guidance on gender-defined social groups, the Department of Homeland Security (DHS) filed a supplemental brief in the case of Ms. L. R., a Mexican woman seeking asylum on the basis of two decades of virtual enslavement and brutal abuse by her common-law spouse. It should be noted that although Rody Alvarado and L. R. were from Latin America, there are numerous cases of women fleeing spousal abuse who are seeking asylum from countries on the African continent (see Bookey 2013).

In its brief, DHS stated that social visibility may be established upon proof that the government and/or the society subjects members of the group to differential (i.e., discriminatory) treatment and that particularity simply requires showing the group is susceptible to being defined in a manner that makes it clear to other members of society just who is included in the group.

DHS suggested two alternate social groups that could—with the submission of appropriate evidence about country conditions—be found to meet the dual requirements of social visibility and particularity. The groups were: (1) Mexican women in domestic relationships who are unable to leave (e.g., if the intimate partner does not accept that the woman has the right to leave and does not recognize that divorce or separation will end his right to abuse), or (2) Mexican women who are viewed as property by virtue of their positions in a domestic relationship. The DHS suggested that the BIA send L. R.'s case back to the immigration court so that she could submit country condition evidence relevant to these social groups.

On remand, L. R. put forth the legal argument that she was a member of the social group of Mexican women in domestic relationships who are unable to leave. She was keenly aware of the framework in the DHS brief, which, as noted, requires a showing of differential treatment to establish social visibility and clear definitional parameters to show particularity.

Toward this end, L. R. submitted the sworn affidavit of expert Alicia Elena Perez Duarte y Norona (Ms. Duarte), a lawyer who has worked in both governmental and nongovernmental positions on woman's rights issues for over thirty years. Duarte attested to the deep-seated patriarchy in Mexico and documented the legal and social norms that assign women a subordinate position in society and cause them to tolerate violence perpetrated against them—including violence in intimate relationships—as natural and acceptable.

Duarte's analysis provided strong support for L. R.'s argument that Mexican women, including those in domestic relationships, are subject to different and discriminatory treatment and are thus socially visible within the framework set forth in the DHS brief. Duarte also provided facts relevant to the finding of particularity, attesting that "partners" who "reside together" or "have children together" are seen as being in a common-law marriage, a group that has clear parameters. Additional documentation (reports of governmental and nongovernmental organizations, press reports, and so on) was also submitted to establish these key requirements.[13] The DHS found Duarte's expert opinion, along with the country conditions evidence, to be persuasive, and it stipulated to a grant of asylum to L. R. on August 4, 2010. Cases involving African women have been successfully brought with the use of evidence that establishes similar cultural norms and conditions.

The use of an expert in L. R.'s case to establish that her proposed group had both social visibility and particularity provides a concrete example of the pivotal role an expert may play in the developing area of social group claims. The existence of L. R.'s social group was not adjudicated in the abstract but was a highly fact-dependent determination, necessitating an evaluation of the proposed group in light of pertinent legal and societal norms. As long as the law continues to require proof of social visibility and particularity, experts will be sought out to provide testimony on the legal and societal attitudes toward and the choate nature of a range of social groups—be they evangelical Salvadorans (Petitioner's Opening Brief 2011, 39), "young Christian males" who resist gang membership (*Perez-Morales v. Holder* 2011, 590), "Jordanian women who, in accordance with social and religious norms . . . are accused of being immoral criminals" (*Sarhan v. Holder* 2011, 654), or Colombian truckers who are opposed to the Revolutionary Armed Forces of Colombia (FARC) and "have collaborated with law enforcement and refused to cooperate with FARC" (*Escobar v. Holder* 2011, 545).

Finally, particular social group claims pose a challenge to proving nexus in that a claimant must show the distinct and unique characteristics that define the particular social group also motivate the persecutor in targeting the claimant for persecution. The challenges in asylum claims of children fleeing incest illustrate the difficulty of proving motivation in relation to social group characteristics, as well as the critical role that experts can fill in establishing the "on account of" element.

Children, like adults, can suffer from a range of persecutory harms.[14] A review of recent cases provides anecdotal evidence that incest is increasingly a central element of child asylum claims arising in a number of Central American and African countries.[15] These cases are consistent with country conditions evidence that demonstrates incest is pervasive and committed with impunity in Guatemala, El Salvador, and Honduras.[16] There is also anecdotal evidence that incest claims arise in cases from the African continent, specifically Egypt, Ghana, Cameroon, and Kenya. Although its victims can be either boys or girls, incest is a form of abuse predominantly committed against girls.

Claims of children fleeing incest have often been framed as "particular social group" cases, with the characteristics defining the group being nationality and status as a girl child in a family (e.g., Honduran girls in families) or nationality and status as a child in a family (e.g., Honduran children in families).

Cases with compelling facts, in which the children had suffered appalling levels of sexual abuse, have frequently been denied. Typically, the adjudicator did not doubt the credibility of the child or question the egregiousness of the harm; rather, he or she denied on the basis that there was no nexus to an enumerated ground. The adjudicator reasoned that the perpetrator was a deviant individual and that the fact that the victim was a girl or child in the family (i.e., a member of the defined social group) was irrelevant.[17] Peculiar to such decisions was the fact that they were apparently not based on the adjudicators' own expertise regarding incest as a behavioral phenomenon, nor were there authorities cited to support the assertion that being a girl in the family was irrelevant to the victimization. These outcomes pointed out the need to consult with an expert to determine whether the basis for the denial of these claims had validity.

The Center for Gender and Refugee Studies, working with the UC Hastings Refugee and Human Rights Clinic, called in an expert—Judith Herman, an internationally renowned authority on incest—to address this issue.[18] Her research proved to be critical in establishing the causes and motives underlying incest. Herman's research has documented that incest is not simply the act of a deviant individual, targeting his victim at random. To the contrary, abusers target "girls in the family precisely because their gender and their perceived role in the family make them vulnerable targets" (Herman 2011, 2). In other words, the social group characteristics of being a girl and being in a family motivate the abuser. Although this holds true across cultures, the more deeply entrenched patriarchal norms are in a society, the higher the level of sexual abuse— including incest—against women and girls (Herman 2011, 6).

Herman's analysis also directly addresses the default analysis of adjudicators, who, refusing to accept that the abuser was motivated by an enumerated ground, seize upon the perceived deviance (i.e., psychological dysfunction) of the perpetrator as the explanation for his actions. Herman flatly rejects that explanation of the cause of incestuous sexual abuse: "Although it is commonly supposed that incest offenders must be mentally ill, in fact, careful psychiatric studies of offenders indicated that very few suffer from major mental illness; in fact, the majority do not qualify for any psychiatric diagnosis" (Herman 2011, 8–9). It is not mental illness or deviance that explains incest but rather "a system of patriarchy [that] prioritizes the desires of men above the needs of girls. . . . The power to abuse is rooted in the family relationship and the ownership over females it confers to men" (Herman 2011, 8).

Herman's affidavit was prepared in the spring of 2011, and there has not yet been an evaluation of the outcomes in incest cases in which it has been submitted.[19] It will be interesting to examine whether, with the inclusion of this evidence, adjudicators have become more readily accepting that there is a causal connection (nexus) between the persecution of incest and membership in a particular social group defined in relation to family and gender.

BECAUSE OF THE unique evidentiary challenges in asylum cases, expert witnesses have become critical to the successful establishment of these claims. Not surprisingly, as the refugee definition has evolved and legal requirements have shifted, the profile of experts and the focus of their testimony have been affected.

In the United States in the early 1980s, many experts were first called to testify regarding cultural or historical conditions that provided a context for understanding the asylum seeker's claim and judging its plausibility—factors that clearly were relevant to evaluating the credibility of the applicant. Experts continue to be called upon to address these factors. Mental health experts also played and continue to play a central role on issues related to credibility, as they explain the correlation between various psychological conditions and the memory, affect, and overall demeanor of the asylum seeker.

The focus of mental health experts expanded after 1996 amendments to the INA imposed a one-year deadline on asylum applications. The deadline can be waived by a showing of extraordinary circumstances, including mental disability. With increasing frequency, psychologists, psychiatrists, and other related mental health experts began to be asked to evaluate asylum seekers who had not met the one-year deadline to determine whether they suffered from a mental condition that could explain the failure to do so.

With the advent of the 1990s, two developments strongly impacted the need for experts. First, the 1992 Supreme Court decision in *Zacarias* required asylum seekers to prove the motivation of their persecutors and to show that it was linked to one of the five statutory grounds. This led to the need for experts who could examine the broader societal context and provide a considered assessment of the persecutor's motivation.

Also in the 1990s, claims arising out of persecution due to gender, sexual orientation, or status as a child started to gain prominence. Although it was not always the exclusive reason, many of these claims were based on the "particular social group" ground of the refugee definition. Initially, the establishment of a social group required proof of defining characteristics that were fundamental or immutable. With these requirements in mind, experts could speak to whether a trait such as being an "uncut" woman (not subjected to FGC) or being a gay man "with a female sexual identity" in Mexico (*Hernandez-Montiel v. I.N.S.* 2000, 1099) was immutable or fundamental.

As the jurisprudence evolved, proof of the fundamental or immutable nature of a characteristic was no longer enough—the group had to also display social visibility and particularity. An assessment of the visibility or particularity of a group within a given society put a premium upon experts who could speak to the prevailing societal attitudes toward group members, as well as the definable parameters of the group.

There is no doubt that the contribution of experts is often pivotal, providing evidence upon which determinative legal conclusions depend. The partnership between lawyers and experts from a range of disciplines has been a fruitful and invaluable factor since the earliest asylum cases were adjudicated under the 1980 Refugee Act. As the law evolves, it will continue to inform the role experts play, and the strongest and most effective attorney-expert collaborations will be those in which the attorney clearly knows what he or she needs to prove and thoroughly assesses the expert's ability to illuminate those issues.

## Notes

I would like to thank my colleague Blaine Bookey for her helpful comments and my law clerks, Annie Daher and Jose Herrera, for their excellent assistance. I also thank my colleague Misha Seay for her research and editing assistance.

1. The primary purpose of the 1967 protocol was to remove the 1951 convention's geographic and temporal restrictions to events occurring in Europe prior to January 1, 1951. In other respects, the protocol is identical to the convention.

2. The Federal Rules of Evidence, which are not binding in immigration proceedings, set forth the parameters for expert witness testimony, stating:

> A witness who is qualified by knowledge, skill, experience, training, or education may testify in the form of an opinion or otherwise if:

(a) the expert's scientific, technical, or other specialized knowledge will help the trier of fact to understand the evidence or to determine a fact in issue;

(b) the testimony is based on sufficient facts or data;

(c) the testimony is the product of reliable principles and methods; and

(d) the expert has reliably applied the principles and methods to the facts of the case. (Federal Rules of Evidence, sec. 702)

3. See Keast (2005, 1237) for an overview of procedural issues regarding the use of experts.

4. The Overseas Refugee Program has often been criticized as being informed more by foreign policy than by humanitarian considerations. During the Cold War, "presidents . . . generously admitted those refugees fleeing Communist countries while largely turning a deaf ear to almost all others" (Legomsky 1995, 676–77). A study of the refugee numbers over the past decades illustrates this bias. For example, even though repression and bloody wars raged throughout Latin America in the 1980s, almost all the refugee slots from that world region were allocated for Cuba (Musalo, Moore, and Boswell 2009, 76).

5. Individuals fleeing persecution may apply for asylum or seek two lesser but related forms of relief: withholding of deportation (also referred to as "restriction on removal") (INA 1980, sec. 1251(b)(3)) or protection under the Convention against Torture (CAT) (Procedures for Asylum and Withholding of Removal 2000, 8 C.F.R. sec. 1208.16(c) and 8 C.F.R. sec. 1208.17).

6. There are two levels of adjudication for asylum claims. First, an individual who is legally present in the United States or who is not legally present but has not yet come to the attention of immigration authorities may apply "affirmatively" and have his or her claim decided by an asylum officer. The Asylum Office is located within the Citizenship and Immigration Services (CIS) of the Department of Homeland Security. Second, an individual who is not present legally and who has been put in removal proceedings can raise a claim for asylum as a defense to removal in immigration court. Immigration judges, who are part of the Executive Office for Immigration Review (EOIR) of the Department of Justice (DOJ), decide these claims. The proceedings are adversarial, with the government represented by trial attorneys who are employees of Immigration and Customs Enforcement (ICE) of DHS. Individuals who apply at the Asylum Office and are not granted asylum are referred to immigration court for removal and may renew their claims there.

7. A long-standing criticism of US refugee policy has been that it is improperly influenced by foreign policy objectives (Silk 1986, 7). This translated into high rates of grants of asylum being extended to individuals fleeing "enemy" regimes and low rates for those fleeing regimes with whom the United States was friendly—regardless of the human rights conditions in the respective countries or the risks of persecution faced by those seeking asylum.

8. For a detailed discussion, see Musalo 2014.

9. For example, Father James Curtin's affidavit focused on three areas affecting the credibility of indigenous Guatemalans: (1) their difficulty in placing events within the context of dates as measured by Western calendars; (2) their reluctance

to contradict an authority figure (such as an immigration judge) because of the historical relationship between authority and oppression; and (3) the potential communication problems arising from their unique native languages and speech patterns, which can sometimes be perceived as "rambling and not getting to the point" (FMCARP 1988, 26).

10. During the civil war in El Salvador, the term *popular organizations* was used to describe groups of students, peasants, workers, and others who had not taken up arms but who shared some of the objectives associated with the guerrilla group, the Farabundo Marti National Liberation Front.

11. *Black's Law Dictionary* provides this definition: "A canon of construction holding that when a general word or phrase follows a list of specifics, the general word or phrase will be interpreted to include only items of the same class as those listed" (Garner 2009, 594).

12. Race and nationality are examples of characteristics that an individual cannot change, whereas religion and political opinion are characteristics that an individual should not be required to change.

13. Additional information about the legal arguments made, the experts involved, or other evidence in this case may be obtained through the Expert Consultation Program of the Center for Gender and Refugee Studies (CGRS), at http://cgrs .uchastings.edu/assistance/request.

14. See, for example, the cases involving the claims of children fleeing forced participation as child soldiers, persecution by gangs, and abuse by both governmental and nonstate actors, which the youngsters suffered as "street child[ren]" (*Lukwago v. Ashcroft* 2003, *Matter of S-E-G-* 2008, *Matter of E-A-G-* 2008, *Escobar v. Gonzales* 2005).

15. The Center for Gender and Refugee Studies maintains a database of cases in which its assistance with an asylum matter has been requested. In cases that CGRS has been involved with over the past two years, twenty-five out of ninety-three of the children's cases from Central America involved incest. Six cases from Africa between 2006 and 2013 involved incest.

16. In Guatemala, "statistics show that seven out of 10 children suffer abuse, generally sexual aggression committed by family members or friends—acts that almost always end in impunity" (Noticias de Guatemala 2009). Out of 5,097 complaints of sexual crimes, only 242 resulted in a conviction (US Department of State, 2010). In El Salvador, "on average, an act of sexual aggression [is] perpetrated against a child every eight hours" (La Prensa Gráfica 2010). Intrafamilial abuse is met with a "lack of rigorous investigations into complaints" by the government, and "recent years have witnessed a steady decline in the number of judicial procedures for cases of intra-family violence initiated in family courts, falling from 4,890 in 2003 to 1,240 in 2007" (Amnesty International 2010). In Honduras, over 4,000 cases of child abuse are reported every year (Committee on the Rights of the Child 2007). Despite multiple plans of action to end sexual violence and incest, the "insufficient allocation of resources" continues to hinder progress (Committee on the Elimination of Discrimination against Women 2007).

17. Many adjudicators take this approach in cases involving domestic violence between intimate partners as well. They reject the argument that the male abuser is motivated by the victim's membership in a social group defined by gender and intimate relationship. Instead, they reason that the male partner's abuse is the result of meanness, drunkenness, or other antisocial behavior. This "explanation" of why domestic violence occurs flies in the face of broadly accepted understandings of the dynamic of partner abuse. As Nancy Lemon, a nationally recognized expert on domestic violence, has observed: "Gender is one of the main motivating factors, if not the primary factor for domestic violence" (Lemon 2011, 1).

18. Herman is a psychiatrist with over forty years of experience researching issues related to incest. She has published extensively on the topic, including two seminal and widely cited books (Herman 1981, 1997). She is currently a clinical professor of psychiatry at Harvard Medical School.

19. The affidavit of domestic violence expert Nancy Lemon (2011) has been cited by immigration judges in cases involving domestic violence. In one case pertaining to a Salvadoran asylum seeker, the immigration judge found a nexus between the abuse and a gender-defined social group, quoting Lemon's opinion that "the male batterer's abuse and violence is motivated by a view that sees men as entitled to beat and control women" (CGRS Case #7571, IJ Dec., at 17).

## References

*Akinwande v. Ashcroft,* 380 F.3d 517 (1st Cir. 2004).

*Akram Qassim Hamid v. Gonzales,* 417 F.3d 642 (7th Cir. 2005).

*American Baptist Churches v. Richard Thornburgh,* 760 F. Supp. 796 (N.D. Cal. 1991).

American Psychiatric Association. 1994. *Diagnostic and Statistical Manual of Mental Disorders.* 4th ed. Washington, DC: American Psychiatric Association.

Amnesty International. 2010. *Amnesty International Report 2010—El Salvador.* Accessed January 15, 2014. http://www.unhcr.org/refworld/docid/4c03a82e50.html.

*Baballah v. Ashcroft,* 367 F.3d 1067 (9th Cir. 2004).

*Beltran-Tirado v. I.N.S.,* 213 F.3d 1179 (9th Cir. 2000).

Bergman, Barbara, Nancy Hollander, and Theresa Duncan. 2010. *Wharton's Criminal Evidence, Common Experts and Expert Testimony.* 15th ed., vol. 3, sec. 13:45.

*Boer-Sedano v. Gonzales,* 418 F.3d 1082 (9th Cir. 2005).

*Bolanos-Hernandez v. I.N.S.,* 767 F.2d 1277 (9th Cir. 1984).

Bookey, Blaine. 2013. "Domestic Violence as a Basis for Asylum: An Analysis of 206 Case Outcomes in the United States from 1994 to 2012." *Hastings Women's Law Journal* 24 (1): 107–48.

*Brathwaite v. I.N.S.,* 633 F.2d 657 (2d. Cir. 1980).

*Canas-Segovia v. I.N.S.,* 970 F.2d 599 (9th Cir. 1992).

*Castillo-Arias v. Gonzales,* 549 U.S. 1115 (2007).

*Castillo-Arias v. U.S. Attorney General,* 446 F.3d 1190 (11th Cir. 2006).

Center for Gender and Refugee Studies (CGRS). Technical Assistance Program of the Center for Gender and Refugee Studies. http://cgrs.uchastings.edu/assistance/.

Chávez, Suchit. 2010. "Tres casos diarios de abuso sexual a niños [Three cases of child sexual abuse per day]." *La Prensa Gráfica.* Accessed January 15, 2014.

http://www.laprensagrafica.com/el-salvador/judicial/104509-tres-casos
-diarios-de-abuso-sexual-a-ninos.html.

*Chen Shi Hai v. the Minister for Immigration and Multicultural Affairs.* 2000. American Law
Reports 170:553.

Cianciarulo, Marisa Silenzi. 2006. "Terrorism and Asylum Seekers: Why the REAL ID
Act Is a False Promise." *Harvard Journal on Legislation* 43:130–31.

Committee on the Elimination of Discrimination against Women. 2007. "Concluding
Comments of the Committee on the Elimination of Discrimination against
Women: Honduras, CEDAW/C/HON/C/6." Accessed January 15, 2014.
http://www.bayefsky.com/docs.php/area/conclobs/treaty/cedaw/opt/o/stae
/76/node/3/filename/honduras_t4_cedaw_39.

Committee on the Rights of the Child. 2007. "Concluding Observations: Honduras,
CRC/C/HND/CO/3." Accessed January 15, 2014. http://www.bayefsky.com
/pdf/honduras_t4_crc_44.pdf.

Culligan, Lawrence J. 1989. *Corpus Juris Secundum, Criminal Law.* Vol. 22A, sec. 1037. St.
Paul, MN: West.

*Damaize-Job v. I.N.S.,* 787 F.2d 1332 (9th Cir. 1986).

*Dandan v. Ashcroft,* 339 F.3d 567 (7th Cir. 2003).

DePaulo, Bella M., Julie I. Stone, and G. Daniel Lassiter. 1955. "Deceiving and
Detecting Deceit." In *The Self in Social Life,* edited by Barry R. Schlenke. New York:
McGraw-Hill, 323–70.

*Dinu v. Ashcroft,* 372 F.3d 1041 (9th Cir. 2004).

Durst, Ilene. 2000. "Lost In Translation: Why Due Process Demands Deference to the
Refugee's Narrative." *Rutgers Law Review* 53:152–56.

*Edimo-Doualla v. Gonzales,* 464 F.3d 276 (2d Cir. 2006).

*Escobar v. Gonzales,* 417 F.3d 363 (3d Cir. 2005).

*Escobar v. Holder,* 657 F.3d 537 (7th Cir. 2011).

Father Moriarty Central American Refugee Program (FMCARP). 1988. *The Impact of
Cultural Factors on Credibility in the Asylum Context.* San Francisco: Immigrant Legal
Resource Center.

*Fatin v. I.N.S.,* 12 F.3d 1233 (3d Cir. 1993).

The Federal Rules of Evidence, sec. 702.

*Fiadjoe v. Attorney General,* 411 F.3d 135 (3d Cir. 2005).

*Fisher v. I.N.S.,* 79 F.3d 955 (9th Cir. 1996).

Fogelson, Steven. 1990. "The Nuremberg Legacy: An Unfulfilled Promise." *Southern
California Law Review* 63:834.

Friedland, Steven I., Paul Bergman, and Andrew E. Taslitz. 2004. *Evidence Law and
Practice.* 2nd ed. Newark, NJ: LexisNexis.

Garner, Bryan, ed. 2009. *Black's Law Dictionary.* 9th ed. St. Paul, MN: West.

*Gatimi v. Holder,* 578 F.3d 611 (7th Cir. 2009).

*Goel v. Gonzales,* 490 F.3d 735 (9th Cir. 2007).

*Gontcharova v. Ashcroft,* 384 F.3d 873 (7th Cir. 2004).

Grahl-Madsen, Atle. 1966. *The Status of Refugees in International Law.* Leiden: A. W.
Sijthoff.

*Hakim v. Attorney General of the United States*, 189 F.App'x. 135 (3d Cir. 2006).

HealthRight International Human Rights Clinic. 2009. *Training Manual for Physicians and Mental Health Professionals*. New York: HealthRight International.

*Henriquez-Rivas v. Holder*, 449 F.App'x 626 (9th Cir. 2011).

*Henriquez-Rivas v. Holder*, 707 F.3d 1081 (9th Cir. 2013).

Herman, Judith Lewis. 1981. *Father-Daughter Incest*. Cambridge, MA: Harvard University Press.

———. 1997. *Trauma and Recovery*. New York: Basic Books.

———. 2011. Affidavit. On file with author.

*Hernandez-Montiel v. I.N.S.*, 225 F.3d 1084 (9th Cir. 2000).

Illegal Immigration Reform and Immigration Responsibility Act (IIRIRA). 1996. Pub. L. 104–208, Div. C, 110 Stat. 3009–546, § 309(a). Codified as amended in scattered sections of 8 U.S.C.

Immigration and Nationality Act (INA). 1980. 8 U.S.C.

*In re A-M-E- & J-G-U-*, 24 I&N Dec. 69 (BIA 2007).

*In re Assicurazioni Generali S.p.A. Holocaust Ins.*, No. MDL 1374, 2007 WL 601846 (S.D.N.Y. Feb. 27, 2007).

*In re Berta Lidia Iraheta*, A24 247 299 (BIA Sept. 10, 1990) (unpublished).

*In re H*, 21 I&N Dec. 337 (BIA 1996).

*In re V-T-S-*, 21 I&N Dec. 792 (BIA 1997).

*I.N.S. v. Cardoza-Fonseca*, 480 U.S. 421 (1987).

*I.N.S. v. Elias-Zacarias*, 502 U.S. 478 (1992).

Kälin, Walter. 1986. "Troubled Communication: Cross-Cultural Misunderstandings in the Asylum-Hearing." *International Migration Review* 20 (2): 236.

Keast, Rachael. 2005. "Using Experts for Asylum Cases in Immigration Court." *Interpreter Releases* 82 (30): 1237.

*Korablina v. I.N.S.*, 158 F.3d 1038 (9th Cir. 1998).

*Laurent v. Ashcroft*, 359 F.3d 59 (1st Cir. 2004).

Legomsky, Stephen. 1995. "The Making of United States Refugee Policy: Separation of Powers in the Post-Cold War Era." *Washington Law Review* 70:676–77.

Lemon, Nancy D. 2011. Affidavit. On file with author.

*Lopez-Umanzor v. Gonzales*, 405 F.3d 1049 (9th Cir. 2005).

*Lukwago v. Ashcroft*, 329 F.3d 157 (3d Cir. 2003).

Lustig, Stuart L. 2008. "Symptoms of Trauma among Political Asylum Applicants: Don't Be Fooled." *Hastings International & Comparative Law Review* 31:726.

Lustig, Stuart L., Sarah Kureshi, Kevin L. Delucci, Vincent Iacopino, and Samantha C. Morse. 2008. "Asylum Grant Rates Following Medical Evaluations of Maltreatment among Political Asylum Applicants in the United States." *Journal of Immigration & Minority Health* 10 (1): 9.

*Maini v. I.N.S.*, 212 F.3d 1167 (9th Cir. 2000).

*Mashiri v. Ashcroft*, 383 F.3d 1112 (9th Cir. 2004).

*Matter of Acosta*, 19 I&N Dec. 211 (BIA 1985).

*Matter of C-A-*, 23 I&N Dec. 951 (BIA 2006).

*Matter of E-A-G-*, 24 I&N Dec. 591 (BIA 2008).

The Evolving Refugee Definition

*Matter of Fuentes,* 19 I&N Dec. 658 (BIA 1988).

*Matter of Kasinga,* 21 I&N Dec. 357 (BIA 1996).

*Matter of R-A-,* 22 I&N Dec. 906 (BIA 1999)(en banc), vacated, 22 I&N Dec. 906 (A.G. 2001), remanded, 23 I&N Dec. 694 (A.G. 2005), remanded and stay lifted, 24 I&N Dec. 629 (A.G. 2008).

*Matter of S-E-G-,* 241 I&N Dec. 579 (BIA 2008).

*Matter of Toboso-Alfonso,* 20 I&N Dec. 819 (BIA 1990).

*Mayo v. Ashcroft,* 317 F.3d 867 (8th Cir. 003).

Meister, Julia Blanche. 1995. "Orientation-Based Persecution as Grounds for Refugee Status: Policy Implications and Recommendations." *Notre Dame Journal of Law, Ethics & Public Policy* 9:275.

Musalo, Karen. 1996. "In Re Kasinga: A Big Step Forward for Gender-Based Asylum Claims." *Interpreter Releases* 73 (25): 855.

———. 2010. "A Short History of Gender Asylum in the United States: Resistance and Ambivalence May Very Slowly Be Inching towards Recognition of Women's Claims." *Refugee Survey Quarterly* 29 (2): 47.

———. 2014. "A Tale of Two Women: The Claims for Asylum of Fauziya Kassindja, Who Fled FGC, and Rody Alvarado, a Survivor of Partner (Domestic) Violence." In *Gender in Refugee Law: From the Margins to the Centre,* edited by Efrat Arbel, Catherine Dauvergne, and Jenni Milbank, 73–97. Oxford: Routledge.

Musalo, Karen, Jennifer Moore, and Richard A. Boswell. 2009. *Refugee Law and Policy: A Comparative and International Approach.* 4th ed. Durham, NC: Carolina Academic Press.

*Ndom v. Ashcroft,* 384 F.3d 743 (9th Cir. 2004).

*Ngure v. Ashcroft,* 367 F.3d 975 (8th Cir. 2004).

*Niam v. Ashcroft,* 354 F.3d 652 (7th Cir. 2004).

*Niang v. Gonzales,* 492 F.3d 505 (4th Cir. 2007).

Noticias de Guatemala. 2009. "Childhood Represents One of the Most Forgotten Populations in Guatemala [La niñez representa uno de los sectores más olvidados en Guatemala]." Accessed January 15, 2004. http://noticias.com.gt /nacionales/20091001-la-ninez-representa-uno-de-los-sectores-mas-olvidados -en-guatemala.html.

*Osorio v. I.N.S.,* 18 F.3d 1017 (2d Cir. 1994).

*Pena v. Canada (Minister of Citizenship and Immigration).* 2000. F.C.J. No. 1550.

*Perez-Morales v. Holder,* 448 F.App'x 585 (6th Cir. 2011).

Petitioner's Opening Brief. *Grande Mercado v. Holder,* No. 10–71311 (9th Cir. 2011).

Physicians for Human Rights. 2001. *Examining Asylum Seekers: A Health Professional's Guide to Medical and Psychological Evaluations of Torture.* Boston: Physicians for Human Rights.

Procedures for Asylum and Withholding of Removal. 2009. 8 C.F.R.

*Quan v. Gonzales,* 428 F.3d 883 (9th Cir. 2005).

*Ramirez-Rivas v. I.N.S.,* 899 F.2d 864 (9th Cir. 1990).

REAL ID Act. 2005. Pub. L. No. 109–13, 119 Stat. 231, 302. Codified in scattered sections of 8 U.S.C.

Rempell, Scott. 2011. "Gauging Credibility in Immigration Proceedings: Immaterial Inconsistencies, Demeanor, and the Rule of Reason." *Georgetown Immigration Law Journal* 25:377–405.

Respondent's Opposition to Petitioner's Petition for Rehearing en Banc. *Henriquez-Rivas v. Holder,* 449 F.App'x 626 (9th Cir. 2011) (No. 09–71571).

Rogers, Richard. 1997. *Clinical Assessment of Malingering and Deception.* 2nd ed. New York: Guilford Press.

*Santos-Lemus v. Mukasey,* 542 F.3d 738 (9th Cir. 2008).

*Sarhan v. Holder,* 658 F.3d 649 (7th Cir. 2011).

Schrag, Philip G. 2000. *A Well-Founded Fear: The Congressional Battle to Save Political Asylum in America.* New York: Routledge.

*Shire v. Ashcroft,* 388 F.3d 1288 (9th Cir. 2004).

Silk, James. 1986. *Despite a Generous Spirit: Denying Asylum in the United States.* Washington, DC: US Committee for Refugees.

Stadtmauer, Gary J., Elizabeth Singer, and Eva Metalios. 2010. "An Analytical Approach to Clinical Forensic Evaluations of Asylum Seekers: The HealthRight International Human Rights Clinic." *Journal of Forensic and Legal Medicine* 17 (January): 41–45.

Statute of the Office of the United Nations High Commissioner for Refugees (UNHCR Statute). 1950. G. A. Res. 428(V). chap. 2, art. 8. December 14.

*Ucelo-Gomez v. Mukasey,* 509 F.3d 70 (2d Cir. 2007).

UN Convention Relating to the Status of Refugees. July 28, 1951. 189 UNTS 2545.

UN High Commissioner for Refugees (UNHCR). 1979. *Handbook on Procedures and Criteria for Determining Refugee Status.* Geneva: UNHCR.

UN Protocol Relating to the Status of Refugees. January 31, 1967. 19 UST 6223, 606 UNTS 267.

US Congress. 1995. *Proceedings of Congress and General Congressional Publications.* 104th Cong., 1st sess., vol. 141, iss. 129.

US Department of State, Bureau of Democracy, Human Rights, and Labor. 2010. *2009 Human Rights Report: Guatemala.*

*Valdiviezo-Galdamez v. Attorney General,* 663 F.3d 582 (3d Cir. 2011).

van Rooyen, Rene, UNHCR Representative, letter to Senator Henry Hyde. August 25, 1995.

*Zhou v. Gonzales,* 437 F.3d 860, 869 (9th Cir. 2006).

*Zolfagharkhani v. Canada* (Minister of Employment and Immigration). 1993. 3 F.C. 540.

# FOUR

## Expert Evidence in British Asylum Courts

*The Judicial Assessment of Evidence on Ethnic
Discrimination and Statelessness in Ethiopia*

John Campbell

AS AN ANTHROPOLOGIST with experience working in and writing about the Horn of Africa, I have been asked by lawyers representing asylum clients to write expert reports for Ethiopians and Eritreans seeking asylum in the United Kingdom, the United States, Canada, South Africa, and Israel, where asylum applicants must navigate their way through policies aimed at preventing them from reaching a country of asylum and where their asylum claims face increasing scrutiny.

In an effort to understand how the British asylum system functions, I secured funding for a two-year study of refugee lawyers, the Home Office/UK Border Agency, refugee communities, and the British courts in order to follow Ethiopian and Eritrean asylum claims through the legal system. This chapter is based on that fieldwork and involves an analysis of legal documents—witness statements, skeletons, Home Office refusal letters, judicial decisions, expert reports, and so on—produced by those who argue and decide claims, as well as interviews with asylum applicants and participant observation in law offices and the courts. In short, I provide a processual analysis that follows asylum claims through the courts.

In this chapter, I examine the decisions of adjudicators in the United Kingdom's Immigration and Asylum Chamber (the Chamber). The

British system is based on the adversarial model, in which the claim of an individual seeking asylum is argued in court before an adjudicator: asylum applicants are normally represented by an independent barrister, and the Secretary of State for the Home Office (the SSHD, or Home Office) is represented by a Home Office Presenting Officer (HOPO), a junior civil servant with limited legal training.

The procedures regulating the work of the Chamber are set out in various rules, legislation, Practice Directions, and Practice Rules.[1] For instance, Practice Directions set out appeal procedures, how evidence should be submitted to the court, and the responsibilities of expert witnesses. It is worth noting that adjudicators believe they possess their "own level of expertise as a special tribunal, not only in the legal issues for its determination, but also in its knowledge of country situations" (Barnes 2004, 357). Their skepticism of country experts means that they frequently set aside the evidence those experts submit.

Notwithstanding the adjudicators' purported expertise, *at least* 20 percent of their decisions are overturned on appeal. However, the labyrinthine nature of legislation, the negative role played by the Home Office, and problematic legal representation also contribute to poor judicial decisions. In this essay, I argue that attention to legal argument, legal procedure, and the wider context of the case allows anthropologists to understand, as Bruno Latour (2010, 192) puts it, how adjudicators "grapple with a file" and, by way of a particular "chain of reasoning," pronounce a decision that maintains a semblance of legal stability.

I focus on legal argument and adjudicator decision making in two Ethiopian "country guidance" (CG) cases. Rule 12.2 of the Practice Directions defines the status of country guidance cases and states that

> a reported determination . . . bearing the letters "CG" shall be
> treated as an authoritative finding on the country guidance issue
> identified in the determination, based upon the evidence before
> the members of the Tribunal, the AIT or the IAT that determine
> the appeal. As a result, unless it has been expressly superseded or
> replaced by any later "CG" determination, or is inconsistent with
> other authority that is binding on the Tribunal, such a country
> guidance case is authoritative in any subsequent appeal, so far as
> that appeal: (a) relates to the country guidance issue in question;
> and (b) depends upon the same or similar evidence.[2]

In short, CG cases are intended to provide guidance to all adjudicators when they hear an asylum appeal that raises the same issues. They are precedents because they are based on a review of all relevant material, and they set out guidance with respect to how adjudicators should assess specific elements of a claim.

In analyzing asylum claims, my principal objective is to assess how adjudicators evaluate evidence. As Anthony Good (2008, 48) has argued, the courts generally "have sought to constrain expert's influence, through such means as the 'hearsay rule' . . . and the 'ultimate issue' rule, which prevents witnesses from giving opinions on the main issues at stake." For instance, "the admissibility of expert evidence is a legal rather than a factual matter, and hence subject to judicial discretion" (Good 2008, 48). However, it is important to note that the standing of experts and expert evidence varies significantly in different jurisdictions—that is, civil, criminal, asylum/immigration, and so forth—and in different legal traditions.

Following Latour (2010, 208), I argue that all evidence is assessed in the same way because facts "do not speak for themselves" (cf. Sweeny 2007; Twining 1994).[3] In asylum and immigration law, as in other jurisdictions, facts must be interrogated, assessed, and detached or distanced from the specific nature of a case by subsuming them under relevant case law. Latour (2010, 216) argues that "however stubborn the facts are, they will never have any real hold on the case as such, whose solidity depends on the rules of law that are applicable." He notes that from the perspective of a judge, "facts are things that one tries to get rid of as quickly as possible, in order to move on to . . . the particular point of law that is of interest" (Latour 2010, 215). Importantly, a fact is "whatever is not contested" (Latour 2010, 131n8), which means that we must attend to the legal procedures at play in judicial proceedings to understand how "facts"—whatever their nature or source—are judged (i.e., as admissible or inadmissible) and the relative weight that is given to them. Problematically, an asylum adjudicator's assessment of the credibility of a claim is often wrongly conflated with his assessment of the material facts of the case (Sweeny 2007).

This chapter is organized as follows. The first section examines the asylum claim of "MA," which I followed through the courts as part of my research; pursuant to the Court of Appeal's (COA's) final decision on this case, I was asked to write an expert report supporting MA's fresh asylum claim.[4] The second section examines the subsequent claim of "ST," which I initially followed. However, midway through this claim, I was asked to write an expert report that was submitted to the Chamber when the case was listed for country guidance (the barrister representing both individuals was a member of the advisory board of my research project). I conclude with some observations on judicial decision making, the judicial assessment of evidence, and my own position in these cases as an anthropologist and country expert.

## The Asylum Claim of MA

Between 1998 and 2000, war between Ethiopia and Eritrea displaced well over 1 million people and witnessed the arrest and expulsion by Ethiopia of tens of thousands of individuals of Eritrean ethnicity (Campbell 2013).[5] Thousands of those expelled by Ethiopia were transformed into stateless persons—their passports and identification documents were taken from them prior to being forced across a war zone into Eritrea. For its part, Eritrea assisted these individuals, but its officials did not necessarily recognize them as Eritrean nationals or as refugees. The situation gave rise to a continuous flow of asylum applicants who have, since 9/11, been confronted by extensive measures intended to prevent them from entering a country of refuge and/or to disqualify their asylum applications (Bohmer and Shuman, in this volume; Walker-Said, in this volume). In the Horn of Africa, the border between Ethiopia and Eritrea remains undemarcated, compensation for war claims has not been paid, troops are still concentrated on the border, and thousands of "Eritreans" remain vulnerable and stateless.

At the height of the expulsion of ethnic Eritreans, friends helped MA leave Ethiopia for Kenya, from where she traveled to the United Kingdom in 1999. On arrival, she claimed asylum, giving her nationality as Eritrean (i.e., the reason Ethiopian officials used to expel her); she claimed to fear persecution in Ethiopia and Eritrea. The Home Office (2001) refused her asylum application on the basis that (1) she had not established a well-founded fear of persecution and (2) she could safely be removed to Ethiopia or to Eritrea. The Home Office set her removal directions to Eritrea. By the time her appeal against the decision was heard in March 2002, Ethiopia and Eritrea had signed a peace treaty.

At her hearing, MA testified that she had been born and raised in Ethiopia to parents who had come from Eritrea when it was a province of Ethiopia. She also testified that she had not been involved in Eritrean politics, nor had she ever been issued Eritrean identity documents. Her husband, an ethnic Eritrean who had also been born and raised in Ethiopia, had been expelled, and her in-laws had taken her twelve-year-old son with them when they, too, were expelled.

The adjudicator accepted her evidence but dismissed her appeal. He found that she had a *formal entitlement* to Eritrean nationality and could "return"—the official euphemism for deportation—to Eritrea without risk. Because she held an Ethiopian passport, he found that she was also a national of Ethiopia and could safely be returned to that country. Her counsel successfully appealed this decision on the basis that even though MA might be entitled to Eritrean citizenship, she would need to apply for it.

Her case was reheard in October 2002.[6] At this hearing, the adjudicator set aside two expert reports: the first was three years old (and had been "recycled" from another case), and the second was considered "too general." She also set aside a note from the UN High Commissioner for Refugees (UNHCR) because it "did not relate specifically to the situation of this appellant." The adjudicator found that (1) the appellant should have made a request for, and received a refusal of, protection from the Ethiopian *and* Eritrean authorities to establish that a given nationality was ineffective (UNHCR 1992, ¶107), (2) she was entitled to citizenship in Eritrea and would face no real risk if she was returned there, and (3) she was also an Ethiopian national and could safely return to that country as well. This decision was successfully appealed on the basis that "a lawful claim to Eritrean nationality meant that she would not be entitled to the protection of the Convention" and that it was not clear "whether she would in practice be afforded protection by the Eritrean authorities."[7]

At this point, the Secretary of State changed MA's removal directions to Ethiopia. At her appeal in August 2004, which was listed for country guidance and "joined" with two other Ethiopian claims that raised the same issue, her barrister argued that:

> 1. She was a former national of Ethiopia who had been deprived of nationality on the basis of ethnic discrimination. She was not an Eritrean national. Therefore she was a refugee under Art. 1(A)2 of the 1951 Convention and could not lawfully be removed to Eritrea.

> 2. Being an Ethiopian of Eritrean descent meant that, if she were returned to Ethiopia she would be transformed from a citizen into a registered alien.

3. Finally he argued that the issue was whether she already possessed a nationality. Citing a Court of Appeal decision, he argued that the failure of an appellant to make enquiries at the embassy for a passport or travel document "was excusable where other credible evidence clearly showed that the result would be negative."[8]

Counsel for the SSHD argued that there was no general risk for Ethiopians of Eritrean descent because hostilities had ended and "the Convention provides that an asylum applicant must seek the protection of any country of which he is a citizen. The principle in *Bradshaw* should apply."[9]

The adjudicators accepted the Secretary of State's arguments en bloc. The court considered and dismissed a substantial body of evidence as having little bearing on the current situation in Ethiopia. Thus, it considered that the reports by Amnesty International and Human Rights Watch provided historical background but were of limited value in assessing the current situation. Two detailed expert reports were set aside for similar reasons. Both experts had argued that "there has been no indication that either country is prepared to bring policies of deportation or repatriation . . . to an end" and that "there is no likelihood that they [deportees and other individuals who fled the country] would be allowed back or given identity documents [by the Ethiopian authorities]."[10]

Accordingly, the court decided that: following the peace treaty of 2000, Ethiopian-born ethnic Eritreans were no longer at risk of being deported from Ethiopia; the Ethiopian Directive of 2004 allowed Ethiopian-born Eritreans to return to Ethiopia; and Ethiopians of Eritrean descent would be recognized by the Ethiopian embassy and would be given travel documents allowing them to return. The tribunal found that "the deprival of citizenship by itself is not necessarily persecutory" and that MA had not been deprived of her nationality. With respect to the question of dual nationality, the court relied on *Bradshaw*, stating, "There is, on the face of the Eritrean legislation an entitlement to nationality. . . . In fact [MA] qualifies for Eritrean citizenship and there are no serious obstacles" to her "being able to apply for and obtain citizenship."[11]

When MA's lawyer appealed to the COA against the Chamber's decision, her case was linked to four related Ethiopian cases that had been refused for the same reason. In the COA, the Home Office and MA's lawyer agreed that her claim and three of the four other claims joined with it should be sent back to the Chamber to be reconsidered. However, the Home Office refused to reconsider the fifth claim, filed by "EB"; her appeal was heard in early 2007 by the COA, which decided that

> Ethiopia will not currently allow EB to be returned but the
> question must be answered now, not as at some date in the
> unknowable future when Ethiopia might change its mind
> and decide to re-admit EB for some reason which cannot be
> currently predicted. Once it is clear that EB was persecuted for a
> Convention reason while in Ethiopia, there is no basis on which
> it can be said that that state of affairs has now changed. I would
> therefore conclude that EB has a well-founded fear of persecution
> for a Convention reason and that she is now entitled to the status
> of a refugee. (¶71)[12]

The decision on EB appeared to tilt the scales in favor of MA because the COA had accepted the same expert evidence and legal argument that the Chamber had dismissed when it decided MA's claim in 2004.

During the period leading up to MA's 2007 reconsideration, the Home Office had the government's Treasury Solicitor instruct a senior barrister to prepare and argue its case before the Chamber. Preparation of the case, which occurred over five months, involved convening a "case management review" with several departments in the Home Office to assess the evidence submitted by MA's counsel, to assess what evidence the Home Office needed to produce to prepare the case, and to file a skeleton brief with the court. The task, as the SSHD's legal team saw it, was to provide a more complete picture of the case and of the situation in Ethiopia, to argue that MA's position was "materially different" from that of EB, and to show that "it shouldn't necessarily follow that a deprivation of nationality should lead to refugee status."[13] The legal team, together with a HOPO and several government solicitors, produced four boxes of evidence for the two-day hearing.

Strengthened by his success with EB's case, MA's counsel prepared "to sweep away" the previous Home Office legal argument on the issue of nationality. He assumed that the Home Office would argue that MA, as someone who had fled Ethiopia in anticipation of arrest or deportation, had not been deprived of her nationality. Based on the COA's findings in EB, he believed that the expert evidence—which had been accepted in EB's case—supported his argument that MA had been deprived of her nationality for a convention reason. Going into the hearing, he made several tactical decisions that may have affected the outcome of the case. First, he relied heavily on international refugee law; second, he refused to call MA to testify (in order to preserve the credibility of findings from her testimony in earlier hearings); and third, he submitted reports by two experts who were not called to give oral evidence.

When the case was heard in September 2007, the central issues were whether Ethiopia had deprived MA of her nationality and whether this action amounted to persecution under the terms of the Convention. If she could not be returned to Ethiopia, she was entitled to refugee status. Submissions were made on Ethiopian law, international law, domestic law, and a wide range of evidence was submitted including arguments about the position of the Ethiopian embassy (the key evidence and arguments are summarized in Table 4.1).

The expert evidence, the SSHD's rebuttal evidence, and arguments about the role of the embassy were critical to the outcome of the case. The expert reports—based largely on interviews with ethnic Eritreans and research—argued that no "Eritrean" deportee had been allowed to return and that Ethiopia had a policy of excluding deported Eritreans (i.e., embassies and consulates refused to issue these persons a travel document). In rebuttal, the SSHD called an official from the Home Office Returns Group Unit who testified that the Ethiopian embassy in London did accept the majority of "Ethiopians" applying to return voluntarily via the International Organization of Migration and would accept a bona fide application from MA.[14]

Conflicting interpretations of the embassy's position on this issue were presented. Counsel for MA argued that the embassy's failure to respond to its queries and to the letters sent by the SSHD reflected a policy of excluding deportees/ethnic Eritreans. In contrast, the SSHD argued that even though the embassy had failed to respond to its letters, this did not constitute evidence that the embassy would refuse to accept MA.

We can see how the court "stitched" the case together to arrive at a decision. It argued that the first test in deciding whether a person was a national of a country was whether that person "fulfils the nationality law requirements" of his or her country. MA was found to possess de facto Ethiopian nationality; for instance, she had reportedly traveled to the United Kingdom on an Ethiopian passport, and under Ethiopian law, she could not have been deprived of her nationality. The question of whether

**Table 4.1** Summary of key submissions at MA's 2007 "CG" appeal

| Submission | Counsel for MA | Counsel for the SSHD |
|---|---|---|
| **Ethiopian law** | | |
| 1994 Ethiopian Federal Constitution | Under Art. 33, MA possessed de jure nationality, but this was terminated by the state. | There is no constitutional provision under which MA cou have lost nationality, nor is the any evidence of an executive a by which it was taken away. |
| **International law** | | |
| Nottebohm (*Liechtenstein v. Guatemala*, I.C.J., April 6, 1955) | Effective nationality went beyond a de jure entitlement. | MA fled Ethiopia without bein deprived of her nationality. |
| *Trop v. Dulles* (1957) 356 U.S. 86, *Canada v. Ward* [1993] | Deprivation of nationality meant that if she was returned, she would have no rights. | |
| **Domestic law** | | |
| EB (Ethiopia) *Revenko v. S.S.H.D.* [2001] Queens Bench 601; *Lazarevic v. S.S.H.D.* [1997] | The case of EB did not provide a direct factual precedent, but it did establish that Ethiopia had practiced de facto deprivation of nationality. | The facts in MA's case differed from those in EB's; MA was no someone likely to have been deported. |
| | Deprivation of nationality was persecutory in itself. | Deprivation of nationality depended on its consequence it had not occurred in this case |
| **Evidence** | | |
| Eritrea-Ethiopia Claims Commission, The Hague | Protection of the Ethiopian Constitution was nugatory; deprivation of nationality was practiced on a wide scale. | Deportation had ceased; the appellant would not have bee deported. It is now safe to retu |
| Ethiopian Directive of 2004 | Offered no support to those expelled or deprived of their nationality; registration extended only to those who had remained resident in Ethiopia. | MA did not need to apply for nationality; hers had not been taken away. If she cooperated with the embassy, she would given a travel document. |
| Evidence of the Home Office Returns Group Unit and a note from International Organization of Migration | The embassy provided little information to the Home Office about reasons for refusing applications; the information was of limited value in clarifying the basis on which specific individuals were documented for return. | The embassy accepted the majority of "Ethiopians" applyi to return voluntarily; if the appellant made a bona fide application, she would be accepted. |
| Objective evidence | Amnesty International and Human Rights Watch reports provided factual background to the arrest, deportation, and denationalization of ethnic Eritreans | Following the peace treaty of May 2000, there was no reaso fear being returned to Ethiopi |
| Expert evidence | No deportee had been allowed to return. | The expert evidence was "larg anecdotal." |

MA had de jure nationality, said the court, rested on the factual question of whether the Ethiopian authorities would accept her. Unlike EB, MA had not had her documents removed by the authorities, which, for the SSHD, meant that she "was not a person who was liable to be deported."[15]

The court rejected expert evidence[16] to the effect that the human rights situation in Ethiopia had deteriorated since the war, that "there was a decline in due process," that the authorities "[applied] the laws in a highly arbitrary manner or openly violate[d] them," and that it was a recurring practice by Ethiopian embassies and consulates to refuse to recognize or assist "Eritreans" (i.e., individuals who had been deported and those who fled the country in anticipation of deportation). It was common ground that from 1998 until 2002–3, "the Ethiopian authorities would not accept an Ethiopian national of Eritrean parentage." However, the court argued that (1) there were no current reports that Ethiopia discriminated against ethnic Eritreans, and (2) the SSHD submitted rebuttal evidence to the effect that "as long as a person said they wanted to go back to Ethiopia and could show that they were *de jure* an Ethiopian national, they would be documented as an Ethiopian national and returned."

Tellingly, counsel for MA relied heavily upon the case of EB to support his argument about deprivation of nationality; in fact, he submitted similar expert evidence in both cases. However, the adjudicators set aside substantial elements of his argument and evidence on three grounds. First, they found that the facts in MA's case were different from those in EB's; in other words, the case of EB did not apply. Second, counsel for the SSHD rebutted MA's expert evidence and submitted evidence that the London embassy accepted applications by Ethiopians wishing to return, that is, she offered the court alternative evidence about the role of the embassy. Third, as MA's counsel later admitted, her solicitor "had blinked" by failing to get her to make a bona fide application to the embassy, which would have countered the SSHD's assertion that she had only approached the embassy for "the purpose of litigation."[17] The court found that if MA applied to the embassy in "good faith," she "would be likely to be issued with emergency travel documentation" allowing her to return. On this basis, the court dismissed her appeal.[18]

MA's barrister appealed this decision, but the COA only agreed to hear his argument on the basis that the lower Chamber "had erected a false distinction between de facto and de jure nationality." After several hours of argument, the panel agreed that the Chamber's approach to

Expert Evidence in British Asylum Courts

deciding nationality was flawed but that it had not erected "any fresh legal analysis."[19] The COA upheld the *Bradshaw* principle, stating that "there is no reason why the appellant should not herself make a formal application to the embassy to seek the relevant documents," which would remove the necessity for the tribunal to speculate about the response of the embassy.[20] On this basis, her appeal was refused. MA's counsel attempted to appeal "on the papers" to the House of Lords, but the appeal was refused; he subsequently advised her that she should make a fresh asylum claim (which succeeded).[21]

During the ten years that MA's case had bounced back and forth in the courts, the judiciary repeatedly erred in deciding it and instead relied upon the *Bradshaw* principle to decide whether an asylum applicant had a *formal entitlement* to nationality in a country other than the one in which he or she was born and raised (i.e., rather than deciding to which country MA had "a genuine and effective link"). In adopting this approach, the court compelled MA—and many others like her—to approach the Ethiopian embassy (whose officials had deported her family) and/or the Eritrean embassy (representing a country she has never lived in) for protection. Rather than examine the arbitrary actions of the Ethiopian state, which had clearly expelled ethnic Eritreans and had subsequently enunciated new norms of citizenship that excluded them from citizenship, the onus was placed on asylum applicants to prove that Ethiopia stripped them of their nationality (Campbell 2013).

### The Asylum Claim of ST

ST was born in Addis Ababa in 1979 to an Eritrean mother and an Ethiopian (Oromo) father. In July 1999, security forces seized his mother and shut down her business. Shortly afterward, armed officers confiscated ST's identity card and detained him for a month, during which time he was repeatedly interrogated about his mother's political activities and tortured before being released on condition that he register with the police.

When ST returned home, he learned that a neighbor had informed the authorities that his mother was sending money to the ruling party in Eritrea (via a rotating savings society) and that she had been deported. At the insistence of his uncle, he went into hiding and was helped to leave for the United Kingdom, where he arrived and claimed asylum in September 1999. However, when officials from the Home Office finally assessed his asylum claim in January 2005, they refused it.

At his appeal in May 2008, the adjudicator[22] accepted evidence about the ethnic/national identity of ST and his parents and his ill-treatment in custody, including medical evidence that he had been physically abused in detention. However, the adjudicator decided that the objective evidence [fell] "short of showing that those of part Eritrean descent [now] face persecution." The judge argued that "there is a [legal] presumption that the appellant will be treated as a *de jure* national" regardless of the refusal of the Ethiopian embassy in London to recognize him. The adjudicator contended that Ethiopia and Eritrea were no longer at war and that "there is an absence of objective evidence that the Ethiopian authorities harbour the same level of suspicion of those of part Eritrean descent now as they did in 1999." On this basis, ST's claim was refused.

ST's counsel appealed the decision on the basis that the adjudicator (1) had to be satisfied that not even a reasonable likelihood existed that the appellant would be persecuted on return, (2) had failed to consider relevant submissions in law, and (3) had failed to address the expert evidence. The Chamber refused the appeal. Counsel made an application on the papers to the COA, which was refused. Following that, he made an oral application to the COA that was accepted on the basis that the Chamber had failed to assess possible persecution in the form of the deprivation of the appellant's Ethiopian citizenship.

The case was reconsidered in December 2008 by an adjudicator who, though noting the grounds for reconsideration, merely reviewed the previous decision without accepting new submissions or evidence. ST's counsel appealed this decision on several bases. First, the adjudicator had failed to assess whether persecution arose from the deprivation of ST's nationality. Second, he also failed to consider legal submissions. Third, he erroneously applied a CG case without examining factual similarities and differences between it and ST's case. And fourth, against a background of continued exclusion of individuals of partial Eritrean descent, the adjudicator had failed to consider evidence that suggested the appellant would not be allowed to return to Ethiopia (and if he was returned, that he would not be allowed to register under the 2004 Ethiopian Directive).

The same adjudicator who had refused the reconsideration in 2008 dismissed the appeal. Counsel appealed on the papers to the COA in January 2009, but this appeal was refused; he made an oral application in March 2009 (amending the grounds to account for the COA decision on MA's case). At this point, the court of appeals stated: "In light of *M.A. (Ethiopia)*

*[2009] E.W.C.A. Civ. 289* there is a real prospect that the applicant will establish that the adjudicator had erred in law in applying a presumption that he was not at risk of being denied status as a national."[23] The case was sent back to the Chamber for reconsideration and was listed as a CG hearing.

Counsel for ST instructed two country experts to prepare reports on related but distinct issues. The first expert, who had submitted evidence in the case of MA, provided a detailed analysis of the political situation in Ethiopia and of the situation confronting Ethiopian-born ethnic Eritreans in Ethiopia for the period 1998 to 2010 (including an analysis of official directives relevant to stateless Ethiopian-born Eritreans). I was instructed to write an expert report that addressed the current situation of stateless "Eritreans." Specifically, my report was based upon recorded interviews with embassy officials in London, interviews with senior officials in Addis Ababa, and interviews conducted in May 2010 with stateless Eritreans in Addis Ababa. Both experts argued that although many thousands of stateless Eritreans were registered in 2004, the process had ended without registering all "Eritreans" who were entitled to register under the 2004 Ethiopian Directive. Furthermore, as the registration process had ended, any "Eritrean" who was returned to Ethiopia would be stateless.

Prior to the hearing, the government cut the Home Office's budget, which restricted the latter's ability to instruct senior legal counsel to represent it at ST's CG hearing; instead, a senior HOPO handled the case. When the claim was heard in January 2011, the key issue was to ascertain whether ST had been denied nationality by Ethiopia.[24] The hearing lasted three days and accepted submissions on the same issues as in MA's appeal.

It was common ground that the appellant was an Ethiopian national at birth and remained so until 1998—99. The adjudicators agreed with ST's counsel that, following Mirna Adjami and Julia Harrison (2008, 101), deprivation of nationality "must be accompanied by important procedural and substantive safeguards," notably, procedural fairness and due process together with a prohibition against ethnic discrimination. The Chamber[25] also reiterated the meaning of "acts of persecution" as defined in Article 1A of the Geneva Convention: that is, such acts must

> (a) be sufficiently serious by their nature or repetition as to
> constitute a severe violation of basic human rights, in particular
> the rights from which derogation cannot be made under Article
> 15(2) of the European Convention for the Protection of Human
> Rights and Fundamental Freedoms; or

(b) be an accumulation of various measures, including violations of human rights which is sufficiently severe as to affect an individual in a similar manner as mentioned in (a).

Further, acts of persecution can take various forms, including:

(a) acts of physical or mental violence, including acts of sexual violence;

(b) legal, administrative, police, and/or judicial measures which are in themselves discriminatory or which are implemented in a discriminatory manner;

(c) prosecution or punishment, which is disproportionate or discriminatory;

(d) denial of judicial redress resulting in a disproportionate or discriminatory punishment.

The adjudicators then assessed the evidence before considering the authorities' treatment of Ethiopian-born ethnic Eritreans in 1998–99. The court found that the removal of ST's identity card constituted an act of persecution for a convention reason. The panel then considered whether events prior to his departure would remain important should he be returned. It also noted that ST had undertaken "all reasonable steps" that could be asked of him in approaching the Ethiopian embassy in London (which had refused to acknowledge his entitlement to Ethiopian nationality). The court accepted the expert's explanation of the embassy's refusal to recognize ST's entitlement to nationality, namely, that officials had an arbitrary view of "ethnic Eritreans," reflected in the manner in which they "blur the issues of ethnicity and nationality." The court accepted[26] that only those ethnic Eritreans who had remained in Ethiopia and had registered with the government could reacquire nationality (and then only in 2004) and that ST had made a bona fide application to the embassy.

Was it possible for the appellant to return to Ethiopia to reacquire nationality? In my expert report, I had argued that large numbers of resident "Eritreans" had not been registered under the 2004 Ethiopian Directive and that it was no longer possible for such persons to register. The other expert argued that the authorities should stipulate a four-year residence rule, which effectively prevents an individual from applying for nationality from abroad. Both of us were unequivocal that the 2004 Directive only applied to "Eritreans" who had been continuously resident in Ethiopia between 1993 and 2004.

In the absence of rebuttal evidence, the court accepted that the appellant was unable to make use of the directive and was unable to reacquire nationality or return. Finally, the adjudicators concluded that "looking at matters overall and acknowledging that the threshold for persecution is a high one, [we] have concluded that the state of affairs would be persecutory for the appellant."[27] ST won his appeal and was granted refugee status, and all previous country guidance cases on the issue of nationality/statelessness in Ethiopia (including MA's) were set aside.

IT IS IMPORTANT to note that had the Home Office taken a decision on the two claims within a reasonable time, both MA and ST would very likely have been granted asylum. As it transpired, however, adjudicators erred repeatedly in deciding their claims: MA's claim was heard six times, and ST's case was heard four times (including the appeal before the COA). A partial explanation for this relates to the fact that adjudicators have limited knowledge of and experience dealing with complex legal issues such as deprivation of nationality. Even so, adjudicators tend to accept Home Office arguments rather than find in favor of appellants.[28]

The success of the SSHD in MA's 2007 CG hearing arose from the fact that her counsel offered the court rebuttal evidence about the role of the embassy, which allowed the court to set aside MA's expert evidence. She also offered the court an alternative interpretation of the principal legal and evidential submissions made on behalf of MA. For instance, the SSHD successfully argued that MA's evidence was historical and did not address the current situation of Eritreans in Ethiopia and that even though the Ethiopian embassy may not have responded to a request for information, it did allow Ethiopians to return. In short, MA's evidence was contested, and the court was given the opportunity to consider alternative interpretations of the evidence placed before it. The SSHD's legal arguments concerning factual differences between MA and EB and the nature of deprivation of nationality also provided grounds for the judges to dismiss MA's appeal.

The situation at the CG hearing of ST was significantly different. At this appeal, the SSHD was represented by an HOPO, who failed to discredit the experts and failed to offer any rebuttal evidence. Once the court accepted the credentials of the experts, it had to address their evidence, which it accepted. In point of fact, expert testimony directly contradicted findings made at MA's hearing about the role of the embassy, the effect of the 2004 Ethiopian Directive, and the likelihood of risk on return.

To those who study the courts, it comes as no surprise that legal and factual arguments are intertwined despite the efforts of legislators to differentiate between the two. To understand the extent to which facts sometimes do exert a hold on a case, it pays to look carefully at the history of the case, the nature of legal argument, whether rebuttal evidence was provided, and how procedural issues affect legal submissions and argument.

This chapter has shown how adjudicators have promulgated decisions that provide a semblance of legal stability when, in fact, they arrive at radically different conclusions, often erroneously, on the same issues. In asylum claims, much of the context explaining how an individual was made stateless is stripped away in the search for the relevant point of law that should guide the proceedings. In addition, all forms of evidence (and without concerns about its "evidential status") are treated in the same fashion by adjudicators. Finally and very unlike proceedings in other legal jurisdictions, the claimant's voice is often of limited significance in an asylum appeal (partly reflecting the efforts of counsel to prevent his or her credibility from being attacked). It is in this way that asylum cases proceed and judges stitch together a decision.

As Tricia Redeker Hepner (in this volume) argues, anthropologists writing as experts are situated in a peculiar "political economy of knowledge" between asylum applicants, lawyers, the courts, and their informants and research communities. As an expert, I "have an overriding duty to help the courts on those matters within my expertise."[29] In short, my obligation is not to the party instructing me to write a report. At the same time, however, the basis of my expertise derives from the trust and rapport I have with my research subjects or informants, some of whom have an interest in my work as an expert. Furthermore, my role in the two cases discussed here came about as a direct result of my research, which raises a potential conflict of interest with respect to anthropology's ethical code of conduct with regard to my professional responsibility to my informants. The pressures that arise in this context compel me to attend to professional ethical standards and the requirements imposed on my by the Civil Procedure rules, while simultaneously acting as a broker by writing expert reports that address the court's "epistemology of ignorance" (Bohmer and Shuman 2007) about Africa and supporting an asylum applicant's right to a fair hearing.

## Notes

I am grateful to the United Kingdom's Economic and Social Research Council for a two-year grant (RES-062–23–0296), which funded the research on which this chapter is based.

1. See http://www.justice.gov.uk/downloads/tribunals/general/consolidated-ait-rules-191211.pdf, accessed December 17, 2013.

2. See http://www.judiciary.gov.uk/Resources/JCO/Documents/Practice%20 Directions/Tribunals/IAC_UT_FtT_PracticeDirection.pdf, accessed December 17, 2013.

3. In part, this reflects the wide scope left to the Chamber. Thus, Procedural Rule 51 (1) states, "The Tribunal may allow oral, documentary or other evidence to be given of any fact which appears relevant to an appeal . . . even if that evidence would be inadmissible in a court of law." See http://www.justice.gov.uk/downloads/tribunals /general/consolidated-ait-rules-191211.pdf, accessed December 17, 2013.

4. The courts assign acronyms to asylum claims in an attempt to provide a degree of anonymity for individuals.

5. I use quote marks to indicate Ethiopians of Eritrean ethnicity who were expelled during the Eritrea-Ethiopia border war and individuals who were stripped of their nationality by Ethiopia ("Eritreans"); when I refer to individuals born and raised in Eritrea, i.e., nationals of that country, no quote marks are used (Campbell 2013).

6. Source: United Kingdom Asylum and Immigration Tribunal determination (27 March 2002) *MA v SSHD*, Appeal no. CC/47612/2001.

7. Source: United Kingdom Asylum and Immigration Tribunal decision: "MA and others (Ethiopia – Mixed ethnicity-dual nationality.) Eritrea [2004] UKIAT 00324" (22 December 2004).

8. Ibid.

9. See Court of Appeal decision: "1994 Imm. A.R. 359," which states that "when a person does not accept that the Secretary of State is correct about his nationality, it is incumbent on him to prove it, if need be by making an application for such nationality" at an embassy (providing such an application does not put the person or their family at risk). Source: ¶42 of United Kingdom Asylum and Immigration Tribunal, "MA and others (Ethiopia – Mixed ethnicity-dual nationality.) Eritrea [2004] UKIAT 00324" (22 December 2004).

10. Source: my notes of the submissions made by MA's barrister during the 2007 appeal.

11. See United Kingdom Asylum and Immigration Tribunal decision: "YL (Nationality-Statelessness-Eritrea-Ethiopia) Eritrea CG [2003] UKIAT 00016."

12. See the Court of Appeal decision "EB (Ethiopia) v SSHD [2007] EWCA Civ 809."

13. Interview with the junior barrister instructed by the Home Office to litigate against MA's appeal.

14. The SSHD produced an e-mail from the International Organization for Migration about applications for Voluntary Assisted Return made to the embassy, but

it was not clear whether some of the individuals who were issued a travel document were deportees/ethnic Eritreans who had fled the country.

15. Source: Fieldnotes taken at the hearing and United Kingdom Asylum and Immigration Tribunal, MA (Disputed Nationality) Ethiopia [2008] UKAIT 00032 (17 April 2008), see ¶56.

16. Source: see note 6.

17. Source: Interview with MA's barrister on September 11, 2007.

18. Source: ¶111 in United Kingdom Asylum and Immigration Tribunal, MA (Disputed Nationality) Ethiopia [2008] UKAIT 00032 (17 April 2008).

19. See the Court of Appeal decision "MA (Ethiopia) v SSHD [2009] EWCA Civ. 289."

20. Ibid.

21. Because I was a recognized country expert and had been following the case, I was asked by ST's solicitor to write a report addressing two issues: "(i) Has Ethiopia recently changed its policies in relation to allowing individuals who were deported and/or who fled in anticipation of deportation during Ethiopia's 1998–2000 war with Eritrea, the right to return? (ii) Would the Ethiopian authorities allow M.A. to return, and if she is allowed to return, would she be at risk of persecution?" My report answered both issues in the negative. In the meantime, MA was escorted to the Ethiopian embassy by a legal caseworker, where officials refused to recognize her as a national.

22. Source: *United Kingdom Asylum and Immigration Tribunal, Samuel Tewolde v SSHD* (1 July 2008) Appeal No. AA/04707/2006.

23. Source: Order made by the Rt. Hon/ Lord Justice Moses, Court of Appeal, 21 July 2009.

24. See United Kingdom Upper Tribunal (Immigration and Asylum Chamber) decision "ST (Ethnic Eritrean—Nationality—Return) Ethiopia CG [2011] UKUT 0025, ¶2 (heard on 18–20 January 2011)."

25. Source: United Kingdom Upper Tribunal (Immigration and Asylum Chamber), *ST v SSHD,* Appeal No. AA/04707/2006 (heard on 18–20 January 2011), ¶74–78.

26. Ibid., ¶116.

27. Ibid., ¶127.

28. The Chamber refuses the majority of appeals, and between 2000 and 2004, "a much larger percentage of appeals brought by the Home Office were allowed" in comparison to appeals made by counsel for the appellant (ICAR 2009, 12–13; more recent data are not available).

29. This obligation is imposed on all experts by the United Kingdom's Civil Procedure Rules; see http://www.justice.gov.uk/courts/procedure-rules/civil/rules/part35.

## References

Adjami, Mirna, and Julia Harrington. 2008. "The Scope and Content of Article 15 of the Universal Declaration of Human Rights." *Refugee Survey Quarterly* 27 (3): 93–109.

Barnes, John. 2004. "Expert Evidence—The Judicial Perception in Asylum and Human Rights Appeals." *International Journal of Refugee Law* 16 (3): 349–57.

Bohmer, Carol, and Amy Shuman. 2007. "Producing Epistemologies of Ignorance in the Political Asylum Application Process." *Identities* 14 (5): 603–29.

Campbell, John. 2013. *Nationalism, Law and Statelessness: Grand Illusions in the Horn of Africa.* Oxford: Routledge.

Good, Anthony. 2008. "Cultural Evidence in Courts of Law." *Journal of the Royal Anthropological Institute.* (ns) S47–60.

Home Office. 2001. Mariam Mohammed Ali. Reasons for Refusal Letter. (14 June).

Information Centre about Asylum & Refugees (ICAR). 2009. *Statistics Paper no. 2: Asylum Decision Making and Appeals Processes—March Update.* Accessed December 17, 2013. http://www.icar.org.uk/ICAR%20Statistics%20Paper%202%20-%20March%2009%20Update.pdf.

Latour, Bruno. 2010. *The Making of The Law: An Ethnography of the Conseil d'Etat.* Cambridge: Polity Press.

Sweeny, James. 2007. "The Lure of 'Facts' in Asylum Appeals." In *Applying Theory and Practice: Issues and Questions for Policy Analysts,* edited by Steve Smith, 19–35. Ashgate, UK: Aldershot.

Twining, William. 1994. *Rethinking Evidence: Exploratory Essays.* Evanston, IL: Northwestern University Press.

UN High Commissioner for Refugees (UNHCR). [1979] 1992. *Handbook on Procedures and Criteria for Determining Refugee Status under the 1951 Convention and the 1967 Protocol Relating to the Status of Refugees.* Geneva: UNHCR.

# FIVE

## "The Immigration People Know the Stories. There's One for Each Country"

*The Case of Mauritania*

E. Ann McDougall

HISTORIANS TELL STORIES for a living. They do it well. They do it convincingly—even to the point of claiming ownership of not only a truth but The Truth. We should, therefore, be of considerable assistance to an asylum lawyer challenged with turning an oral, personal experience into a written, chronological text for consumption by a multilayered legal system such as that of the United States. However, this particular story must convince an immigration court not only of its past veracity but also of its contemporary relevance; in conjunction with a presentation of current country conditions, it must make it evident why this person, given this history, would be in danger should he or she be deported. Anthony Good (2004, 114) explains the challenge in terms of the legal definition of a refugee and specifically whether a claimant's "well-founded fear" should prevent him or her from returning to the country of origin:

> The focus is thus on the future, but one important consideration is their experience before leaving their home country . . . the court must decide, largely on the basis of "objective evidence" [of this past] whether their story is credible and how they are likely to be treated if returned.

The story here has to become a narrative that ties past to future and simultaneously reveals to the court the exceptional situation of this particular claimant, even as its credibility is argued in terms of nonexceptional, publicly shared perceptions of home country conditions (Shuman and Bohmer 2004, 396–410). Countries that generate refugees also generate contextual metanarratives, complete with their own dynamics and metonyms that become a kind of language over time. "The immigration people know the stories. There's one for each country," Suketu Mehta observes in her case study of "Caroline" (2011a, 32). It is perhaps less widely understood how such stories are constructed, how they become "the" narrative, and what role the refugee asylum process plays in both.[1]

In this chapter, I draw upon my experience as an expert witness in about a dozen cases involving Mauritanians seeking asylum in the United States. Case documentation allows us to see something of how the metanarrative is created. Who is involved? Where does history play into the process? How is it engaged to translate a claimant's personal history into a public story? Again, who is involved? How is the language of the narrative employed in its (re)telling? What role does the expert witness play in these processes? What role should he or she play, ethically speaking? And whose ethics should prevail—the expert's or the lawyer's? Given that in the end, even the most objective affidavit has been commissioned and presented to the court by one side—the claimant's—in a clearly adversarial situation is there really any way to be totally neutral?

## Mauritania: The Historical Roots of "The Story"

Mauritania, like its Saharan-Sahelian neighbors, straddles the white-black West African divide—the Arab/Berber desert and the African/black Sahel. And like its neighbors, it has long practiced slavery. During the half century of French colonial rule, interregional slave trading was suppressed, but domestic slave use, integral to Saharan society, was permitted. It was argued that without supplies of new slaves, the institution would die a natural death. However, in Mauritania, slave marriage and reproduction were widely encouraged; slave children belonged to masters and became future parents of yet more slaves. Also, there was a formally recognized category of freed slave, the *hratani* (*hartaniyya,* f.; *haratine,* pl.), that remains an inherited status (McDougall 1988, 366–69).

Mauritania was home to both white/Arabs (Moors) and black/Fulbe (Fulani, Eng.; Peul, Fr.) slave masters. The latter, comprising a mostly francophone elite in the south of the country, prospered under colonial rule but were bitterly disappointed in 1960 when power was handed to

Moors. As the new government actively pursued Arabization policies, disappointment became anger and, eventually, resistance. In the 1980s, the African Liberation Forces of Mauritania (FLAM) threatened to overthrow the government. It was driven into exile in Senegal, where its membership drew strong support in the local Fulbe community (McDougall, Brhane, and Ruf 2003, 67–75).

Mauritania's white Arab society was feeling its own tensions. The extended Sahel drought of the late 1960s and early 1970s drove thousands out of the desert and into a few urban centers; most were haratine or slaves whose masters could no longer support them. By the mid-1970s, the voice of the political party El Hor (The Freeman) demanded improved conditions for haratine and slaves; by 1980, its success in publicizing their plight domestically and internationally forced the government to formally abolish slavery (McDougall 2014; ould Ahmed Salem 2009).

But as the practice continued in spite of the 1980 proclamation, El Hor's campaign became increasingly international.[2] Mauritania's complex racial and social mosaic was simplified in presentation to resonate in the United States and Europe. It was translated, literally, into black and white for its transnational audiences. By the late 1980s, Mauritania was known to the West as an "apartheid" regime in which white elite slave masters exploited black oppressed slaves.

In 1989, a war with Senegal was sparked when Mauritanian guards killed two Senegalese peasants along the countries' shared river. This not only brought tensions to a head but also gave rise to new political voices over the next decade. Between 1989 and 1991, approximately 80,000 to 90,000 black Mauritanians were forced to flee, some to Mali, the majority to Senegal. Their possessions were stolen, their identification papers destroyed, their women raped, and their men tortured.[3] This genocide did not respect social class; rich and poor were victimized. Among the perpetrators were haratine, who comprised a large percentage of police and army personnel.

Internationally, the tale was told differently. FLAM's strategy to seek support for the exiled refugees was to characterize them as black slaves being driven from their homes by white masters. Mauritania's war with Senegal was increasingly presented by the media as one fought over slavery; the distinction between slave and refugee became permanently blurred (McDougall 2010, 265–67).

In 1993, disillusioned El Hor members launched a new organization called SOS Slaves. Although it helped those still in domestic bondage, its priority was garnering an international audience, as its name implies (Messaoud 2009; Bullard 2005, 759–60). It argued (then, as now) that the distinction between hratani and slave obscures the fact that both were slaves at one time to the Moors and, consequently, that they should be united in their resistance. But this remains a hard sell among haratine, who have long seen themselves as semiautonomous extensions of former masters' families, immersed in their Moorish *hassaniya* culture.[4] They are reluctant to associate themselves with those of recent slave status who claim "black" identity but remain largely poor and dependent (McDougall, Brhane, and Ruf 2003, 71–74).[5]

This admittedly simplified history reveals how and when the metanarrative came into being as a response to Mauritania's internal and international politics of slavery; the United Kingdom and the United States were the principal audiences toward which it was addressed. John Mercer's well-publicized report on slavery in Mauritania (Mercer 1981; published 1982) gave it initial voice; fifteen years later, the late Samuel Cotton reiterated it powerfully in the United States. In 1995, Cotton was a Columbia University PhD student studying social services. From an undercover, fact-finding mission in Senegal and Mauritania (December 23, 1995, to January 12, 1996), he brought back material on slavery that formed the basis of: (1) presentations to American congressional subcommittees on international operations and human rights and on Africa, as well as international relations, in the House of Representatives (March 1996); (2) a documentary, *Mauritania and the African Slave Trade* (n.d.); and (3) a book, *Silent Terror* (1999). Cotton had already founded the Committee against Slavery in Mauritania and the Sudan (CASMAS) in 1995, complete with a web page where these and other published materials were advertised.[6] And months before he actually traveled to Senegal and Mauritania, he published newspaper articles railing against Arab slave traders (Moors) and black slavery. In Senegal, his principal informants were FLAM officials (Kinne 2001, 612) and "black Mauritanians" in refugee camps; in his ten-day, secret visit to Mauritania, he interviewed only the leaders of El Hor and SOS Slaves. These observations raise questions as to the scientific quality of his research, but there is no doubt that his subsequent public activities hugely raised the profile of the black-white, slave-master image of Mauritania.[7]

The war of 1989 with Senegal that served as a catalyst for many refugee cases was embraced within this narrative for political reasons, rooted in the historical moment. But these political realities have been successfully rendered invisible by the power of "The Story." And to a large extent, so have the refugee experiences themselves. I turn to the cases of Yusuf, Saidou, and Nana (pseudonyms). Each is presented to the extent necessary to develop the questions posed at the outset of this chapter; each is an actual case with material quoted from the claimant's declarations, lawyers' correspondence (with me), and my submitted affidavits. Briefer references to the cases Abdel, Maloud, and Fatmatou (also pseudonyms) follow in my discussion of ethical issues.

## Deconstructing Stories: In Search of History

By the time expert testimony is sought, the claimant has constructed his or her story in such a way as to engage someone at a law firm; where immigrant communities exist, the claimant has probably also consulted a local adviser to new refugees from his or her country of origin (Mehta 2011a).[8] These preliminary consultations are generally unknown to the potential expert, whose introduction to the case usually begins with an e-mail or telephone contact from an office intern, followed by copies of the claimant's statement or declaration and, finally, direct communication with his or her lawyer.[9]

By this time, the lawyer has worked with the client to prepare a statement that is clear but also legally effective: a specific terminology and discourse need to be introduced to the case if it is to resonate with the case adjudicators who will soon be involved (Good 2004, 114; Bohmer and Shuman, in this volume). Depending on the nature of the claim and the general understanding of the larger country narrative (discussed later), there is often a set of required arguments to be made or motifs to be referenced. The statement needs to simultaneously engage potential expert witnesses conversant with the narrative and court officials responsible for implementing legal arguments consistent with it—all within the context of an extant public perception of that country. Jan Blommaert (2001, 438) calls these "remouldings" and "renarrations"—"text trajectories": "[W]hat happens in the institutional processing of asylum seekers' stories is often a battle with unequal arms, and the confrontation of different narrative conventions creates a huge problem of justice and fairness" (436). Amy Shuman and Carol Bohmer (2004, 398) address the issue even more emphatically: "Lawyers and others who provide assistance to claimants fill a crucial role in reframing the claim not only to be consistent with the law, but also, to correspond with current Western social values."

Yusuf, who had been expelled from Mauritania to Senegal in 1989, contextualized his declaration by noting that "Fulani have been treated like slaves in Mauritania. The white Moors are the majority and they consider that the Fulani are not even considered to be citizens of Mauritania. [In Senegal] the police would also beat me and call me names, bad names, like . . . harthani, which is a bad name for someone that is Fulani, it means like a slave." Although Yusuf's deportation case focused on an entirely unrelated issue, Mauritanian slavery was evoked to suggest Fulbe oppression—"like slaves," Fulbe lacked citizenship in the eyes of the Moors.[10] In observing that Mauritanians generally "reference themselves in terms of an ethnic 'divide' . . . [perceived] 'to be slavery,'" Shuman and Bohmer (2004, 397) note that they are like all asylum seekers needing "to prove that . . . persecution . . . [is] politically motivated," explaining the motivations of their oppressors vis-à-vis their personal "group affiliation." In Yusuf's case, this proof was facilitated because Americans still associated Fulbe ("blacks") being expelled with "slaves" in their long-held, distorted understanding of 1989.

Yusuf's resentment at being called hratani by the Senegalese police, which seems to have bothered him even more than being beaten, is revealing of precisely the racial and social complexity his statement attempts to gloss. He wishes to distance himself from this métis social class not because they are "like slaves" but because they or their ancestors probably were slaves (of the Moors). In introducing haratine to his story, Yusuf reveals both the contradictions inherent in trying to portray Mauritania in paradigmatic black-and-white terms and his personal role in creating what will become his public history.

Similarly, Saidou, a Fulbe who was abducted, imprisoned, tortured, and then expelled to Senegal in 1989, had clearly shaped much of his own declaration to the court. He was well educated and active in FLAM, aware of its history and rhetoric, and knowledgeable about the differences between them. Though he self-presented as being from a middle-class family whose father had been a regional administrator, his group affiliation was to the Fulbe, who were known as persecuted blacks with "no right to government or public service jobs . . . usually relegated to

*E. Ann McDougall*

agricultural work . . . [and] precluded from owning herd animals or working as herdsmen."[11] Blacks who are educated, [or] hold positions of authority or respect in their villages, or who speak out against the government have long been imprisoned, tortured, and killed. My [relative] who was killed was one of these." The government charged FLAM with plotting a coup d'état and began imprisoning its members. Saidou characterized this in terms of 'being black': "The government simply saw any black who held a position of respect or authority in his community as a threat, and invented the coup as an excuse to silence them."

Historically, FLAM was a real political threat, first from within and then from outside, as the country sought political support and arms to overthrow the regime. Saidou was fully aware of this. He even went on to explain that he and his relative were active FLAM members and that FLAM had access to police information that they did not hesitate to exploit. But to effectively situate his personal experience in the publicly recognized story, he drew upon the rhetoric of dramatic white-black racism that FLAM itself had successfully promoted. This was most evident in Saidou's account of the April 1989 conflict. Remembering that the actual spark involved Senegalese peasant-herders who strayed across the border and were shot by Mauritanian soldiers, Saidou's account is strikingly misinformed:

> The conflict between Mauritanian blacks and Moors erupted into battle in April of 1989. Moorish Mauritanian herdsmen led their animals into the fields belonging to black farmers, to graze. The animals destroyed the crops. The farmers finally revolted against decades of oppression and abuse at the hands of the Moors, and captured the animals. The hostility between the two groups led to an eruption of ethnic violence, during which the government brutalized and eventually expelled thousands of blacks from Mauritania.

Saidou undoubtedly knew the actual circumstances. Interestingly, what he describes was an everyday occurrence in the region (pastoralist-cultivator tensions inherent in such border zones, here overlaid with racial dynamics), but he concludes that this was an expression of long-standing, deep hostility on the part of Moorish oppressors and blacks. That this rendering of events remained in his sworn statement is testimony to the power of the metanarrative.

A third case involves Nana, a woman who suffered imprisonment, beatings, and multiple rapes in 1989 and, like Yusuf and Saidou, was then expelled to Senegal. This is the only case in which I received an original declaration (in handwritten French—hereafter Document A), and an English "Memorandum of Law and Facts" (hereafter Document B) prepared for the court. There is little question of the lawyer's substantial intervention in the latter.[12]

For example, Document B reads: "The government police told Nana that she was not Mauritanian—they told her she was Senegalese (i.e. Black)." Though this is plausible, Nana actually said nothing of the kind in Document A; this elision of "Senegalese" and "Black," however, resembles Saidou's characterization (mentioned earlier). It is not the last such echo. Introducing the events leading to Nana's expulsion, Document B explains that

> attempts by Black Mauritanians to penetrate the predominantly
> Arab-Berber government and social structure were rebuffed by
> White Maurs [sic], who resorted to increasingly brutal tactics to
> retain their social and political hold over Black Mauritanians. All
> attempts by Black Mauritanians to advance in society were met
> with hostility, prefacing the large-scale white Maur [sic] retaliation
> that culminated in the violent expulsion of 1989–1990.

And playing the slavery card explicitly, it continues by noting, "The Mauritanian government has historically encouraged discrimination against Black Mauritanians and Haratines [haratine] through enslavement, which reportedly continues today." But in Document A, slavery plays no role whatsoever. Moreover, in providing context for Nana's repeated rapes, Document B states that "both white Maurs [sic] and Haratines [haratine] raped Black Mauritanian women, subjecting them to systematic degradation, humiliation, and torture." So were haratine victims "like black Mauritanians" of white Mauritanian discrimination? Or were they Moors—collaborators, raping black Mauritanian women? Document B is riddled with misunderstandings; the lawyer not only translated the claimant's testimony into English, she articulated it in a slavery-racism discourse she felt would resonate with the court.

In reality (Document A), Nana identified five ethnic groups. The first was the "*Maures*" (Moors), consisting of "white *Maure, bidan*" and "black *Maures, haratine*": "These two have the same culture and speak the same language, *hassanyia.*" The other four were the "Fulany [*sic*], Wolof, Soninke and Bambara," each defined by language. She never referred to herself as black, only belatedly adopting a French shorthand, *les Noirs,* to juxtapose these groups against *les Maures.* She never referred to black Mauritanians or to their enslavement by Moors. Nor did she speak of the enslavement of the haratine; on the contrary, she placed them in the ethnic category of "Maures." In applying a race-based perception of Mauritania to her (re)presentation of Nana's personal story, the lawyer distorted it to the extent that parts are rendered incoherent to anyone familiar with the actual situation.

There are also instances of blatant misrepresentation. Document B contextualized 1989 in a gloss of increasing racial oppression and discrimination. Nana very clearly distinguished between the issues that presented themselves in the 1960s and those of the 1980s; none was couched in the racial terms of Document B. "The first years after independence were difficult," Nana wrote:

> The tensions between the Moors who effectively controlled
> the country and the Blacks who occupied most middle-level
> management within the government, were exacerbated. The Blacks'
> fear of Arab domination was accentuated with the introduction
> by the government of a vision to Arabize the country. And most
> notably by the decision taken in 1966 to render schooling in Arabic
> compulsory. The Blacks preferred to study in and speak French in
> order to maintain their relations with French Black Africa. Although
> the Moors and the Blacks are both Muslims, the Blacks do not
> accept the assimilation made between Islam and Arabism and seek to
> preserve their own cultures and heritages [my translation].

She used the "Blacks" here as shorthand for the four non-Moor ethnic groups.

The issues presented were clearly language and culture—resistance to Arabic and Arabization, not to whites per se. And at that moment in time, black Moors (haratine) were integral to the government's vision of Arabizing the country—they spoke hassanyia and embraced hassanyia culture.

As to the years culminating in the violent expulsions of 1989, Nana wrote:

> From 12 December, 1984, the country was under military law.
> There was no freedom of expression [or] activity. The conditions
> of life became worse for the Negro African people, especially
> for the Fulani people. The movements and activities of the

opposition [political] parties were under high surveillance. Since 1986, I supported all the activities and participated at all the demonstrations to speak to the unjust decisions of the government of President Maouya Sid Ahmed Taya. I officially became a member [of FLAM] in 1987.

This is a straightforward account of the growing political tension between FLAM and the Mauritanian government that also became a story of ethnic persecution as the Fulbe increasingly became the characters associated with the exiled party. Nana asserted unequivocally that it was her involvement in FLAM that resulted in her horrendous experience in 1989. As with Saidou, it was that political involvement that provoked her arrest and expulsion. And like Yusuf, she rendered a nuanced account of her history with FLAM. The comparison between Document A and Document B could not be more revelatory of the impact the public metanarrative has when it frames both the content and the language of the personal story.

## The Elephant in the Room: The Question of Ethics

So, we arrive at a troubling question: what should the expert do with this understanding? In the case of Nana, I engaged primarily with Document A, ignoring the more egregious efforts at statement crafting evident in Document B. Where necessary, I drew the two together with some crafting of my own. To address the central slave-race distortion, I wrote that although it is true that Mauritania has "an unusual social structure" and that historically it has been the white Moors and their black slaves and former slaves (haratine) who have captured international attention,

> there is a third group that confounds these simplified Western images of Mauritania . . . the large, black free population living mostly in the south and belonging primarily to the Halpulaar (Peul) ethnic group. The politics of Mauritania since independence have been shaped largely by the intersecting dynamics of these groups as each attempted to redefine and position itself relative to Mauritania's resources.

This was an implicit correction to Document B.

With the "Arabization question," I tried to bridge the gap between what Nana had said and what the lawyer had constructed. Acknowledging government attempts to replace the most offensive colonial legacy, the French language, I wrote,

[The policy of Arabization] had roots in the 1960s but it was really the 1980s that bore the brunt of the policy. [During this decade,] the government made a concerted effort to court support from wealthy Middle Eastern countries. It became truly "Arab" and Islamic, introducing Sharia law, enforcing Arabic education and ensuring a government run in Arabic, by Arabic speakers. This is the social context in which black [African] Mauritanians . . . found themselves increasingly economically marginalized. Positions for which they were clearly qualified in terms of training were going to non-educated *hassanyia*-speaking Moors (and even *haratine*), while degree-holders drove taxis or remained unemployed— thus a complete reversal of the early post-colonial years. Nana's personal history clearly places her within this group of increasingly disenfranchised and frustrated citizens.

Similar negotiation was required in the affidavit for Saidou. With respect to the disconnection between his own familial situation and the oppressed Fulbe group identity he claimed, I suggested that

French-educated Halpulaar (and other blacks) were represented in the government and civil service in the late 1970s; what this man is remembering is the 1980s and 1990s, when political opposition emerged clandestinely in parties like F.L.A.M. . . . and the government became sensitive to both international scrutiny and internal political actions arising in the wake of the 1980 decree abolishing slavery.

Put another way, I created a historical elision between two truths.

As for Saidou's evocative imaging of the 1989 river valley incident, I acknowledged that

it was precisely the localized conflict over pasture he describes but it would be more accurate to portray it as a consequence of the ethnic tensions plaguing the valley region rather than its cause. The official international conflict was but yet another articulation of long-standing problems [between Mauritania and Senegal].

This discrepancy of fact should have provided an easy target for cross-examination, but it was never mentioned. The narrative proved stronger than the historical truth.

These efforts produced an already somewhat negotiated affidavit, which, in my experience, still required more discussion with the lawyer.

In Abdel's case, for example, a point "mentioned but not stressed" in my draft provoked the question, "[Has] there has been a crackdown on opposition groups since the failed coup? . . . If so, that would help our client." My initial submission in Maloud's case raised nine additional questions, each requiring further research. One pushed me to address a weakness in the original statement: "[Lawyer ]: 'Have you heard of the U___ Party of which his [relative] was a part? Does that ring true? Maloud said it was in the 1980s.'" I had indeed heard of it; the problem was it did not exist until the 1990s. After providing some background to the party, I attempted to establish an acceptable middle ground:

> [It] could be argued that Maloud's [relative] might have been politically active—he said his [relative was a professional] and [professionals] are among those named as politically active during this era. . . . [They] saw themselves as the only ones capable of challenging the regime. Although Maloud must have been mistaken about the party being the U___, it could well have been the M___. The fact that it [the latter] has been part of the U___ since 199x might well explain Maloud's mistaken impression.

Maloud's case also involved information about a detention in 199y. "[Lawyer]: 'Are these detention conditions e.g. paragraph 8, consistent with descriptions of Nouakchott cells/prisons?'" Unfortunately, I had not been able to find information for that particular year, so I provided the following evidentiary gymnastic:

> According to reports referring to the 1990–91 situations [*Africa Watch*], methods of torture mention being beaten frequently and describe cold water being poured over the head. . . . [The] report says at J'reida (north of Nouakchott) most detainees were tortured [which was also true of most detention centers, according to Amnesty International]. A 1999 report on the Human Rights situation . . . indicated much attention had been given to improving conditions within prisons; lack of sanitation, poor food, poor-to-no medical care—were all listed as "issues" that had been improved during [the] year covered by the report (1998–9). This might be taken as proof that conditions were as bad in 199x as the client suggests.

This gathering of additional, potentially helpful evidence generated more than five pages of documented information and plausible hypotheses stitched together with conditional qualifiers such as "could," "would," "might have," and "may have."

Shuman and Bohmer (2004, 408) note that "[the] law states that the story is sufficient, if credible, yet we have never come across a case in which asylum was granted without corroboration." If we need only to show that a story is credible, such qualifiers are not a problem. But if our information is being used "to corroborate . . . an individual's story," seeking an ethical middle ground with fancy wordsmithing may still be problematic (as in the case of Fatmatou, which will be discussed).[13]

Finally, we return to Nana. Another problem emerged as I examined the court submission. The slavery and racism framework the lawyer used to contextualize Nana's case was none other than Samuel Cotton's. The lawyer wrote that "the Mauritanian government has historically encouraged discrimination against Black Mauritanians and Haratines [*sic*] through enslavement, which reportedly continues today," citing Cotton's online newspaper articles as references. This FLAM-inspired statement resonated precisely because it was already part of the publicly accepted race-slavery discourse, thanks in large part to Cotton's earlier propaganda. As I had already criticized his research and his rhetoric in print (McDougall, Brhane, and Ruf 2003, 78–79), to what degree could I now ethically support a statement framed by both? To what degree should I knowingly reinforce this caricature of Mauritania's genuine racial problems? What Nana's case really brought home was that once in play, the narrative dynamic acquires a life of its own.

Let us return to the ever-present ethical "elephant in the room." In legal terms, it does not exist; in reality, its presence is palpable.[14] Preparing an affidavit does not depend solely on one's expertise. It often requires a willingness to compromise with a lawyer's advocacy. One can argue that lawyers should ask expert witnesses for objective statements and remain hands-off; one can also argue that expert witnesses should understand they are not meant to corroborate, advocate for, or attest to the claimant's credibility. However, it is naive to assume that in real situations, these neat legal categories do not bleed into each other.[15]

Good (2004, 119–20) illustrates this fine line between theory and practice in his discussion of the British scholar George Joffe, a specialist in North African politics. A judge chastised Joffe for seeming to assess a client's credibility and then extrapolate what might happen if the client were deported to Egypt. Only the court or tribunal is entitled to address "credibility." But an appeal judge accepted Joffe's explanation: "I must . . . within the context of my expertise, indicate whether or not such statements are consonant with what I know of the objective circumstances

[and] I must also comment upon the consequences that would follow if such statements were to be correct—but that . . . is not to determine or comment on their accuracy or veracity." Good concludes, "For experts to assess an applicant's credibility is one thing; for them to express 'opinions as to what is likely to happen to him' is another. Such opinions are precisely what solicitors seek." Yet in a continuing case (1999–2004), I was asked directly in 2004, "How likely it is [that the client] is telling the truth?" Would the government's assertion that his birth certificate was falsified "[now] affect my opinion of his truthfulness/credibility?" The original affidavit would stand; the lawyer wanted me "to give the judge [my] sense of what has happened in Mauritania since [I] last wrote (1999) and [my] opinion of [the client's] credibility." Good's and Joffe's distinctions notwithstanding, they can indeed become blurred in practice. And apparently judges' interpretations of these unclear boundaries can vary significantly as well.[16]

The ethical dimension that technically should not exist also presents itself when claimants' statements are not, as Joffe says, "consonant with what is known of the objective circumstances"—when, for example, credibility was factored into a previous denial and the lawyer now wants to be sure relevant issues are addressed on appeal. As Maloud's lawyer put it after first apologizing for "plaguing [me] with even more questions," "the client's judge has a 98 percent denial rate and we need to provide all the documentation to fight for an appeal."[17] Though never asked to change my information or even nudge my ethical boundaries (that pressure is self-inflicted), I have been asked to simply not address something in the claimant's statement if what I can say is not helpful. These discussions also take place when going over questions lawyers will ask me if I am called to testify. Like any good lawyers, they do not want to pose a question to which they do not know the answer—and they do not want answers that will hurt their clients. This complicated, multifaceted process draws the expert witness into the very construction of narratives that in turn become "history." It raises issues of ethics as much as expertise.

### "In Your Expert Opinion, What Would Happen to the Claimant Should She Be Deported?": The Ultimate Bottom Line

If the story rings true, it is likely that expressed fears about deportation are also well founded; the expert witness can lay an effective base for this conclusion. But even such a base may not satisfy the needs of the claimant.

The affidavit has to transform history into a probable future, one that suggests to the court the strong likelihood that the claimant's human rights would be violated if he or she were deported. This is a problematic scenario given the rapidity with which many African countries change and the tortoise-like pace with which cases move through the courts. From the early 1990s, Mauritania has transitioned from a military dictatorship to a pseudodemocracy, then to several alternating military coup d'états and so-called democratic regimes. Asylum cases I have been involved with have experienced court delays of (on average) two to five years.

In Nana's case, such delays necessitated a new affidavit. The regime in power at the time of her expulsion had been overthrown, and a transitional government was promising elections. On the face of it, this normalizing of the political situation undermined my initial submission significantly. Genuinely doubting that appearances would translate into reality, I tried to sustain the original case. I argued that consecutive United States' Country Reports on Human Rights Practices (Mauritania) covering the former government and the transitional regime had not changed. Therefore, conditions had probably not changed, which meant the claimant's safety would still be a concern if she returned. The reports repeated themselves verbatim, which actually suggested a lack of new data more than deliberately reiterated commentary. However, saying this when the magic words *democratic elections* were in the air was not likely to be effective.

Yusuf's case was postponed twice over five years. One of his identity papers had been declared fraudulent by the US government; Mauritania's government had changed, and international policy regarding the 1989 refugees had moved on—camps were closed, the situation considered resolved.[18] Rewriting the affidavit was a challenge. The following passage reflects my attempt to marry my previous affidavit with largely unknown country conditions. With respect to earlier violence directed at returnees, I noted:

> While I am not clear on what the government is doing about
> those claiming citizenship without proof, I can say that the stories
> surrounding the experiences of those who have been permitted to
> return in the past are not encouraging. As to the current situation,
> I am not sure the reports of attacks are as frequent as they were
> just a few years ago, but there has been no effort on any legal
> front to restore property or compensate for losses and damage.
> With respect to F.L.A.M. and his [Yusuf's] earlier membership:

In all honesty, I am not sure how significant that association would be regarded given the government's current preoccupation with so-called "Islamists." That said, returning without proper papers would automatically subject Yusuf to an investigation and his previous activities, arrests and possibly expulsion would be a matter of record. I suspect the greater danger would be the "unofficial" reception he might receive locally, were he to attempt to recover any of the property taken from his family, or seek legal restitution for his treatment or that of his family.

And I continued in that vein.

In both instances, initial affidavits had been relatively strong from the claimants' perspective. I believed fully in the dangers deportation would bring. However, with Mauritania appearing to be proceeding along a committed democratic path, the arguments became increasingly difficult to support. The extent to which I felt morally obligated to step beyond my comfort zone of compromise grew commensurately.

But in at least one case, it was not far enough for the claimant. Fatmatou's case was on appeal. The military transitional government marked a significant change in the country's political conditions since she had first been refused, but as with Nana and Yusuf, there was nothing concrete one could yet say about its impact. The decision, a denial of appeal, read:

> The respondent has included evidence indicating that in August 2008 a military coup d'état occurred in Mauritania restoring, to some extent, military power. It is the respondent's burden to show that changed country conditions would likely change the outcome of her case. [No evidence has been presented] other than an affidavit from the director of the MEAS program at the University of Alberta Canada [McDougall], which acknowledges the change in government but does not establish how the change . . . affects the respondent's claim for relief. . . . A mere showing of a change in government is not sufficient. Accordingly, the appeal will be dismissed and the motion will be denied.

At that moment in time, it would have been impossible for anyone to say conclusively whether conditions would deteriorate or improve, let alone how the changes would affect "the respondent's claim for relief." But having my information singled out by the judge as "not being sufficient" left me feeling a victim of that supposedly nonpresent elephant. Rightly or wrongly, for the sake of the claimant, I wished I had been able to wrestle it more effectively.

### Concluding Reflections: In Court and Beyond

The asylum process rarely concludes with the submission of documents; the affidavit is usually examined under oath. After responding to the lawyer's prepared questions, the expert is subject to government cross-examination.[19] This alone renders moot any arguments that he or she is not understood to be implicitly part of the claimant's case. Moreover, even though the legal responsibility for advocacy lies with the claimant's lawyer, the expert's affidavit may determine the outcome.[20] How does one weigh professional ethics against moral responsibility in such situations?[21] Why should historians, indeed academics in general, even try?[22]

To my mind, there are two compelling reasons. Academic training and experience allow scholars to see where contemporary reality and asylum stories intersect. In Mauritania, the dominant metanarrative has been one of slavery and racism.[23] In other countries, it takes on its own local colors— "a story for every country."[24] What is important is to recognize the discourse embedded in the claimant's initial, often oral statement and the lawyer's subsequent, written court submission. Scholars can bring specialized country knowledge to bear on what they see and hear in these documents, ultimately presenting a reasoned and defensible vision of what deportation would mean for the claimant. The process is flawed, but it remains the best hope asylum seekers have to forge their own futures.

And there is something else at stake. As we have seen, the process by which refugee claims are constructed constitutes a kind of circular dynamic, reinforcing the most dramatic and traumatic moments in the country narrative. Its controversial role in facilitating asylum aside, its impact on how Africa as a whole is perceived—and how Africans in general are received in American society—may be far less sanguine and far more enduring.[25] For the scholar, understanding why he or she should become part of this narrative ultimately may be less difficult than learning to do so effectively.

### Notes

1. Bohmer and Shuman (in this volume) also explore "the story"; they emphasize its cultural components and role as documentation in the asylum process.

2. Legislation in 1981 rendered the declaration practically meaningless (McDougall 2014).

3. Missing identity documents later pose serious problems for asylum stories needing corroboration (Shuman and Bohmer 2004, 395).

4. *Hassaniya* is an Arabic-Berber dialect spoken by Moors and most haratine; the term also applies to culture.

5. Nor do they associate with "blacks" (Fulbe, Soninke) of higher social status who were themselves slave owners.

6. The website is no longer accessible.

7. Berger's contribution (in this volume) traces the evolution of a similar narrative around female genital cutting. She discusses journalistic "research" much like Cotton's, which had comparable impact; her case studies (like mine that follow) illustrate how the narrative influences asylum adjudicators.

8. See also Blommaert (2001, 414–15) for a comparative Belgian situation. He speaks specifically to "home narratives": "Home narratives are often long . . . involving usually very detailed information on local events, the crises from which refugees fled and so on. Home narratives are contextualizing accounts, and the particular contextualization trajectories they follow require close inspection" (Blommaert 2001, 415; developed further 428–36).

9. In a recent appeal, I was told the initial lawyer suspected his client "may have unnecessarily embellished certain parts of [his declaration], perhaps at another alien's suggestion." Being privy to such information is unusual in my experience.

10. The issue was that his Senegalese relatives would force his daughters to undergo circumcision.

11. To my knowledge, this is not true.

12. An anonymous reviewer questioned whether "the basis of the statement is a document written by the claimant him or herself, which the lawyer then edits." I do not believe Nana's case was unusual in this sense. I cannot speak to "edits"; I assume there was a process of discussion with the client, resulting in a lawyer preparing the final, written version.

13. Shuman and Bohmer (2004, 409) argue that lawyers want expert witnesses "to corroborate specific details of an individual's story"; this has also been my experience. An anonymous reviewer disagrees.

14. This is inherent in the dynamics Tricia Redeker Hepner (in this volume) argues are irreducible either to legal procedures or political-economic contexts.

15. Redeker Hepner (in this volume) conceptualizes this reality as the "asylum-advocacy nexus"—the "interface" where objectives of academic experts, advocates (lawyers, activists), and asylum seekers intersect.

16. In spite of doubt expressed by both the initial judge in the Joffe case (Good 2004, 120) and an anonymous reviewer that such reports could or should be inadmissible, my affidavit in this case was accepted.

17. Apparently, this kind of discussion between lawyer and expert witness is unusual in the United Kingdom (according to an anonymous reviewer).

18. Bohmer and Shuman (in this volume) discuss the issue of "fraudulent/missing" documentation.

19. Good (2004, 124–25) argues that the vulnerability of the "undefended expert witness statement" should outweigh cost savings in deciding on witness presence; my experience, nevertheless, has been uniquely telephonic testimony, as the cases are usually being handled pro bono.

20. This can work negatively, as in Fatmatou's case, or positively, as in a 2013 appeal where on the basis of my affidavit establishing country conditions and a few minutes of establishing the claimant's credibility, the judge decided the case in the claimant's favor.

21. In Good's discussion of credibility (2004, 118–20, quotation at 118), he notes that one textbook characterized expert witnesses "as close to being professional liars."

22. J. Leigh Lawrence (1991, 522–23) questioned the pros and cons of political scientists setting foot in the courtroom, concluding that "[a]ny would-be witness should always ask himself or herself, 'Why am I an expert in this area?'" The question remains relevant and not only for political scientists.

23. On the one hand, this may be changing. I have been told that recently, claims tend to be based on homosexuality because Mauritania's sharia law condemns homosexuals to death and constitutes an unambiguous danger to a deportee's safety. But on the other hand, my most recent case (2013, referenced earlier) was an appeal in exactly such a case; the simple existence of the law is no longer sufficient (if it ever was) to prove its application, let alone its application in a given case. It remains to be seen if this particular story gains long-term currency. Moreover, the recent activities of internationally recognized antislavery activist Biram ould Dah Abeid, awarded human rights honors in Europe and by the United Nations in 2013, may well ensure the longevity of a reinvigorated slavery and racism metanarrative after all.

24. See Shuman and Bohmer (2004, 410).

25. Iris Berger (in this volume) develops this point in terms of anthropologists' concerns in particular.

## References

Blommaert, Jan. 2001. "Investigating Narrative Inequality: African Asylum Seekers' Stories in Belgium." *Discourse and Society* 12 (4): 413–49.

Bullard, Alice. 2005. "From Colonization to Globalization: The Vicissitudes of Slavery in Mauritania." *Cahiers d'études africaines* 45 (179-180): 751–69.

Cotton, Samuel. 1996. "Testimony and Statement: Slavery in Mauritania and Sudan." Joint Hearing before the Subcommittees on International Operations and Human Rights and Africa and on International Relations, US House of Representatives, 114th Cong., 2nd sess., March 13. Accessed January 20, 2014. http://www.archive.org/stream/slaveryinmauritaoounit/slaveryinmauritaoounit_djvu.txt.

———. 1999. *Silent Terror: A Journey into Contemporary African Slavery*. New York: Writers and Readers Publishing.

Good, Anthony. 2004. "'Undoubtedly an Expert'? Anthropologists in British Asylum Courts." *Journal of the Royal Anthropological Institute* 10 (1): 113–33.

Kinne, Lance. 2001. "The Benefits of Exile: The Case of F.L.A.M." *Journal of Modern African Studies* 39 (4): 597–621.

Lawrence, J. Leigh. 1991. "Political Scientists as Expert Witnesses." *Political Science and Politics* 24 (3): 521–24.

McDougall, E. Ann. 1988. "Topsy-Turvy World: Slaves and Freed Slaves in the Mauritanian Adrar, 1910–1950." In *The Ending of Slavery in Africa,* edited by Richard R. Roberts and Suzanne Miers, 362–88. Madison: University of Wisconsin Press.

———. 2010. "The Politics of Slavery in Mauritania: Rhetoric, Reality and Democratic Discourse." *Maghreb Review,* Special Issue on Mauritania, 35 (1–2): 259–86.

———. 2014. "Affirming Identity in the *Islamic* Republic of Mauritania: The Abolition Crisis of 1980–1983." *Maghreb Review.* 39 (2): 191–207.

McDougall, E. Ann, Meskerem Brhane, and Urs Peter Ruf. 2003. "Legacies of Slavery, Promises of Democracy: Mauritania in the 21st Century." In *Globalizing Africa,* edited by Malinda Smith, 67–88. Trenton, NJ: Africa World Press.

Mehta, Suketu. 2011a. "The Asylum Seeker." *New Yorker* 87 (22): 32–37.

———. 2011b. Short version of "The Asylum Seeker." Accessed January 24, 2014. http://www.newyorker.com/reporting/2011/08/01/110801fa_fact_mehta.

Mercer, John. 1981. "Slavery in Mauritania in 1980. Intervention on behalf of the Anti Slavery Society for the protection of Human Rights." Commission on Human Rights. United Nations Economic and Social Council (August, Geneva). Also published as *Slavery in Mauritania Today* by London: Anti-Slavery Society, 1982 and Edinburgh: Human Rights Group, 1982.

Messaoud, Boubacar (founder, director, and spokesperson for SOS Slaves). 2009. Interview with the author. Nouakchott, Mauritania, December.

ould Ahmed Salem, Zekeria. 2009. "'Bare-Footed Activists': Transformations of the Haratine Movement in Mauritania." In *Social Movements in Africa,* edited by Stephen Ellis and I. Van Essel, 156–77. Leiden: Brill.

Shuman, Amy, and Carol Bohmer. 2004. "Representing Trauma: Political Asylum Narrative." *Journal of American Folklore* 117 (446): 394–414.

# SIX

## Cultural Silences as an Excuse for Injustice

*The Problems of Documentary Proof*

Carol Bohmer and Amy Shuman

THE PURPOSE OF a political asylum hearing is to get to the truth of what happened in order to differentiate between fraudulent and legitimate applications. As in an inquisition, the questioners control the line of inquiry as well as the determination of what counts as evidence. As Carlo Ginzburg (1980) discovered in his study of the fifteenth-century case of a peasant accused of blasphemy, an inquisition can impose its own script on the proceedings, and the petitioner may be in the position of trying to guess what the questioner wants to hear. Political asylum officials would be dismayed to be compared to such a disregard for justice, but when they overlook cultural circumstances, they can make neutral application of the law impossible. In particular, they too often do not acknowledge either the rhetorical dimensions of the trauma narratives told by the applicants or the cultural differences in how people establish, utilize, and manipulate social networks in conflict situations.

Asylum applicants face scrutiny based on the immigration officials' prior knowledge and assumptions about the conditions in particular countries. This situation has been described as "refugee roulette" because asylum applicants' acceptance can depend as much on where they come from and where they apply for asylum as on the legitimacy of their cases (Ramji-Nogales, Schoenholtz, and Schrag 2009; Tsangarides 2010). The authorities are often misinformed about whether a particular government is protecting its citizens against human rights abuses (Pirouet 2001, 51–52), and beyond that, they may also misunderstand cultural customs, which can result in the perception that an applicant's testimony is either unclear or inconsistent (Bohmer and Shuman 2007b). In the United Kingdom, Home Office (HO) officials are often slow to update country conditions; as we will discuss, the result can be that an applicant's testimony is considered incredible because the official is inadequately informed. Alternatively, officials may know that a civil war has been resolved but may not be aware of ongoing human rights abuses. Several asylum scholars have documented the seeming arbitrariness or misunderstanding of asylum decisions, not only in the United Kingdom but also in other countries accepting victims of persecution (Pirouet 2001; Ramji-Nogales, Schoenholtz, and Schrag 2009; Spijkerboer 2000).

The interrogation process produces silences and gaps that that the asylum applicants rarely can fill with the necessary documentary evidence. Some documents do not exist; others cannot be procured. In some cases, the various authorities' cultural misunderstandings about what is documented and the availability of those documents (for example, visits to a doctor or time spent in prison) result in false expectations and unwarranted suspicions. Here, we examine the role that this need for documentation (and the absence of documentation) plays in asylum applications. The documents of the asylum application create a "text" that matches the interrogation in certain ways but actually produces some of the gaps.

Asylum law requires that applicants prove they have a well-founded fear of persecution, based on race, religion, nationality, membership in a particular social group, or political opinion. The law always attempts to be culturally neutral, but in the case of asylum, cultural difference plays a crucial role. Bonny Ibhawoh (2003, 63) argues that political asylum procedures require a "weak cultural relativism" in which understanding cultural practices is critical but does not undermine universal human rights. In practice, however, it is difficult for asylum officials to avoid making prejudicial judgments that disparage some cultural practices and favor others.

Our research represents a collaboration between a lawyer and sociologist (Carol Bohmer) and a folklorist specializing in the study of narrative (Amy Shuman). We began our work at an agency in central Ohio, the Community Refugee Immigration Services, that provided a range of services, including housing, language instruction, employment, and legal services, to new refugees. Bohmer served as a pro bono lawyer, and together, we helped individuals prepare political asylum applications. In our publications (unless requested to do otherwise by the applicants), we have referred as much as possible to already published cases that match the issues faced by the applicants with whom we worked, to protect their privacy and guard against any danger that might come to them or their families as a result of recognition. When we have referred specifically to people we interviewed, we have obtained permission and changed the names and identifying details. We have never considered the people we worked with to be research subjects; instead, in our publications, we have reflected on all that we have learned about the political asylum process in law, as narrative, and as what Mary Louise Pratt (2007) has described as a "contact zone."

Even more familiarity with local cultural customs would not resolve fundamental problems in the political asylum process itself. In the absence of documentation or other supporting evidence, the process depends on preexisting information, and the immigration officials are often unaware of the limits of this information or of the ways that they impose their own assumptions and expectations on the narratives told by the applicants. Because the adjudicators regard the applicants' narratives as insufficient, they sometimes pressure the applicants to produce documentary evidence, which the officials consider more "reliable." However, the lack of evidence is itself a part of the condition of seeking asylum. The narratives told by the applicants are about displacement and disembodiment. The larger context is the age of globalized mobility in which some people, especially asylum applicants, cannot stay where they are and are prevented from relocating elsewhere. Marco Jacquemet (2009, 428) describes the asylum process as "a crucial nexus for understanding late modern technologies of power. It constitutes a site where questions of identity and the traumatized body; law, credibility, and the production of evidence; language ideology; national and transnational belonging; and intercultural communication come to the fore in a context defined by asymmetrical power relations."

The political asylum process is distorted, in part, by the positions of the interrogator and the interrogated, the official and the petitioner, which implicitly reference the power relations but do not directly map onto the categories of knower and the known. The official can never know; he or she can only recognize the limits and benefits of the available instruments of inquiry. Nor do the petitioners stand in the role of knower, for they have vast gaps in terms of the things known only by their persecutors. The political asylum process, like other forms of inquisition, is vulnerable to "cultural silences," which comprise one form of excuse for inaccurate communication between the inquisitors and the people they question (Rosaldo 1986, 82). Cultural silences can refer to what people tell or fail to tell their inquisitors, whether those inquisitors are ethnographers, historians, or judges. The inquisitor demands that the narrator of a personal story be the same person he or she was when experiencing the events, but of course, a person who suffers trauma is never the same person again. We are not arguing that there is no objective truth: that would be the last thing the asylum applicants would say. To the contrary, we are arguing that the instrument used in an investigation is always part of the truth it finds. The instrument is part of the production of knowledge. And in this case, the instrument, the political asylum process, is implicated in the production of cultural silences. The political asylum process produces gaps in knowledge as well as knowledge. It is engaged in epistemologies of ignorance (Bohmer and Shuman 2007a). The cultural silences—or the vast gaps in who knows what and what information is missing—are also part of the truth.

Asylum applicants often have only their stories as evidence of the atrocities they have suffered. They may be able to supplement their personal stories with public accounts of the persecution of a particular religious, political, or ethnic group, but they still need to prove that they were members of those groups. How people tell their stories can be as important as what they say. And what applicants do not say can damage their chances of obtaining asylum. As Louise Pirouet (2001, 50) points out, "The glib liar with a good story who sticks to it may have an easier ride than a traumatized person who is inarticulate and so easily tripped up. The inarticulate and muddled always find bureaucracies difficult to deal with." Often, officials rely on other sorts of details, such as family histories or histories of contact with individuals, to determine whether an applicant's story is credible. Trauma narrative is characterized by an inability to recount certain kinds of details (Cochrane 2010). However, immigration officials often search for these inconsistencies, as well as for other discrepancies, in their assessments of an applicant's credibility. The officials sometimes rely on their own familiarity with other cultural customs regarding marriage, support of children, and social obligations, and

*Carol Bohmer and Amy Shuman*

on finding a discrepancy with the applicant's narrative, they may mistakenly perceive an account as inconsistent. For example, Thomas Spijkerboer (2000) describes the strong gender bias in asylum cases in which Dutch officials dispute a woman's claim because they find it incredible that she would leave her children behind when fleeing persecution.

## The Power of Documents

Documentation and narrative are intimately connected in political asylum cases. Applicants need to prove that they are who they say they are and that their stories are true. In the absence of documentation, applicants rely on their narratives of what happened as the primary form of evidence. As Caroline Moorehead (2005, 165) notes, "Their story is their only real passport." The narratives people tell are, in a sense, stand-ins for missing or suspicious documents (and the officials cast suspicion on many documents). Documents are no more neutral than personal stories. We acknowledge the subjectivity of narrative but sometimes imagine documents to be neutral, when in fact, like narratives, they are dependent on the conditions of their production. Documents function very differently in asylum cases than in other areas of law. There is very little standardization, predictability, or reliability in the evaluation of and use of documents in political asylum hearings. Further, applying Western legal methods to understand the political asylum documents (or absence of documents) only exacerbates a situation already complicated by the lack of standardization of documents, the risk applicants take in acquiring or traveling with documents, and the motivation to use fraudulent documents in life-or-death situations. Ethnographers further complicate our understanding of the production and use of documents as cultural artifacts not only with no singular meaning but importantly variable in their significance and use (Riles 2006). Here, we are suggesting that paying attention to this complexity would be a means of creating more accurate assessments of asylum applications.

One problem is that in asylum hearings documents are often used for purposes other than that for which they were intended. A second problem is that forms are not standardized. A passport may be a universal document, but a birth certificate is not. Even in the United States, birth certificates are contentious documents, prompting arguments about race and ethnicity data, birth defect data, and parents' education and occupation data. One group recommended that sex be indicated by designating "male," "female," or "not yet determined" (Report of the Panel to Evaluate the U.S. Standard Certificates 2003). Third, documents may not exist. This is of particular relevance for political asylum applicants: in addition to the fact that forms are not standardized, not all places even provide forms for birth, death, medical visits or hospitalizations, or police interrogations, all of which may be crucial to supporting the asylum narrative.

A classic example of the way in which such documentation is expected but not available can be seen in the following exchange from a case we observed in London in 2008.

> H.O. (Home Office): Between April 2006 and November 2007, this period of sustained beatings, did you ever visit the hospital or a medical doctor?
>
> A.P. (applicant): Yes, I did attend a private hospital for bruises and the pain I had due to the beatings I sustained.
>
> H.O.: And you haven't provided any medical evidence or documents or evidence relevant to these visits?
>
> A.P.: They used to give me slips of prescriptions that I obtained but I didn't bother to keep them.

In this case, the HO official assumed that a person would retain prescriptions as "evidence" that would support a narrative; the applicant, however, did not understand the necessity of retaining such evidence.

In the West, we assume a correspondence among identities, events, and documents. Further, we regard documents as a relatively neutral representation of identities and events, and we therefore give greater credibility to a document than to a personal account. Also, along the same lines, forged or fraudulent documents are considered to taint the character of anyone using them, no matter how legitimate the reason for the deception. The acceptability (or lack thereof) of the use of fraudulent documents is itself a cultural matter. For the asylum officer, such an act attracts moral opprobrium. But in other cultures, individuals are aware that government officials misuse documents and that, first, one cannot assume the neutrality of written evidence and, second, the production of fraudulent documents may be necessary for survival in a corrupt society.

In *Discipline and Punish,* Michel Foucault (1977) demonstrated how documentation can be understood as part of a history of institutionalization and control of bodies as part of regulatory practices. The documents that asylum officials seek are far from neutral but rather are at the core of the persecution asylum applicants face. Denying access to travel documents is a primary means of controlling people, and requiring documents of people who have not had that access is also discriminatory. Subjecting documents to scrutiny to determine their authenticity—and thus the authenticity of the applicant—is a way of bureaucratizing the political asylum experience and thus denying applications as bureaucratically, rather than substantially, flawed. In *The Archaeology of Knowledge,* Foucault (1972, 7) wrote, "The document is not the fortunate tool of a history that is primarily and fundamentally memory; history is one way in which a society recognizes a mass of documentation with which it is inextricably linked."

A reconsideration of the role of documents in the political asylum process requires rethinking the relationship among history, memory, and documentation for ordinary individuals. Except in the rare case where someone is publicly known, the experiences of individuals in political events are rarely documented and then only by oral historians who assert the value of an alternative, on the ground, everyday experience (Portelli 1991). Political asylum applicants' ordinary lives have been disrupted; not only are they are being asked to produce documentation of lives not ordinarily documented, they are also being asked to produce the part of life experience that is outside the purview of historical records.

People who flee their homelands in fear for their lives are likely to leave quickly, in the middle of the night, and in ways that attract as little attention as possible. So most asylum seekers take with them as little as possible and especially avoid carrying identifying documents, in case they are caught. The asylum adjudicators acknowledge this; indeed, it is expected, as proof that the fear the individuals experienced was well founded. However, the adjudicators also expect that an asylum seeker will be able to provide them with documentary material to corroborate his or her story of persecution. This is true in practice, even though asylum law explicitly recognizes the possibility that an applicant may have only a narrative on which to base his or her claim. A British report argues that without corroborating evidence, a person does not have much hope of getting asylum, even though the law expressly allows for such a possibility:

> Documentary evidence to support the asylum claim is, in practice, not an option but a pre-requisite. The standard of proof is thus

already set at a level that is hard to achieve in circumstances of flight, and often well-nigh impossible at long-distance. It can be extremely hard for asylum-seekers to obtain any sort of documentary evidence from war-torn or unstable countries where mail may be monitored and official records of (for instance) police activities are more or less non-existent. Indeed, if an asylum-seeker were to come equipped with all the necessary documentary evidence, he or she would might [*sic*] be said to be more, not less, suspect. (AsylumAid 1999, 23)

Although this report dates back a number of years, the situation may be even more problematic now, given the constant pressure on the system to respond to the surge of people claiming asylum and the necessary effort by those evaluating claims to determine which claims are valid and which are not.

Not only do some asylum applicants lack documentary evidence because they left in a hurry, but it is also possible, as mentioned earlier, that such evidence simply does not exist. In the countries from which many asylum seekers come, persecuted individuals are rarely given documents that could prove the facts of their persecution. Such documents as arrest records or prison records are not likely to be available from those who do their persecuting in the shadows, even if the country has a general tradition of providing paper, which many do not. So much depends on where the applicant comes from. As one US lawyer told us, "It's much easier with Ethiopians, they have a document which says 'detained in reeducation camps' so he can be reeducated . . . then you have a slam dunk case. A right wing regime might just slap him in jail for trespass. The left wing guys would sometimes generate paper [labeling him an] 'enemy of the regime'" (Quinn 2002). It is an exception when someone can produce documents proving arrest or detention, yet applicants are routinely asked for such evidence, and its absence is judged negatively. We argue that in the asylum process, the lawyers are as much a part of the system of creating and disrupting expectations as are the asylum officials. Patrick Quinn's story about Ethiopians and right-wing regimes is an example.

In their reports, nongovernmental organizations (NGOs) often use narrative to influence asylum policy. One AsylumAid report (1999, 24), for example, describes the case of a Colombian "whose claim included three attempts by the police to kill him, and whose friend was killed,

[who] was told 'you have not produced [name of friend's] death certificate.' To which the common-sense reply is the one constantly in mind when faced with the Home Office's demands: 'How could he?'"

Unlike the US and UK officials, the Italians assume it is likely such documents will be forged and simply disregard them altogether (Furlan 2005). By contrast, the United States has an elaborate system of authenticating documents. One of the methods used is to send a document back to the country of origin for the embassy there to authenticate it. Even though the embassy staffers are supposed to be careful about what they do with the documents, there is a risk entailed in asking the very authorities who are accused of persecuting an individual to say that a document is authentic (UNHCR 2005). The process may also make public the asylum seeker's location and intentions, which he or she is likely to have worked hard to keep private for fear of retribution against family members by the persecutors.

Even obtaining documents from abroad after the asylum seeker has fled and is claiming asylum can be risky to those left behind. Many asylum seekers are extremely reluctant to contact family or friends to help them obtain documents in support of their claims because they are afraid doing so will be dangerous. For instance, the adjudicators encouraged Henri, an asylum seeker from the Central African Republic, to obtain death certificates for his wife, his children, and his father—important pieces of evidence to show that they had, indeed, died when he said they did—to support his claim that they had died because of his political activities. We tried to procure the documents through the International Red Cross, but it did not have an office in the Central African Republic so it could not help. Finally, Henri asked a friend to get him the documents. Later, he learned that the friend had disappeared. He may have been killed, and Henri worried that he was responsible for his death.

Efforts to corroborate the story itself also can be dangerous for the applicant and his or her family and illustrate either cultural insensitivity or unwillingness on the part of the adjudicators to recognize these risks (or both). A recent report in the United Kingdom describes the Home Office practice of using officials from the Sudanese embassy to corroborate the story of an asylum seeker: "Sadiq Abakar, 29, who fled Darfur for Britain in 1999, said he was asked questions about his background and tribe by a Sudanese official when he attended an appointment at the Home Office last month. He said he was asked to go into a side room, where a

Sudanese embassy official questioned him in Arabic about his tribal background. He said, 'it's like somebody taking you to see your killer. Since then, I have not felt safe. It's just not right at all. It is really, really scary'" (Russell 2007, 28).

People seeking asylum face the double problem of, first, trying to narrate unspeakable events and, second, translating those personal stories into a different sort of narrative that conveys the information needed by the asylum officials (Shuman and Bohmer 2004). The stories people told us when we first met them in the central Ohio immigration agency often focused more on the trauma of loss and the struggle to survive than on the details of persecution. However, it is these details about the persecutors and their interrogations, incarcerations, and torture, as well as the individual's role in a larger political, religious, or social conflict, that interest the asylum officials. Asylum law and the expectations of the adjudicators who are hearing the claims have narrowed the range of possible narratives that can result in a grant of asylum. They have also injected the need for claimants to prove their claims through the use of documents, a process that is alien to them. It is often necessary to explain to an applicant how and why documents are valued above the narrative. The claimant must walk a narrow line to fit his or her story into the confines of a suitable narrative, as well as support it with material he or she may not be able to obtain.

## Documents and Multiple and Changing Identities

As we mentioned, in the absence of identity documents such as birth, marriage, and death certificates or passports, asylum officials rely on narratives to assess identity. When documents are presented, they, too, are subject to being challenged as fraudulent, just as narratives also are evaluated for credibility. Inconsistencies are a source of suspicion in regard to both documents and narratives. Both are scrutinized for missing pieces. Questioning an applicant's lack of documents often shows the same absence of cultural awareness as questioning the applicant's failure to recount a particular incident. Yet an applicant's behaviors that appear unusual or inexplicable to the official (such as leaving a child behind) or the applicant's reliance on bribery or forgery may be easily explained as matters of expediency in terrible situations. Moreover, as Meredith Terretta describes elsewhere in this volume, corruption and bribery are "a reality in daily life" in some places.

Documents and narratives do very different kinds of work in terms of establishing identity and proof of the events recounted. Obviously, establishing one's identity is crucial in an asylum hearing. And on the surface, documents can establish identity in a particular group or nation. Narratives, in contrast, establish identity by accounting for familial or community relationships. Identity cards confirm that a person is a member of a nation, tribe, or political organization. Narratives might report how one became a member or what one knows about being a member.

Providing proof of important details of identity can be difficult for asylum seekers. Many Somali applicants, for example, base their claims on membership in a minority clan, for which the adjudicators are always seeking proof. They often use language and culture as ways of proving nationality or clan membership. In the case of minority clans, this is considered strong evidence in support of the claim. The authorities in the United Kingdom and elsewhere have used Sprakab, a Swedish company that has "experts" listen to tapes of applicants' voices to determine where they are from. But there is serious concern about the accuracy of these assessments, and the matter has been litigated in the UK and Scottish courts, with different results. The English case decided that if a Sprakab report concluded that the person's native language was "with certainty not" that of the claimed country of origin, Somalia, then "little more" than that opinion was required to conclude that the person was not Somali (*R.B. [Somalia] v. S.S.H.D.* 2012). The Scottish cases, by contrast, disapproved of the use of anonymity for those who make the assessments, as being in violation of normal practice with experts in court cases (*M.A.B.N. and K.A.S.Y. v. Adv. Gen. for Scotland* 2013). The Home Office appealed this decision and a similar one, but lost; the case has been sent back to the Upper Tribunal for interpretation of the judgment. Like so many issues, it is at least in part a matter of money. Because of the reluctance of the UK Border Agency (UKBA) to pay for highly specialized services, Sprakab and other similar companies use people who are often insufficiently qualified as linguists to undertake the careful analysis required in such cases, as Fallou Ngom's afterword outlines (see also Campbell 2013; Eades 2005; Kam 2015; Patrick 2012).

Asylum officers assume that identity is a fixed category, but in reality, people have multiple and changing identities throughout their lifetimes; for asylum seekers, this may be out of necessity. The law wants the kinds of things one finds in a document: names, dates, and other details;

individuals, however, see the definition of who they are as based on their social networks. Asylum applicants are asked to produce identity in a system that produces ignorance, a system that erases identity systematically and then asks for forms of identity that further obliterate their sense of who they are.

Political asylum applicants are asked to both produce a stable identity and describe its destabilization. Their identities are not fixed entities but instead are part of a process. As Liisa Malkki (1997, 71) writes, "Identity is always mobile and processual, partly self-construction, partly categorization by others, partly a condition, a status, a label, a weapon, a shield, a fund of memories, and so on. It is a creolized aggregated composed through bricolage." In our research, we found many examples of multiple identities produced by changing contexts. Timothy Longman (2001) describes a young Rwandan woman, whom he calls Claudette, who grew up as a Hutu. During the Rwandan genocide (in which the Hutu militia killed more than six hundred thousand Tutsi in six months), it was discovered that her grandfather had been known as a Tutsi before he moved to the area where Claudette was raised. He had received an identity card stating his ethnicity as Hutu, which he passed down to his descendants. As a result of her father's Tutsi identity becoming public knowledge, Claudette and her family were the target of ethnic violence, and several family members were killed. Claudette's "new" identity as a Tutsi is now suspect, as she and her family had enjoyed the "benefits" of being Hutu before the genocide. Now she says, "I do not really know what I am. I do not know what it means to be Tutsi" (Longman 2001, 346).

The exigencies of escape often require deceptive or concealed identities. Asylum seekers routinely use false passports because they are afraid to apply for their own, because they know they will not be given one, or because they need to flee using someone else's identity so as not to be detained at the border. Even obtaining a passport can be too dangerous, as it alerts the authorities to the possibility that they may be about to leave. In most countries from which asylum seekers come, there is also less emphasis on the identity documents we take for granted in the West. In some, most notably Somalia, even such basic documents as birth certificates are not available because of the turmoil that has existed in that country for so long or because people never had them in the first place. In Somalia and other African countries, people born or married in rural areas are unlikely to have birth certificates; many of them do not even know their date of birth. It has been estimated that each year, approximately 48 million children are not registered by the age of five (UNICEF 2005). Similarly, many children born in the border area between Myanmar and China have no birth certificates; this provides the loophole through which militias recruit child soldiers. And in Egypt, "Baha'is and certain other nationals have been unable to obtain birth certificates, identity cards, marriage certificates, death certificates and other vital records because the government requires all such documents to list religious affiliation and restricts the choice of religion to the three officially recognized religions: Islam, Christianity and Judaism. Many persons have been unable to obtain identification papers because they refuse to lie about their religious affiliation and have been denied the possibility of leaving the entry about religious affiliation blank" (Massey 2010). In the United States, many refugees have been given January 1 as their birth date by the authorities to provide a detail that is important in the United States but not in the country they fled.

Many people who flee persecution use agents to help them, and often, the same people who help genuine asylum seekers flee persecution also provide the means whereby others can enter the country illegally. They provide sets of false documents on which the asylum seekers enter the country, which they often take back immediately to reuse; the applicants are kept ignorant of whose passports are being used. Because of this ignorance, anything the applicants may tell the authorities about their identity or about details of their arrival is simply more of their uncorroborated story and becomes a major barrier to their asylum claims.

Asylum seekers also face the risk of being charged with fraud for using forged passports, perhaps the only way they could flee. Using a false passport was not previously a particular problem either in the United States or the United Kingdom as the authorities recognized its necessity, but now, with the widespread securitization measures implemented after the attacks of 9/11, it has become a bigger issue. If someone enters the United States on a false passport, the case is immediately referred to the Immigration Court, without the more informal hearing with an asylum officer. In 2004, UK legislation made it a crime to enter the country without a passport or with a false passport, unless the person had a "reasonable excuse" for doing so (Asylum and Immigration [Treatment of Claimants, etc.] Act 2004, sec. 8). This move was intended to prevent people from deliberately destroying their passports before arriving; it was also intended to be a response to those who claim to come from a country other than their real country of origin, as part of a false claim (Neumayer 2006). The authorities, especially in the United Kingdom, argue that many applicants claim to be from a different country of origin—one where persecution is more common—in the hope that this deception will go unnoticed. Language analysis is used here, also, in an effort to determine which country the claimant is actually from. Critics claim that the authorities are actually using private companies, such as Sprakab, to discredit the applicant. However, a decision by the Court of Appeal subsequently allowed the courts to disregard the use of false documents when assessing credibility ( *JT (Cameroon) v. Secretary of State for the Home Department* 2008).

The paradox here is that although it is supposed to be acceptable for someone to seek asylum even if it means using a false passport (and it is even acknowledged in the law that it might be necessary to do ), in practice a false passport is a barrier to asylum. As C. Peter Erlinder (2008, 228) reports, though the 1967 UN Protocol Relating to the Status of Refugees stipulates that an asylum applicant who declares the use of false documents cannot be prosecuted, the fact is that in the United States, applicants are indicted and detained and face felony criminal prosecution for the use of false documents. The difficulty stems, in part, from the undoubted fact that some people do destroy their passports so that the adjudicators cannot find proof of their country of origin. They may use false documents to claim they are from an adjacent country where the chances of getting asylum are greater or to prevent being sent back to the country from whence they came. The general rule is that a person can only be sent back to his or her own country when that is known and as long as he or she would not be at risk of persecution (the principle of nonrefoulement). At present, some countries seem to be willing to violate both of these rules (Human Rights Watch 2005).

There is often a class bias here. People with more education and greater resources are more likely to own passports, so they need not risk the exposure when applying for one. They are also more likely to be able to find ways of getting to the United States or the United Kingdom on their own passports and a visitor's visa, a student visa, or a short-term business visa. Those with fewer resources have to fall back on illegal means to enter a country before applying for asylum. We assume that persecution knows no class boundaries, but the process of seeking asylum is easier for more sophisticated and better-off applicants.

Immigration adjudicators expect that an asylum seeker will tell exactly the amount of the story required to convince them that the claim is valid and genuine but no more. Applicants are punished for what they do not tell as well as for telling too much or for giving details the adjudicators think are irrelevant. For many asylum seekers, some things, especially rape (the classic example of this phenomenon), are just too terrible to describe, at least in the early stages of the asylum process. The applicants risk being refused because they failed to mention something early but bring it up later. New details may provide the impetus for denying a claim on the grounds that it is not credible. One UK refusal letter stated, "The Secretary of State notes that during interview you failed to mention rape. The Secretary of State also believes that it would be reasonable to expect that you would have mentioned this at the earliest opportunity. Furthermore the Secretary of State concludes that the fact that you did not undermines the veracity of your claim" (Amnesty International UK 2004, 36). This issue has received enough publicity that one might well think the asylum adjudicators would know by now what is going on; this, in turn, raises the possibility of a willful lack of understanding on their part.

Marthe, a Cameroonian woman whose case we observed in London in 2006, was asked in court by the Home Office representative why she did not mention that her escape had been announced on the radio in her initial statement. She replied, rather perceptively, "When you are giving a statement through questions, sometimes details can go unnoticed and you don't dwell on them."

Henri, the political activist from the Central African Republic mentioned earlier, applied for asylum in the United States after his family was killed, and he narrowly escaped being killed himself. At the asylum hearing, the officer was not interested in Henri's political observations. The asylum officer wanted to hear about his personal role in the coup and his position in his political party. Henri kept insisting that some of the details of the political situation were important, such as the role of outside intervention in the political situation. These details, however, were of no interest to the officer, who kept asking him to describe in extensive detail what he did in the coup and how he managed to escape. We have often had applicants who insisted on fleshing out the political details of their country of origin, even when they are not "relevant" in their claims for asylum.

Cultural Silences as an Excuse for Injustice

Some missing details are not about humiliation but instead are about more ordinary matters. A Zimbabwean woman was interrogated for inconsistencies in her account of when she last saw her parents and whether or not they attended her "marriage ceremonies."

H.O.: In your interview you were asked if your parents attended the marriage ceremonies. Did they attend?

A.P.: Yes. What dates? The dowry was the first one. The dowry celebration was in December 2007.

H.O.: You then went on to say it was a mistake, you had not seen your parents. You said in your interview why?

A.P.: The interview was too much for me; I lost my head.

H.O.: You initially said you didn't know where your parents were.

A.P.: That was a mistake; that is why I corrected it to 2008.

Later in the interview, it became clear that her husband traveled without her to Zimbabwe to arrange the dowry and to have the dowry celebration. The husband and the parents did attend this part of the marriage ceremonies, although she did not. This was unfathomable to the HO officials. Also, they did not understand why her husband, who had asylum, risked traveling to Zimbabwe to ask permission to marry her. The following is from an interrogation of the husband (W.).

J. [Judge]: You said you couldn't live together until you'd gone to Z. Whose permission were you looking for?

W.: Her parents.

J.: People live together all the time in the U.K. Why should you get permission?

W.: I am a descendant of a tribal chieftain, if I had offspring I . . .

J.: Different tribal background?

W.: We're all from different tribal background.

Officials interviewing an asylum seeker are looking for a coherent and consistent narrative, and any inconsistency is considered a possible sign that the entire narrative is fraudulent. However, missing details can sometimes be attributed either to cultural difficulties in reporting humiliating or horrendous experiences or to the asylum officials' inability to make connections that depend on cultural knowledge. Further, the interrogation itself can produce some of the gaps.

One of the problems that adjudicators face involves when to believe a story that they have heard before. E. Ann McDougall, in this volume, discusses the construction of these narratives: "Countries that generate refugees also generate contextual metanarratives, complete with their own dynamics and metonyms that become a kind of language over time." People who are persecuted are often treated similarly, so the stories sound similar. As Kai Erikson (1976) discovered in his study of flood victims whose stories too closely resembled each other (according to the insurance company that reviewed their claims), trauma victims often borrow from others the language they use to describe their experiences. In addition, psychologists working with trauma victims, among them Dori Laub (1995), emphasize the role of everyday communication in shaping memory and thus its dependence on language, social discourses, and the relationships people have established. Consequently, the stories asylum seekers tell are, like those of everyone else, socially constructed in ways that may make them seem more similar to the narratives of others who were also persecuted.

There is, nonetheless, the possibility that asylum seekers will share false stories that they believe (or have been told) will likely to lead to success. As one lawyer put it, "A lot of the same stories are starting to come out. Obviously you get successful with one client and the client has shared the affidavit, so the new affidavit looks similar" (Hohenstein 2002). Another lawyer described three Ethiopians in three days all telling exactly the same story; he recalled that "we called them back in. How is it possible that all three of you have exactly the same claim? They kept saying 'it happened to us . . . '; they didn't speak English" (London 2004). In such situations, the paradox is that asylum seekers are expected to report a story of societal persecution rather than individual trauma, but they are challenged for representations that appear too similar to other stories.

We asked officers in the Home Office how they reacted to stories they had heard before, and we got the following reply: "If a person makes a common claim I don't think that has an impact. In Zimbabwe it is membership in the M.D.C. I wouldn't look more or less favorably on it (if I had heard it before)." From another officer, we learned that "it depends on the merits of the individual claims, for example, the Jamaican labor party-people have said they were an active member, so you ask who was the candidate at the campaign you worked on . . . if they don't know . . . it helps to have heard it before, the more you deal with it, the better you know what to ask" (Avery 2004). This tolerance for similar stories may be true in theory, yet we have also heard that the adjudicators are very skeptical of stories that sound similar, on the ground that they have been learned rather than actually experienced. As is so often the case in asylum matters, there is some truth behind this concern; some stories are, indeed, fictions. We are told that for an appropriate price, a trafficker will provide (in addition to the usual travel arrangements and false documents) a boilerplate asylum story to be presented to the immigration officials on arrival.

In some cases, false stories are even used by people who have valid claims. According to Jason Dzubow, a lawyer interviewed by journalist Suketu Mehta, asylum seekers are persuaded to embellish their stories. "If they go to the asylum coaches, or 'case builders,' in the immigrant community, they will be likely be urged to embellish their stories with tales of torture and beatings, because it is thought that being arrested alone will not make a strong enough case for asylum" (Mehta 2011, 36). The lawyers we have spoken to who represent these clients after the failure of the false stories spend quite a lot of their time repairing the damage caused by such fabrications. This problem came to public attention in an article in the *New Yorker* triggered by the revelation that the woman who accused Dominique Strauss-Kahn of rape in a New York hotel room had lied in her asylum claim. The author of the article tells the story of a woman he calls Caroline who claimed that she had been raped (though she had not) because so many women in Africa had been raped. In fact, her house had been broken into by soldiers, and she and her family had been beaten by them because they were supporters of the opposition, all details that she did not report but that indicated a well-founded fear of persecution (Mehta 2011).

## Cultural Silences in the Bureaucratic Process

The immigration officials' misunderstandings of cultural difference can lead to inaccurate expectations both of the use and availability of documents and in the assessment of narratives that stand in the place of documents. The political asylum hearings are bureaucratic events governed by the genre of interrogation, a genre that always does violence to personal narrative. The expectations for consistency and coherence are impossible for anyone to meet, but with people recovering from trauma, disrupted lives produce disrupted stories. In other words, consistency and coherence are not the hallmarks of a reliable trauma narrative. To thoroughly and more accurately assess reliability, the adjudicators would do better to attempt to get explanations for the inconsistencies. In our experience, many of these can be explained satisfactorily, and in any case, the inconsistencies are not a good measure of credibility.

It is understandable that adjudicators try to find ways to determine who is telling the truth via the use of "tools" such as consistency and coherence. Without them, there is very little on which the adjudicators can base their assessments. The whole procedure is an effort to make sense of the narratives of lives that are vastly different from the lives of those judging the asylum process—and to do so as consistently and fairly as possible. We are not claiming that the adjudicators are dishonest; rather, we are critiquing the methods by which they work in determining which asylum seekers are telling the truth and which are lying. We should also point out that, especially in the United Kingdom, cases are initially heard by young "caseowners" who appear under considerable pressure to produce arguments to refuse claims, for any reason, as part of the UKBA's efforts to cut the numbers of those granted asylum. The pressure seems to be less intense in the United States, where asylum is less of a hot-button issue than it is in the United Kingdom. Cases that are appealed to judges often fare better, but fewer and fewer cases are now appealed, especially in the United Kingdom, where the ability to appeal is circumscribed by financial and legal constraints.

In addition to differences in the political situations, the response to conflict, and the resources people use to escape, we have seen the cultural differences in how people talk about trauma and escape. Individuals rely on cultural resources when they talk about persecution, especially when they try to manage talking about unthinkable experiences, whether humiliations or tragedies. Documents, including public documents such as passports and private documents such as personal letters, also depend on cultural resources, especially in the official assessments of the conditions that explain missing documents. We have also seen that what they do not say—the cultural silences—can also be significant in the asylum process. What is not said is interpreted differently depending on the cultural context.

The paradoxical role of documents in the political asylum process is not only a problem of cultural difference in the production and use of documents or a problem of the lack of documentation of persecution. Rather, the paradox is symptomatic of a more general problem in the political asylum process, which attempts to impose rigid national categories of language, culture, and even persecution on people whose identities and lives have been disrupted. Jan Bloomaert (2009, 425) argues, "Not just their cases are harmed, but their subjectivity is as well, because they are deterritorialized people whose existence cannot be squeezed into the modern frame of national units and institutions." Cultural silences in these circumstances can result not only in misunderstanding but also in injustice.

## References

Amnesty International UK. 2004. "Get it Right." London: Amnesty International UK.
AsylumAid. 1999. "Still No Reason at All." London: AsylumAid.
Avery, Miranda. 2004. Interview with the author. London, November 19.
Bloomaert, Jan. 2009. "Language, Asylum and the National Order. *Current Anthropology* 54 (4): 415–41.
Bohmer, Carol, and Amy Shuman. 2007a. "Producing Epistemologies of Ignorance in the Political Asylum Application Process." *Identities* 14 (5): 603–29.
———. 2007b. *Rejecting Refugees: Political Asylum in the 21st Century.* New York: Routledge.
Campbell, John. 2013. "Language Analysis in the United Kingdom's Refugee Status Determination System: Seeing through Policy Claims about 'Expert Knowledge.'" *Ethnic and Racial Studies* 36 (4): 670–90.
Cochrane, Clare. 2010. "Trauma and Credibility in the Asylum Process: Evidence to Help Women Asylum Seekers." *Women's Asylum News,* no. 92: Asylum Aid, 1–3. http://www.refworld.org/pdfid/4c0f430e2.pdf.
Eades, Diane. 2005. "Applied Linguistics and Language Analysis in Asylum Seeker Cases." *Applied Linguistics* 26 (4): 503–26.
Erikson, Kai T. 1976. Everything in Its Path. New York: Simon and Schuster.
Erlinder, C. Peter. 2008. "When 'Fear of Persecution . . . ' Requires Deportation: 'Catch-22' False-Document Prosecutions after a Grant of Asylum." *William Mitchell Law Review* 35 (1):226–46.
Foucault, Michel. 1972. *The Archaeology of Knowledge.* Translated by A. Sheridan Smith. New York: Pantheon Books.
———. 1977. *Discipline and Punish: The Birth of the Prison.* Translated by Alan Sheridan. New York: Vintage.
Furlan, Simonetta. 2005. Interview with the author. Florence, Italy, May 17.
Ginzburg, Carl. 1980. *The Cheese and the Worm: The Cosmos of a Sixteenth Century Miller.* Baltimore, MD: Johns Hopkins University Press.
Hohenstein, Joe. 2002. Interview with the author. Philadelphia, May 1.

Human Rights Watch. 2005. Call for Action against the Use of Diplomatic Assurances in Transfers to Risk of Torture and Ill-Treatment. Accessed March 8, 2008. http://hrw.org/english/docs/2005/05/12/eca10660_txt.htm.

Ibhawoh, Bonny. 2003. "Defining Persecution and Protection: The Cultural Relativism Debate and the Rights of Refugees." In *Problems of Protection: The UNHCR, Refugees, and Human Rights,* edited by Niklaus Steiner, Mark Gibney, and Gil Loescher, 61–75. London: Routledge.

Jacquemet, Marco. 2009. "The Search for Rigid Designators: How Asylum Authorities Deal with Transidiomatic Confusion." Paper presented at the Annual Meeting of the Anthropological Association, Philadelphia, PA, December 1–5, 2009.

*JT (Cameroon) v. Secretary of State for the Home Department.* [2008] EWCA Civ 878, United Kingdom: Court of Appeal (England and Wales), 28 July 2008, available at: http://www.refworld.org/docid/488edbed2.html (accessed August 31, 2014).

Kam, Noé M. 2015. "Interpreting the Sociological Identity of Asylum Seekers: A Critical Analysis of Language Analysis for Determining Origin in the European Union." In *Adjudicating Refugee and Asylum Status: The Role of Witness, Expertise, and Testimony,* edited by Benjamin N. Lawrance and Galya Ruffer. Cambridge: Cambridge University Press.

Laub, Dori. 1995. "Truth and Testimony: The Process and the Struggle." In *Trauma: Explorations in Memory,* edited by Cathy Caruth, 61–75. Baltimore, MD: Johns Hopkins University Press.

London, Judy. 2004. Interview with the author. Los Angeles, June 22.

Longman, Timothy. 2001. "Identity Cards, Ethnic Self-Perception, and Genocide in Rwanda." In *Documenting Individual Identity: The Development of State Practices in the Modern World,* edited by Jane Caplan and John Torpey, 345–57. Princeton, NJ: Princeton University Press.

*M.A.B.N. and K.A.S.Y. v. Adv. Gen. for Scotland* [2013] C.S.I.H. 68.

Malkki, Liisa H. 1997. "National Geographic: The Rooting of Peoples and the Territorialization of National Identity among Scholars and Refugees." In *Culture Power Place: Explorations in Critical Anthropology,* edited by Akhil Gupta and James Ferguson, 52–74. Durham, NC: Duke University Press.

Massey, Hugh. 2010. "UNHCR and *de facto* Statelessness." UNHCR Legal and Protection Policy Research Series. Accessed August 31, 2013. http://www.refworld.org/pdfid/4bbf387d2.pdf.

Mehta, Suketu. 2011. "The Asylum Seeker." *New Yorker,* August 1, 32–37.

Moorehead, Caroline. 2005. *Human Cargo.* New York: Henry Holt.

Neumayer, E. 2006. "Unequal Access to Foreign Spaces: How States Use Visa Restrictions to Regulate Mobility in a Globalized World." *Transactions of the Institute of British Geographers* 31 (1):72–84.

Patrick, Peter. 2012. Interview with the author. London, October 1.

Pirouet, Louise. 2001. *What Ever Happened to Asylum in Britain? A Tale of Two Walls.* New York: Berghahn Books.

Portelli, Alessandro. 1991. *The Death of Luigi Trastulli and Other Stories: Form and Meaning in Oral History.* Binghamton, NY: SUNY Press.

Pratt, Mary Louise. 2007. *Imperial Eyes: Travel Writing and Transculturation*. New York: Routledge.

Quinn, Patrick. 2002. Interview with the author. San Diego, CA, February 1.

Ramji-Nogales, Jaya, Andrew I. Schoenholtz, and Philip G. Schrag. 2009. *Refugee Roulette: Disparities in Asylum Adjudication and Proposals for Reform*. New York: NYU Press.

*R.B. (Somalia) v. S.S.H.D.* [2012] E.W.C.A. Civ. 277 (C.A. (Civ. Div.)).

Division of Vital Statistics, National Center for Health Statistics. 2003 "Report of the Panel to Evaluate the U.S. Standard Certificates, National Center for Health Certificates." Accessed August 31, 2013. http://www.cdc.gov/nchs/data/dvs/panelreport_acc.pdf.

Riles, Annelise, ed. 2006. *Documents: Artifacts of Modern Knowledge*. Ann Arbor: University of Michigan Press.

Rosaldo, Renato. 1986. "From the Door of His Tent: The Fieldworker and the Inquisitor." In *Writing Culture: The Poetics and Politics of Ethnography*, edited by James Clifford and George E. Marcus, 77–97. Berkeley: University of California Press.

Russell, Ben. 2007. "Home Office 'Collaborating with Sudan over Refugees.'" *Independent*, April 13.

Shuman, Amy, and Carol Bohmer. 2004. "Representing Trauma: Political Asylum Narrative." *Journal of American Folklore* 117 (466): 394–414.

Spijkerboer, Thomas. 2000. *Gender and Refugee Status*. Burlington, VT: Ashgate.

Tsangarides, Natasha. 2010. "The Refugee Roulette: The Role of Country Information in Refugee Status Determination." Research, Information and Policy Unit, Immigration Advisory Service, London.

UNHCR. 2005. Advisory Opinion on the Rules of Confidentiality Regarding Asylum Information. UNHCR Representation in Japan. March 31. Accessed August 31, 2013. http://www.refworld.org/docid/42b9190e4.html.

UNICEF. 2005. "The 'Rights' Start to Life: A Statistical Analysis of Birth Registration," 3. Accessed August 31, 2013. http://www.unicef.org/protection/BirthReg10a_rev.pdf.

# SEVEN

## Between Advocacy and Deception

*Crafting an African Asylum Narrative*

Iris Berger

IN THE SUMMER of 2011, two high-profile stories spotlighted the issue of falsified claims for asylum. First, in July of that year, Nafissatou Diallo, a hotel housekeeper from Guinea, accused Dominique Strauss-Kahn, director of the International Monetary Fund, of sexual assault. After Strauss-Kahn's attorneys began digging into her background, Diallo admitted to reporters that, as part of her asylum application, she had lied about being gang-raped. The *New Yorker* then followed up with an article detailing how a woman from central Africa had crafted her story of rape and torture to substantiate an asylum claim (Mehta 2011). Both women drew on stereotypical portrayals of Africa as a continent of rampant military violence against civilian populations (including rape) and, in Diallo's case, of painful female genital cutting (FGC), often portrayed as a primitive, patriarchal practice. The women admitted that they had tailored their stories to fit the requirements of US asylum law.

Analysis of such cases by legal scholars and anthropologists reflects surprisingly different attitudes toward African asylum seekers and their quest to remain in the United States. Although the accounts of both groups focus heavily on female genital cutting, legal experts, concerned to expand the definition of political persecution to include gender-specific maltreatment, have argued that genital cutting should be treated as a human rights violation. Karen Musalo's chapter in this volume explores some of these issues. Anthropologists, by contrast, have reacted against the images of Africa conveyed in these cases—as tribal, traditional, patriarchal, unchanging—and have focused more on exposing the stories of women who have relied on (and sometimes manipulated) these images to create fraudulent claims for asylum.

I was drawn into the life history of one asylum applicant in 2006 when I was asked to serve as an expert witness for Chantelle Koyango (a pseudonym), a young woman from the Central African Republic (CAR) married to a man from the Democratic Republic of Congo (DRC) who had received asylum in the United States. She had two children living with her parents in a refugee camp (a daughter and a stepson) and a son born in the United States. Brought up in a prominent political family, she described herself as "a victim of genital mutilation," an advocate for woman's rights, and a victim of torture by soldiers as she fled to the States. According to her attorney's brief, the government was targeting her along with her family and other members of her ethnic group. She and her husband had been trying to obtain asylum for her since March 2002, soon after she arrived in the United States, but the applications were denied twice on technical grounds. Without legal counsel, they had no way of knowing that there was a one-year deadline for filing her own application.

Koyango's personal story explained other aspects of her case. Just before her fifteenth birthday, she "was forced to undergo genital cutting," after which her parents planned to compel her to marry an older man. To escape this forced union, she fled to Kinshasa in the DRC to live with an aunt, where she went to school and met and married another student, her current husband. When his opposition to the authoritarian government of Congolese president Laurent Kabila put his life in danger, he escaped to the United States, where he received political asylum in June 2000. The month after his exile, Koyango made a "long, dangerous escape" from Kinshasa and returned to Bangui, the capital of the CAR, with her husband's son by another woman. Her first child was born four months later. Upon returning home, she began her "political work to stop [the] abuse of women." Her original asylum application gave her occupation as undersecretary in the opposition party headquarters in Bangui, in charge of mobilizing women to join the party and to oppose such practices as circumcision, wife beating, and polygamy.

Following a failed coup d'état in the Central African Republic on May 28, 2001, Koyango's group and their political party, the Central African

Democratic Assembly (RDC) were blamed. In the attacks that followed, Koyango and her family were forced to flee to a refugee camp in Zongo, just across the border in the Congo. Her uncle and three of his sons were attacked and killed, and the government issued an arrest warrant for Koyango. Because of the past attacks on her family, she remained in hiding with a close friend, whose high-ranking husband helped her obtain a visa to the United States. When she arrived at the airport in Bangui on February 24, 2002, she and her friend were stopped and detained by authorities; her hands were tied, and her hair was burned with lighted cigarettes. Only her friend's intervention saved her.

After her arrival in the States, her husband filed form I-730, the Refugee/Asylee Relative Petition, for his wife and children in March 2002 and again in July 2003. Immigration officials denied both petitions, the first time because he had not mentioned the marriage on his own application, the second time because the documents were filed more than two years after he had received asylum. While these petitions were pending, he "insisted" that his wife did not need to file her own asylum application or seek legal counsel. According to the document, Koyango "deferred to her husband in these decisions, as is customary in her culture." Without speaking English, she had little way to challenge his decision. The attorney's brief then underscores her husband's domination of the procedures, noting that Koyango "anxiously tried to arrange for legalization of her status" despite her husband's insistence that she did not need to do so.

Meanwhile, Koyango's situation and that of her family grew worse. Her parents were once again forced to flee Bangui in October 2004, and a friend informed her that security forces had issued a warrant for her arrest. She also learned that her parents' house had been attacked and her nephew killed. On receiving this information, she finally convinced her husband that she needed to file her own asylum application (I-589). He still refused to get legal assistance and only agreed to do so after his second I-730 petition was denied.

When their attorney contacted me in spring 2006, I had little asylum experience. The case appealed to me as a historian of African women and a feminist scholar. I agreed to write a statement of support without considering the veracity of the claim. Although I had read extensively in the anthropological and social science literature that criticized extreme portrayals of female genital modification, I had also followed the case of Fauziya Kasinga; I was drawn to the lawyer's description of a young woman who came from a political family in a highly repressive, militarized country and who faced a high probability of arrest, torture, and even death if returned to her country of origin.[1] I had not done research in the Central African Republic, but the attorney was unable to locate anyone who had due to high levels of repression, violence, and terror in the country. Her judgment that my extensive research in African women's history would be appropriate for a case built around issues of genital cutting and advocacy of women's rights raises questions about how to define appropriate expertise.

Since my role as an expert witness was primarily to confirm and document the client's account of the brutal conditions in the CAR and the likelihood that she would face imminent danger if she were expelled from the United States, I only began reading the scholarly literature on women's asylum claims in the wake of the Diallo case and the *New Yorker* article. I sought to understand how scholarship in law and anthropology—and my own background as a historian—might lead me to a more nuanced understanding of the Koyango case and the broader issues it raised.

## Legal Scholars as Advocates

The highly publicized case of Fauziya Kasinga, a woman from Togo who was granted asylum in 1996 based on her fear of genital cutting if she were deported, initiated a wave of scholarly articles in both legal studies and anthropology, each with a distinct set of concerns. Predating the Kasinga decision but strongly influenced by the movement in the early 1990s to extend the discourse of human rights to include violations of the rights of women (Bunch 1990), Daliah Setareh (1995–96) published an article on women seeking asylum in the United States. The title, "Women Escaping Genital Mutilation," announced the author's intent to advocate that US courts expand the definition of persecution to encompass cruel, inhumane, and degrading actions against women that amounted to forms of torture. Her chief concern was to promote policy changes that would designate women as members of a distinct social group, victims of the "horrors of female genital mutilation" (Setareh 1995–96, 123). She argued that more concerted action was needed to follow the first step: the Immigration and Naturalization Service (INS) publication of a memorandum on May 25, 1995, entitled "Considerations for Asylum Officers Adjudicating Asylum Claims from Women." In order to promote a radical transformation of US asylum policy, it was in Setareh's interest to portray genital cutting in the most extreme and barbaric light possible, as a form of mutilation of women designed to impose male domination. This interpretation reflected much of the feminist writing of the period, including the work of both Western and African scholars and of some African women who had suffered from genital cutting themselves. Estimating that some 110 million girls and women in Africa, the Arabian Peninsula, the Middle East, India, and East Asia had been genitally mutilated, Setareh went on to discuss only its most extreme form, infibulation, which she deemed the "most prevalent" form without making any effort to document this claim.[2] Citing only anticircumcision literature such as Hanny Lightfoot-Klein (1989), Olayinka Koso-Thomas (1987), and Asma El Dareer (1983), Setareh described the purpose of circumcision as keeping women subordinated and dependent on their husbands and other men.

The following year, Amy Stern (1997) made a more sweeping argument. She advocated broadening the legal definition of persecution to include maintaining and perpetuating the subordination of women. Under this new definition, "females who flee their native countries after having undergone FGM [female genital mutilation] may be granted asylum so long as they fear contributing to the preservation of patriarchal structures if forced to return to their homelands" (Stern 1997, 89). Stern addressed the legal dilemma arising from the Kasinga case—that since women who had suffered the "past persecution" of circumcision could not face the procedure again, they would no longer have a "well-founded fear of persecution" as required by US law. Stressing this point, Stern argued that a woman's mutilated body in itself contributes to the maintenance of patriarchal structures in her own society by perpetuating an ideology of women's subordination. Like Setareh, one of her major sources, Stern distinguished three types of genital cutting (see note 2), but she made no distinction among them when she reviewed their "devastating" physical consequences. Furthermore, her estimate of the number of girls undergoing the procedure annually came not from an academic source but from *USA Today*. Finally, her examples made no reference to specific societies on the continent but simply generalized them all as "African," thus implicitly tarring all African communities with extreme forms of gender oppression. Like Setareh, then, Stern borrowed heavily and not always critically from the anti-FGC literature in the interest of advocating for change in US law.[3]

Also writing in 1997, Arthur C. Helton and Alison Nicoll began with the Kasinga case. Rather than focusing exclusively on circumcision, however, they listed a series of gender-specific forms of persecution, including rape, sexual assault, coerced prostitution, infanticide, gender violence, and forced marriage. Confronting the reluctance of the courts to condemn societies that have different cultural practices than those in the United States, the authors cited "internationally recognized standards regarding basic human rights" (Helton and Nicoll 1997, 379) as the appropriate starting point for asylum inquiries. They argued that international condemnation and the criminalization of female genital cutting under federal law should form a basis for judging these cases. Like Stern, Helton and Nicoll were writing to evaluate the legal significance of the Kasinga case and to recommend ways to make asylum policy more gender sensitive. By placing genital cutting within a broader spectrum of discriminatory practices, they removed its taint as a uniquely horrific form of persecution. The article also included a nuanced discussion of the issues of consent, cultural relativity, and cultural diversity.

Taking a similarly measured stance, Connie M. Ericson (1997–98) analyzed the grounds on which the Kasinga case was decided, evaluated the impact of the decision, and suggested the issues that were left unresolved. Her description of FGC relied on legal sources and was restricted to the practices of Kasinga's ethnic group in Togo. She argued that in granting asylum to Fauziya Kasinga based on her fear of FGM if she returned to Togo, the Board of Immigration Appeals (BIA) expanded the reach of asylum law for women by defining "extreme FGM" as persecution (Ericson 1997–98, 693; see note 2). She also observed that the decision was less successful in showing that "punitive intent" is not a necessary element of persecution, although the court appeared to find "punitive intent in the use of FGM to control or repress the woman's sexuality" (Ericson 1997–98, 693–94). The main issues left for future decisions were the validity of applications by adults seeking to protect their minor children from FGM, whether less severe (non-life-threatening) forms qualify as persecution, and whether there are grounds to argue (as Stern sought to do) that past FGM should qualify as persecution under asylum law.

Two important legal articles examine additional implications of the Kasinga case. Karen Musalo (1998), who successfully argued *In Re Kasinga,* has credited the case with clarifying and broadening the interpretation of two key terms in refugee statutes: *punitive intent* and *social group.* First, the BIA accepted Musalo's argument that punitive intent was not a necessary aspect of persecution, thereby opening the door to many claims of gender-based injustice in addition to FGC. Second, the case was the first published decision that included gender as part of the "particular social group" to which a claimant had to belong—in this case, also defined by ethnicity and opposition to FGM. Finally, Musalo argued that the intense media coverage of the case increased public awareness of the ongoing controversy between advocates for the universality of human rights and those advocating cultural relativism, a controversy reflected in the differing perspectives of legal scholars and anthropologists. In a later contribution, Lindsay M. Harris (2012) explored in greater detail the grounds for gender-related claims based on membership in a particular social group; she also offered practical tips for attorneys and expert witnesses, whose knowledge as "country conditions experts" is often crucial to validating and explaining these cases. The chapters in this volume by Joanna T. Tague, Karen Musalo, John Campbell, E. Ann McDougall, and Tricia Redeker Hepner also address this issue.

Although legal scholars in the 1990s differed in their approach to female circumcision and in terms of the balance between advocacy and analysis, they agreed that the key issue left unresolved from the Kasinga decision was whether there were legal grounds for granting asylum to women who had already experienced genital cutting. In addition, they all used identical language to discuss genital modification—with the abbreviation FGM becoming the norm in both legal scholarship and in decisions of the INS and the BIA.[4] They disagreed, however, in the way the practice was portrayed.

The authors strongly advocating for broadening asylum law drew heavily on feminist writing that condemns these procedures and emphasizes their harmful effects on women's health and sexuality. These articles are also prone to generalize about all of "Africa" and to highlight the most drastic practices as the norm. The more analytical articles, by contrast, discussed female circumcision in the context of broader human rights abuses against women and restrict their discussion of FGC to the practices of the Togolese group that Fauziya Kasinga was fleeing. These articles also focus exclusively on the law and human rights without any consideration of possible individual manipulation of the asylum process or of the media context in which the Kasinga trial took place.[5]

In a closely reasoned follow-up, Valena Elizabeth Beety (2008) has traced more recent developments in asylum law, particularly the need for claimants to show a fear of future persecution, something that is impossible if circumcision has already occurred. She notes that in some jurisdictions (the Eighth, Ninth and Tenth Circuits), judges were beginning to compare genital cutting to other sexual harms (forced sterilization and abortion) and to argue that this was, in fact, an ongoing injury, even if it could not recur, because women would suffer the loss of sexual autonomy and fulfillment for the remainder of their lives. Beety argues that if these applicants were perceived as individuals who have suffered persecution because of their identity as women in a specific culture, then the case could be made that they would be persecuted in the future on the same basis. She cites as a promising precedent the argument of the Tenth Circuit in *Niang v. Gonzales,* which saw FGM as part of a broader range of harms against women, such as domestic violence, forced marriage, child marriage, rape, and sexual slavery.

### Anthropological Skeptics

Anthropologists open up another world of asylum analysis that boldly confronts the arguments and the attitudes toward Africa that are prevalent in legal scholarship; they also echo the concerns of recent articles drawing attention to fraudulent claims. Although concerned with legal precedents, anthropologists raise the question of manipulation and deception, which is absent from the world of legal writing but often at the center of media discourse on asylum seekers, an issue that Meredith Terretta's chapter in this volume also addresses. More culturally relativist than the legal scholars, they are also troubled by the image of Africans as primitive, barbaric, and patriarchal at the basis of many asylum cases. The anthropologists' language and their arguments also challenge the views of FGC that have provided the foundation for legal decisions.[6]

Richard Shweder (2002) provocatively disputes the underlying assumptions of feminist legal scholarship. His argument rests on the research of Carla M. Obermeyer, a medical anthropologist and epidemiologist at the Harvard School of Public Health who in 1999 published an article entitled "Female Genital Surgeries: The Known, the Unknown, and the Unknowable."[7] In an effort to arrive at a more scientific understanding of genital modification, Obermeyer reviewed 435 articles about FGM, seeking evidence for the prevalent views of its harm to women. She discovered that most work on the devastating effects of these procedures presented "no evidence . . . at all" for this claim (Obermeyer 1999, 219). When she examined the small number of studies that passed minimum scientific standards, she found that widely accepted medical complications were the exception, not the rule; that female genital alterations were not incompatible with sexual enjoyment; and that the evidence failed to support the assertions about large numbers of related deaths.

Using Obermeyer's findings as the basis of his critique, Shweder (2002, 219) is struck by the fact that normally skeptical and critical liberals so readily accept anti-FGM representations of African family life as "dark, brutal, primitive, [and] barbaric." After doing his own review of the anthropological literature, he concludes, "Fifty years after the end of colonial rule, many First World intellectuals still think of Africa as the Dark Continent and imagine that genital cutting is a Dark Age practice supported mainly by those who are unenlightened, uneducated, ignorant, and unsophisticated" (Shweder 2002, 229–30). He also contrasts anthropological accounts that portray circumcision as "controlled, performed and . . . upheld by women" (Shweder 2002, 227) with journalistic portrayals of FGC as a form of mutilation and patriarchal oppression. Advocating a relativistic approach, he argues that rather than assuming that our own perceptions of beauty and disfigurement are universal, we should consider the possibility of a "real and astonishing" cultural divide in "moral, emotional, and aesthetic reactions" to female genital cutting (Shweder 2002, 222). Instead, he contends, "saying 'yuck' to the practice has become a symbol of opposition to the oppression of women and of one's support for their emancipation" (Shweder 2002, 225).

Although he takes a more measured approach to asylum as it applies to women fearing or having experienced FGC, Shweder fails to give gender difference the same respect he accords to cultural difference. Ignoring the insights of feminist scholarship that persecution might have different meanings for women than for men, he questions whether family practices lacking government involvement qualify as persecution and, in line with his earlier arguments, cautions against characterizing other people's "valued customs" as "political persecution" (Shweder 2002, 244). Nonetheless, he concedes that fear of being forcibly circumcised might be grounds for an asylum request.

Shweder does advocate for change. But rather than appealing to government and immigration authorities to widen the basis for granting asylum to excised women, he calls on knowledgeable "cultural pluralists" to ensure that this critical public policy debate follows the "highest standards of reason and evidence" (Shweder 2002, 248).

Other anthropologists share Shweder's outrage at the portrayal of Africa in these asylum cases as primitive and unchanging, and they show how the press (particularly Celia Dugger's articles in the *New York Times*) exploited these images to influence the outcome of the Kasinga case. Perhaps most challenging, they also highlight the efforts of individual claimants and their lawyers to exploit such images—in some cases, in order to deceive immigration authorities, and in others, simply to win a favorable decision. In their effort to defuse the inflammatory language around circumcision, these anthropologists differ from the legal scholars, using the terms *genital modification, cutting,* or *surgery* rather than *mutilation.*

Charles Piot (2007, 157), who played a minor role in the Kasinga case, examines the court transcripts and articles in the *New York Times* to verify his concern that they glossed over complex local realities, reinforced racist stereotypes, and "fictionalized and fetishized Africa as the West's other." He makes a number of arguments that relate directly to the way asylum law is formulated. Because the law required that Kasinga be portrayed as a member of a recognized social group that has experienced persecution, her lawyer (Karen Musalo) was forced to narrow the definition of the relevant social group to an invented social category that might have as its only members "uncircumcised Tchamba women who resist cutting and justly fear they will be persecuted countrywide" (Piot 2007, 160–61).[8] Another difficulty the case encountered was the legal need to show "malicious and punitive intent" on the part of the persecutors, which Musalo successfully argued was "purely for the purpose of gender subjugation . . . to control women, sexuality and reproduction" (Piot 2007, 161).[9] Piot concludes that the images and stereotypes that dominated the discussion went uncontested, with the only major issue being whether the case would enable Kasinga to fit into the "rigid, albeit ill-defined" categories of asylum law (Piot 2007, 162).

Like Corrine Kratz (discussed later), Piot expresses outrage that Celia Dugger, whose articles in the *New York Times* attracted millions of readers, spoke neither French nor Tchamba and spent only a few days in Togo yet wrote widely read articles that purported to show the "truth" not only about Kasinga but also about the entire continent. This supposed truth included photos of "dirt roads and submissive women, with heads bowed before male patriarchs" all depicting the "immutable nature of patriarchal tradition in a timeless Africa" (Piot 2007, 162–63).

Finally, Piot poses the dilemma that faces anthropologists. Now that a more "robust and nuanced" literature has begun to emerge that, though not supporting genital modification, complicates any "simple-minded" reading of the practice, how are anthropologists and feminists to think about their role in this debate? (Piot 2007, 164).[10]

Like Piot, Corrine Kratz (2002) addresses the relationship between asylum and genital modification as part of a complex intercultural dialogue in which collisions between different values, social organizations, and religious and aesthetic convictions undergo further translations into specialized legal language and procedures. She analyzes two asylum cases, that of Kasinga in 1994–96 and that of Adelaide Abankwah in 1997–99. As portrayed in the US media, both cases seemed to provide dramatic examples of young women being threatened and oppressed by "tribal customs." Whereas Kasinga's case centered on whether and how her claims could be made to fit into the parameters of US asylum law, Abankwah's case introduced the issue of fabricated claims—regarding whether genital modification was practiced in the area she came from and whether it ever was used, as she alleged, as punishment for not being a virgin.[11] As it turned out, despite heavy celebrity involvement on Abankwah's behalf, her claims were totally fraudulent, once again resting on and perpetuating Western stereotypes of Africa. A commentator in the *Ghanaian Chronicle* wrote: "With Adelaide's case all doubts I had before about the ignorance of many Americans about Ghanaian and other African societies have evaporated. It requires a lot of education to correct the jaundiced view of many on the other side of the ocean . . . they should know that people on this side of heaven also live in skyscrapers, drive cars, wear Calvin Klein and Gucci and watch television" (Kratz 2002, 191).

Kratz, like Piot, points out the ambiguity of such cases for those (herself included) who generally support "broadly tolerant" decisions about immigration and asylum. Abankwah, she argues, turned her case into a "Rashomon tale and Rorschach test" for American ideas about Africa and genital modification. In an ironic conclusion, investigators recommended in 1999 that Abankwah be prosecuted for fraud, but the Justice Department was reluctant to do so for fear of embarrassing the politicians and administration officials who had supported her.

Between Advocacy and Deception    **173**

Jennifer Coffman's analysis (2007) of another deceptive case raises additional questions about how asylum seekers represent themselves, how they use and perpetuate stereotypes about Africa, and whether and how anthropologists and other social scientists should intervene. After reviewing the precedents of Kasinga and Abankwah, Coffman introduces a third case—that of a twenty-three-year-old woman from Kenya who arrived in the United States in 1999 seeking asylum. She purported to be Mary Gachumi, a Maasai woman who argued that she would be forcibly circumcised and made to marry an older, polygamous man if she were compelled to return to her country.

Gachumi had an implausible identity, however. Coffman was first alerted to the "troubling inconsistencies" in her account by Gachumi's name, which sounded more Kikuyu than Maasai. She also claimed falsely that the Maasai practiced infibulation and that Maasai women must undergo virginity testing on their wedding nights. Finally, she alleged that after her mother, the only wife of a wealthy and powerful man, died, the man never remarried—which was, in the author's view, an "unheard of" situation for a Maasai male. When Coffman discovered that Gachumi was unable to speak the Maa language, her case fell apart.

In addition to feeding into all the other stereotypes of Africa, this one had a particular bent, resting on the widespread imagery of the Maasai as fierce, noble, aristocratic warriors who stubbornly resisted change. When the attorney dropped the case and Gachumi filed an appeal in 2006, the lawyer said it was clear that Gachumi had modeled her statements on what she had read about Kasinga and Abankwah, fashioning herself as a member of a social group—"Maasai women and girls in Kenya who oppose forced female genital mutilation and forced polygamous marriage" (Coffman 2007, 74).

These cases, Coffman argues, draw attention to the limited investigative capacity of both pro bono and government representatives; the tendency to draw on stereotyped, colonial images of Africa; and the need to establish a "well-founded" fear of persecution based on membership in a particular group or sharing a particular political opinion rather than on an individual situation. In view of this context, Coffman questions the appropriate role of anthropologists and whether their courtroom activities can help to overcome the reliance on a rigid narrative that opposes "us" versus "them" and "tradition" versus "modernity" and "human rights."

Coffman also argues that when an asylum seeker attempts to establish her claim, she usually relies on pro bono representation. The attorney who accepts and believes in the case begins to work with the claimant "to craft convincing affidavits and collect compelling supporting materials." And then, the author adds, "the dance begins" (Coffman 2007, 64).

## The Asylum Dance

The legal writing on asylum cases clarified the reasons for the attorney's narrative in the Koyango case: the emphasis on her "past persecution," on resistance both to genital cutting and marriage to an older man, and on membership in "two particular social groups" that were "fundamental" to Koyango's identity. Specifically, these were politically active members of her ethnic group and members of her family, as well as women who worked to stop violent and discriminatory practices against African women.

On these grounds, Koyango's claim for asylum seemed strong. But a close reading of the documents suggested two potential problems—how closely her own application fit the legal requirements for asylum (particularly on the question of resistance) and how the behavior of her husband, which was responsible for the multiple denials of their claims, could be understood. Although these questions went beyond my role as an expert witness, the anthropological articles detailing deception on the part of applicants prompted me to examine these narrative threads more carefully, with an eye to evaluating the plausibility of the claims.

On the issue of Koyango's opposition to FGC and women's oppression, there is mixed but inconclusive evidence. Koyango's discussion of her life history in her 2004 application, before she had an attorney, detailed her reservations about excision from the time of her own cutting, together with the growth of her doubts about the procedure during her short time in Kinshasa. These questions, according to her account, led her to work against excision and the oppression of women when she returned to Bangui. Given the tense atmosphere in the country and the ongoing fear of coups and violence, I could not help wondering whether the opposition party would have hired her specifically to work with women. A letter on her behalf from the party's general secretary affirmed that she was responsible for recruiting women and mobilizing them in the campaign to fight violence against women. Yet learning that resistance was viewed favorably in asylum claims increased my doubts. Still, if that part of the story was not true, how would Koyango have known to emphasize it in her application? One clue might pertain to a friend from her community who was living in the United States, had "survived the female circumcision," and agreed to testify on Koyango's behalf.

Another testimonial letter came from a Congolese woman, then a US citizen, who had written a BA dissertation on the place of women in African society. Her depiction of women's lives in the Congo and the CAR showed strong parallels with the description provided in Koyango's application. Like Koyango, she discussed "harmful traditional practices such as women circumcision, wife beating and . . . young women given too early to marriage to the rich old men for money" and parents "who do not do much to help their daughters to go to school as they do to their sons." It is impossible to determine whether these parallels indicate deception on the part of Koyango or simply coaching on how to make a successful claim.

It is similarly difficult to gauge whether Koyango's husband, Jean Ngonde (also a pseudonym), was deliberately hindering the progress of her application or if he had simply made an unintended error that was exacerbated by his evident need to control his wife's actions. A close reading of Koyango's statements, however, suggests that his reluctance to act decisively on her behalf may have been related to the complicated circumstances of their marriage. The month before they married, her husband had a pressing dilemma. He was in the process of divorcing his first wife and coping with a newborn son by another woman who had just died in childbirth. Wishing to keep the child, Ngonde arranged for Koyango to be listed on the birth certificate as the infant's mother. They married several weeks later, less than a year before he fled to the United States, and she returned to her parents' house with her husband's son. After the couple engaged an attorney, a new difficulty surfaced—Ngonde had not only failed to include Koyango on his original application, he had listed the name of his first wife.

After the attorney who contacted me took the case, I agreed to attend a hearing along with a translator who was fluent in French and Sango, the official language of the Central African Republic. The immigration judge never called any of us to testify, a source of frustration both for me and for the attorney, given our extensive preparation; in the end, the Immigration and Customs Enforcement (ICE) counsel proposed a joint petition to close the case administratively so that the US Citizenship and

Immigration Services (USCIS) could rule on a new I-730 petition filed by her husband, requesting an extension of the two-year filing requirement on humanitarian grounds. In 2009, after this application had again been turned down, a new hearing was scheduled. This time, the judge ruled that if genital cutting was documented, the claim would be approved; if not, the outcome was questionable. She also agreed to hear testimony only from an expert witness who could verify the claimant's story first-hand. This decision forced Ngonde to allow a doctor to examine his wife. Her cutting was verified.

Not having heard from the attorney since then, I assumed that the case had been resolved, particularly after learning about the circuit court decisions in 2005 and 2007 cited in Beety's article. When I contacted Koyango's attorney for verification, however, she informed me that her client had hired another law firm—which would not have been necessary had the outcome of the final appeal been positive.

## Narrative and Memory

Despite the stark differences between the narratives of legal scholars and anthropologists, the reflections of both groups contribute, albeit in different ways, to understanding the Koyango case. Rather than confirming either of these divergent approaches to asylum, however, this case seems to verify the pattern documented in the *New Yorker* article regarding asylum seekers, family members and friends, and the applicants' attorneys collaborating to create a convincing story. To do so, they draw on relevant aspects of the applicants' background and stereotypes of Africa that have become embedded in US popular culture, along with possibly fabricated or exaggerated claims that conform to the requirements of asylum case law.

For Koyango, the well-documented violence against members of her ethnic group and members of her own family and the warrant for her arrest might have been sufficient to confirm her justified fear of being sent home. But with genital modification now established as part of the process of asylum claims, her personal life became relevant: it was the saga of a woman whose family, though Catholic, expected that she would quietly undergo circumcision and an arranged marriage to an older man. Instead, she ran away to Kinshasa to escape this predetermined fate. Yet despite the burns on her head (physical evidence of past persecution), the warrant for her arrest, proof of her excision, and the new legal precedents, she apparently still failed to win a favorable decision. And despite the skepticism of the anthropologists based on individual fraudulent claims, as well as their worry about negative stereotyping of African societies as primitive, patriarchal, and unchanging, only Shweder seems to challenge the legitimacy of excision as a basis for asylum.

The anthropologists' close attention to the individual stories of asylum seekers was critical to my understanding of the case, however. When I agreed to be an expert witness, I interpreted my role as a historian and women's studies scholar as confirming the repressive, violent, dictatorial behavior of successive governments in the Central African Republic and the effects of this brutality on members of Koyango's ethnic group, especially those who were active in the opposition party. I also needed to substantiate the applicant's account of her personal experience of genital cutting and forced marriage as part of the cultural fabric of the country and her region. The materials I consulted were unanimous in verifying the applicant's narrative about the chaotic, repressive situation in her homeland, although whether she as an individual was telling the truth was difficult to document.

Given my instinctive sympathy for Koyango and without the probing anthropological literature and the recent publicity given to the falsification of asylum claims, I (perhaps naively) would have accepted her claims at face value. Instead, I returned to the case as a historian, rather than an advocate, scrutinizing Koyango's and Ngonde's personal histories more closely and looking for inconsistencies and possible fabrication. Rather than finding evidence of outright deception or fraud, this review left me with questions about why Ngonde failed to list his current wife on his original asylum application, how much Koyango relied on the advice of friends in constructing her own story, and whether Ngonde was in some ways ambivalent about having his wife join him in the United States.

To decode the "asylum dance" more fully, however, also may require an understanding of African traditions of narrative and storytelling. When I was first preparing my statement, I received an e-mail from the attorney, indicating some of the "extraordinary circumstances" I should emphasize. She mentioned in particular Koyango's difficulty in understanding the need to tell a story in chronological order and be precise about when particular events occurred. Carol Bohmer and Amy Shuman, in this volume, also explore applicants' difficulty in shaping a suitable account, particularly one that can be supported with documents.

Thus, in order to craft a legally acceptable story, asylum attorneys have to learn to make sense of African narratives. A recent *New York Times* article by the Swedish writer Henning Mankell, who has lived off and on in Mozambique since the mid-1980s, drove home this point. He wrote:

> If we are capable of listening, we're going to discover that many African narratives have completely different structures than we're used to. . . . Western literature is normally linear; it proceeds from beginning to end without major digressions in space or time. That's not the case in Africa. Here, instead of linear narrative, there is unrestrained and exuberant storytelling that skips back and forth in time and blends together past and present. (Mankell 2011, SR 4)

Koyango's case seems to verify Mankell's assertion, although literature on memory—and memory and trauma—might provide another explanation for the complex stories of some asylum seekers (Personal Narratives Group and Barbre 1989), an issue that Karen Musalo also discusses. But Koyango's experience raises other questions as well. Since expert witnesses are normally able to verify only the general conditions in a given country, not (apart from high-profile cases) the particular life story of any individual, is there any way to guard against fraud, while giving serious consideration to those truly in danger? Is FGC in all its forms a unique harm more detrimental than other forms of gender oppression? How does one weigh the benefits to individual claimants of making genital cutting a basis for asylum claims against the perpetuation of negative stereotypes about African primitiveness that make these claims successful? Answering these questions is beyond the scope of this chapter. But for too long, the concept of human rights was restricted to abuses in the public political arena, neglecting violations in the private sphere that are more difficult to track and confirm unless genital cutting is accepted as evidence of ongoing harm. Although accepting private violations of human rights as grounds for asylum may complicate further the documentation of these cases, from women's perspectives taking them into account represents an unquestionable advance in asylum law since the mid-1990s.

## Notes

1. The correct spelling of her last name is Kassindja, which the INS rendered incorrectly as Kasinga. This error was reflected in all official documents and thus in most of the legal writing about the case.

2. Female "circumcision" takes many forms, from pricking or removing a small part of the clitoris (clitoridectomy) to excision (the removal of the clitoris and most or part of the labia minora) and infibulation (in which all of the external genitalia and all or part of the labia majora are removed, leaving a tiny opening for urinating and menstruation). For an introduction to the fraught politics surrounding these issues, see Nnaemeka (2005) and James and Robertson (2002).

3. I prefer FGC, or female genital cutting, but I will employ the acronym FGM, female genital mutilation, when discussing authors who have used this term.

4. Although the term *mutilation* has helped to make women's circumcision a global political and legal issue, it conveys the idea of evil intent to practices that were an integral part of many African coming-of-age ceremonies; it also perpetuates the stereotypes about Africa, discussed in the next section of the chapter.

5. One legal article that is fully sensitive to cultural nuance is Obiora (1997).

6. Ellen Gruenbaum's sensitive study (2001) briefly mentions the inclusion of FGC as grounds for asylum in France and Australia.

7. His thinking was also prompted by the findings of Fuambai Ahmadu, an African scholar originally from Sierra Leone who grew up in the United States; she does not accept critical accounts of FGM because the emphasis on adverse effects contradicts her own experience and that of most Kono women in Sierra Leone.

8. Karen Musalo challenges this statement, asserting that the definition of the group is "susceptible of including many women" and that the fear of countrywide persecution is necessary in all cases involving nonstate actors (personal communication, October 2012).

9. He also draws attention to the inflated figures on the level of genital modification in Togo, the lack of discussion of how Tchamba elders would respond to resistance to undergoing accepted rituals, and decades of scholarship establishing the fluid nature of group identity in Africa.

10. He also points out that the INS had been renamed US Citizenship and Immigration Services (USCIS) under the Bureau of Homeland Security, a deeply conservative arm of the US government—another fact that may complicate the participation of anthropologists in these cases.

11. Kratz uses the original spelling, Kassindja, rather than Kasinga.

## References

Beety, Valena Elizabeth. 2008. "Reframing Asylum Standards for Mutilated Women." *Journal of Gender, Race & Justice* 11 (239): 1–29.

Bunch, Charlotte. 1990. "Women's Rights: Toward a Revision of Human Rights." *Human Rights Quarterly* 12 (4): 486–98.

Coffman, Jennifer E. 2007. "Producing FGM in U.S. Courts: Political Asylum in the Post-Kasinga Era." *Africa Today* 53 (4): 59–84.

El Dareer, Asma. 1983. *Woman, Why Do You Weep? Circumcision and Its Consequences.* London: Zed Books.

Ericson, Connie M. 1997–98. "In RE Kasinga: An Expansion of the Grounds for Asylum for Women." *Houston Journal of International Law* 20 (3): 671–94.

Gruenbaum, Ellen. 2001. *The Female Circumcision Controversy: An Anthropological Perspective.* Philadelphia: University of Pennsylvania Press.

Harris, Lindsay M., Esq. 2012. "Expert Evidence in Gender-Based Asylum Cases: Cultural Translation for the Court." *Bender Immigration Bulletin* 17 (22): 1811–26.

Helton, Arthur C., and Alison Nicoll. 1997. "Female Genital Mutilation as Ground for Asylum in the United States: The Recent Case of RE Fauziya Kasinga and Prospects for More Gender Sensitive Approaches." *Human Rights Law Review* 28 (2): 375–92.

James, Stanlie M., and Claire C. Robertson, eds. 2002. *Genital Cutting and Transnational Sisterhood: Disputing U.S. Polemics.* Urbana: University of Illinois Press.

Koso-Thomas, Olayinka. 1987. *The Circumcision of Women: A Strategy for Eradication.* London: Zed Books.

Kratz, Corrine A. 2002. "Circumcision Debates and Asylum Cases: Intersecting Arenas, Contested Values, and Tangled Webs." In *Engaging Cultural Differences,* edited by Richard A. Shweder, Martha Minow, and Hazel Rose Markus, 309–43. New York: Russell Sage Foundation.

Lightfoot-Klein, Hanny. 1989. *Prisoners of Ritual: An Odyssey into Female Genital Circumcision in Africa.* Binghamton, NY: Harrington Park Press.

Mankell, Henning. 2011. "The Art of Listening." *New York Times,* December 10: *Sunday Review* 4.

Mehta, Suketu. 2011. "The Asylum Seeker." *New Yorker,* August 1, 32–37.

Musalo, Karen. 1998. "Ruminations on In Re Kasinga: The Decision's Legacy." *Southern California Review of Law & Women's Studies* 7S: 357–71.

Nnaemeka, Obioma. 2005. *Female Circumcision and the Politics of Knowledge: African Women and Imperialist Discourses.* Westport, CT: Praeger.

Obermeyer, Carla Makhlouf. 1999. "Female Genital Surgeries: The Known, the Unknown, and the Unknowable." *Medical Anthropology Quarterly* 13 (1): 79–106.

Obiora, Leslie. 1997. "Bridges and Barricades: Rethinking Polemics and Intransigence in the Campaign against Female Circumcision." *Case Western Reserve Law Review* 47 (2): 275–378.

Personal Narratives Group and Joy Webster Barbre, eds. 1989. *Interpreting Women's Lives: Feminist Theory and Personal Narratives.* Bloomington: Indiana University Press.

Piot, Charles. 2007. "Representing Africa in the Kasinga Asylum Case." In *Transcultural Bodies: Female Genital Cutting in Global Context,* edited by Ylva Hernlund and Bettina Shell-Duncan, 157–66. New Brunswick, NJ: Rutgers University Press.

Setareh, Daliah. 1995–96. "Women Escaping Genital Mutilation—Seeking Asylum in the United States." *UCLA Women's Law Journal* 6: 123–59.

Shweder, Richard A. 2002. "'What about Female Genital Mutilation?' and Why Understanding Culture Matters in the First Place." In *Engaging Cultural Differences,* edited by Richard A. Shweder, Martha Minow, and Hazel Rose Marcus, 216–51. New York: Russell Sage Foundation.

Stern, Amy. 1997. "Female Genital Mutilation: United States Asylum Laws Are in Need of Reform." *American University Journal of Gender, Social Policy and the Law* 6 (1): 89–111.

# EIGHT

## Allegations, Evidence, and Evaluation

*Asylum Seeking in a World of Witchcraft*

Katherine Luongo

IN THE SPRING of 2012, Ashabi Rebecca Fatoyinbo, a Nigerian asylum seeker, sought a judicial review of the decision made a year earlier by the Immigration and Refugee Board (IRB) of Canada stating that she was neither a "convention refugee" nor "a person in need of protection" (*Fatoyinbo v. Canada* 2012, 1). In the original proceedings, Fatoyinbo had argued that her son-in-law's accusation that she was a witch, together with the abuse she suffered at his hands and the likelihood that the accusations of witchcraft he leveled against her would incite antiwitchcraft vigilante violence by members of their community, rendered her a member of a particular social group subject to persecution and thus eligible for refugee protection. She further asserted that there was nowhere in Nigeria where she, as an accused witch, could be protected from current and future persecution of a potentially lethal character.

Several years earlier, in 2006, a male asylum seeker from Nigeria (unnamed by the court but hereafter identified by the pseudonym Adams Enofe Ezomo) made a claim for protection to the IRB.[1] He argued that if he was returned to Nigeria, he would be murdered for being a witch. Ezomo elaborated that the residents of his hometown believed his success in farming, along with the mysterious killing by a swarm of bees of a person who had contested his ownership of a parcel of land, had resulted from Ezomo's witchcraft prowess. He explained that such perceptions rendered him a ripe target for lethal antiwitchcraft vigilantism. Ezomo maintained that there was nowhere in Nigeria where he, as an alleged witch, could hide or escape from the potentially deadly persecution that a mob of his fellow townspeople could inflict upon him, as the Nigerian state offered alleged witches no protection from antiwitchcraft vigilante violence.

In the same year that Ezomo presented his case, Sarah Gideon Mwakotbe, an asylum seeker from Tanzania, applied to the IRB of Canada for a judicial review of the decision made the previous year in which she was "determined not to be at risk in her country of nationality"; it was also found that her fear of persecution had "no nexus to the Convention refugee definition" (*Mwakotbe v. Tanzania* 2006, 4). Mwakotbe had originally argued that in Tanzania, her safety was imperiled by her affinal relatives who regularly practiced witchcraft against prosperous members of the extended family such as herself. She also maintained that as the Tanzanian state offered no protection from witchcraft, there was no place in Tanzania where she could escape from the threat posed by her relations.

During the preceding year, Magdalena Mhando and Gibbons Johannes Mlowe, a married couple from Tanzania seeking asylum, requested a judicial review of the decision made a year earlier by the IRB that neither husband nor wife was a refugee or a person needing protection (*Mhando v. Canada* 2005). The couple argued that if they were returned to Tanzania, elders from Mlowe's tribe who were infuriated by the couple's refusal to have Mhando undergo female circumcision—a practice typically undertaken in the husband's community but not in the wife's—would use witchcraft against them. The couple asserted that there was no place in Tanzania where they could go to escape from witchcraft attacks carried out by elders from Mlowe's community because the Tanzanian state did not provide protection from violence perpetrated through witchcraft.

At first glance, these claims that the threat of violence driven by witchcraft—whether it be violence engendered by accusations of witchcraft or violence carried out through witchcraft practices—constitutes grounds for refugee protection appear extraordinary, yet such allegations are by no means atypical. Rather, the cases presented here derive from a broader inquiry into the persistence of witchcraft as an engine of violence in contemporary Africa that undertakes close readings of records of asylum proceedings in several Commonwealth countries, namely, Australia, Canada, and the United Kingdom.[2] Analysis of these records clearly demonstrates that increasing numbers of African asylum seekers claim they have been alleged to be past, present, and/or potential witchcraft practitioners in their countries of origin, whereas other African asylum seekers claim that they have been, currently are, or will be the victims of witchcraft in their home nations. It also shows how African asylum seekers have engaged the official rhetoric of refugee protection to argue that their relationships to witchcraft, whether as (alleged) victims or (purported) perpetrators, together with the absence of protection in their respective countries of origin, imbue them with a particular transnational, legal identity—that of "member of a particular social group" subject to legally constituted persecution. Such an identity, in turn, renders African asylum seekers eligible for protection in a receiving state and opens the door to resettlement in a host nation.

In assessing such claims about the perils of "living in a world with witches" (Ashforth 2001, 206), immigration authorities in both the state and the nongovernmental arenas have mobilized "expertise" about witchcraft and associated violence. Those involved in state systems—immigration lawyers, justices, refugee tribunal members, and so on—have relied on various modes of expertise. As this volume demonstrates, expert testimony, typically rendered in person or through affidavits or reports by social scientists engaged by the asylum seeker's counsel, is more and more significant in refugee status determination processes. Immigration authorities have also turned to other genres of documents, most often those generated by various national-level documentation centers and information services in response to requests for information from courts, refugee boards, and the like, and occasionally have taken recourse to academic texts. Examining witchcraft-driven asylum cases indicates how such documents are produced in a sociohistorical vacuum and regularly recycled across asylum systems at the state level, rendering nuanced, context-centered expert testimony even more critical to the equitable adjudication of asylum claims.

This chapter explores the various legal instruments through which asylum claims are constituted and the analytic lenses through which they are adjudicated. It traces how expertise about witchcraft is brought to bear—or not—by immigration authorities in assessing witchcraft claims like those made by asylum seekers such as Ashabi Rebecca Fatoyinbo, Sarah Gideon Mwakotbe, Adams Enofe Ezomo, and Magdalena Mhando and Gibbons Johannes Mlowe. This chapter argues that efforts to assess witchcraft claims using expert knowledge falter on two levels—that of analysis and that of ethos. First, immigration authorities struggle with the unit of analysis. On the one hand, if they use expert knowledge to develop a broadly applicable rubric for understanding witchcraft, they risk reifying what counts as witchcraft in ways that dangerously overlook the locally contingent aspects of witchcraft and associated violence. On the other hand, if they take witchcraft as very locally specific, they risk eliding the important commonalities and continuities in witchcraft and concomitant violence that span national and even community borders. Second, working within squarely evidentiary-based systems, immigration authorities tend to view both allegations and expertise about witchcraft with institutionalized incredulity.

Indeed, as Carol Bohmer and Amy Shuman point out in this volume, immigration authorities often overlook the cultural circumstances that make the neutral application of the law impossible. In general, immigration authorities approach claims about witchcraft from the standpoint that the problem of witchcraft-driven violence could be solved if only victims and perpetrators alike could be persuaded to substitute empirical reasoning for magical thinking.

## What Is Witchcraft?

Witchcraft has engaged the attention of anthropologists from the early twentieth century forward. In his classic text, *Witchcraft, Oracles, and Magic among the Azande,* E. E. Evans-Pritchard, one of the founders of modern anthropology, developed lexical categories for discussing the supernatural situation of the Zande people of Sudan: witchcraft, sorcery, and magic. Witchcraft, according to Evans-Pritchard, involves the use of embodied, supernatural power to do malevolence. Sorcery entails the employment of paraphernalia invested with supernatural power in order to pursue malevolence. And magic is the use of benevolent supernatural power to remedy witchcraft and sorcery (Evans-Pritchard 1976, 176–78).

Evans-Pritchard's approach to supernatural power among Zande people was not merely descriptive; it was also analytic. Challenging the conventional, contemporary (and enduring) view that beliefs in witchcraft, sorcery, and magic were markers of irrationality and primitiveness, Evans-Pritchard explored the work that such beliefs did in Zande society. According to him, their function was not to offer a simplistic, unscientific explaining away of incidences of misfortune that could, in reality, be accounted for "scientifically" or "reasonably." Instead, it was to make sense of why a specific person had experienced a particular kind of misfortune at a given moment. He wrote, "There is an analogy between the Zande concept of witchcraft and our own concept of luck. When in spite of human knowledge, forethought, and technical efficiency, a man suffers a mishap we say it is his bad luck, whereas the Azande say that he has been bewitched" (Evans-Pritchard 1976, 67). This early work then begins to suggest how witchcraft, sorcery, and magic were ways of being and knowing that involved both analytic and affective registers.

Recent scholarship has engaged the distinction drawn by Evans-Pritchard between external and somatic supernatural power, but generally speaking, this scholarship has used *sorcery* and *witchcraft* interchangeably, more often relying upon the latter to designate malevolent supernatural power whether it is wielded through an embodied capacity or by using paraphernalia. Engaging Evans-Pritchard's categorization of *magic,* this literature has explored the ambivalence of supernatural power—its efficacy in both harming and healing—and in doing so, it has used *witchcraft* and *sorcery* to denote a continuum ranging from supernatural malevolence to supernatural healing. For example, in the context of Mozambique's Mueda plateau, Harry West (2005, 77) underscores how "the Muedan world of sorcery has been filled with shades of gray whose contrasts and textures derive . . . from the overlay of myriad Muedans' voices, perspectives, and judgments." West's comment suggests the ways in which scholars have come to regard witchcraft as an evolving process rather than as a fixed set of practices, as situated in a resonant history rather than in an anthropological present, and as a lived experience rather than an abstract imaginary.

Recent work has also established that since the 1980s, witchcraft has become a much more public, open matter in many parts of Africa; it is increasingly the subject of personal conversations and political debates (Geschiere 2008; West 2007). This work has shown the interpenetration of witchcraft, law, and politics at the both the local and the state levels. This literature analyzes how witchcraft-driven violence has challenged the maintenance of sociopolitical order and given rise to the development of legal methods that endeavor to combat it, addressing as well how witchcraft offers avenues to political power (Ashforth 2005; Comaroff and Comaroff 1993; Geschiere 1997; Luongo 2011; Niehaus 2001).

In the global arena of asylum, where refugee protection cases turn on the articulation and assessment of past, present, and potential persecution, no ambiguity about witchcraft or witches exists. Both terms are accepted by all parties to immigration proceedings as speaking to supernatural harm. Here, witchcraft figures as "an individual's use of an embodied capacity or an object or practice that mobilizes an invisible, malevolent power in order to harm the person, psyche, property, or kin of another" (Luongo 2011, 9). In witchcraft-driven asylum cases, which illustrate the "constantly changing" ways "witchcraft manages to articulate the global with the local" (Geschiere 2013, 36), much of the knowledge mobilized figures witchcraft with an uncomfortable ahistoricity and an awkward detachment from institutions, deficits in understanding that expert testimony aims to remedy.

## Who Is a Refugee?

Refugee status determination—the process through which asylum seekers such as those discussed here are designated refugees or not according to an applicable definition—is carried out by state immigration authorities in the countries where asylum has been sought or by UN High Commissioner for Refugees (UNHCR) protection officers around the world. This process is rooted in a range of criteria established in the 1951 UN Convention Relating to the Status of Refugees, which was stimulated by the refugee crisis in Europe following World War II and flowed from provisions in Article 14 of the 1948 Universal Declaration of Human Rights that set forth "the right to seek and enjoy in other countries asylum from persecution" (United Nations 1948). Asylum seekers who are determined to meet the criteria articulated in the 1951 convention are subsequently classed as "convention refugees."[3]

The 1951 convention was broadened in 1967 by a protocol that expanded its applicability to asylum seekers fleeing from countries outside Europe and from events not related to World War II. Two years after the establishment of the 1967 protocol, the Organization for African Unity (OAU), the institution founded in 1963 to promote political and economic cooperation among the newly independent states on the continent, produced an Africa-specific instrument pertaining to refugees. The OAU's Convention Governing the Specific Aspects of Refugee Problems in Africa introduced local situations into the matrix of asylum seeking and refugee status determination (OAU 1969). Its expanded definition of displacement criteria spoke to particular types of refugee problems that were present across Africa, explaining in Article I(2) that, in addition to the criteria stipulated by the 1951 convention, "the term 'refugee' shall also apply to every person who owing to external aggression occupation, foreign domination or events seriously disturbing public order in either part or the whole of his country of origin or nationality, is compelled to leave his place of habitual residence in order to seek refuge in another place outside his country of origin or nationality" (OAU 1969). The OAU convention thus began to suggest how insurmountable insecurity could derive not only from aggression wielded by the state but also from the absence of sufficient state protection from aggression emanating from another source.

The UNHCR has a competence, or concern, through which it extends international protection to asylum seekers who meet the criteria for refugee status laid out in the 1951 convention or who fall under an extended refugee definition that echoes the OAU criteria in its attention to expansive, broad-based violence that need not be of a state-sponsored or political nature. Asylum seekers fall under the UNHCR's mandate when "they are outside their country of origin or habitual residence and unable or unwilling to return there owing to serious and indiscriminate threats to life, physical integrity or freedom resulting from generalized violence or events seriously disturbing the public order" (UNHCR 2011b, 19).

Finally, states have their own legislation for use in refugee status determination. For example, *Fatoyinbo v. Canada, Mwakotbe v. Canada,* and *Mhando v. Canada* were adjudicated with direct reference to Canada's Immigration and Refugee Protection Act (IRPA) of 2001. As long as state legislation conforms to the international principle of nonrefoulement, which stipulates that no person should be returned to a place where his or her life or liberty will be threatened, state legislation can include eligibility criteria and applicable refugee definitions that are broader than those of the conventions discussed here.[4]

## Affect, Belonging, and Culture

As eligibility criteria and applicable refugee definitions have become more expansive and witchcraft has become more and more a public subject, it is unsurprising that witchcraft allegations are being increasingly mobilized as grounds for refugee protection. As indicated earlier, asylum seekers making witchcraft allegations do so with the aim of establishing that they belong to a "particular social group" and that membership in such a group inspires in them a "well-founded fear" of being persecuted.

In contrast to the more clearly categorical reasons that asylum seekers can cite as engendering their realistic fears of being persecuted—belonging or subscribing to a particular nationality, race, religion, or political opinion—the broadness of "particular social group" renders it challenging to work with both for asylum seekers, who must establish the bounds of the group to which they belong, and for immigration authorities, who must assess if and how such a group exists in the asylum seekers' countries of origin (United Nations 1951).

The UNHCR's *Handbook and Guidelines on Procedures and Criteria for Determining Refugee Status* parses the term *particular social group* to mean "a group of persons who share a common characteristic other than their risk of being persecuted, or who are perceived as a group by society. This characteristic will often be one which is innate, unchangeable, or which is otherwise fundamental to identity, conscience or the exercise of one's human rights" (UNHCR 2011a, 92). Asylum seekers making claims about gender-based forms of persecution have readily mobilized the category of particular social group.

Karen Musalo's and Iris Berger's chapters in this volume illustrate how, among African asylum seekers, women from communities in which female circumcision—typically referred to in asylum cases with the more loaded language "female genital mutilation" or "FGM"—is taken for granted have argued that FGM is itself a form of persecution. Moreover, they note that women in such communities must live with the expectation that they will be forced to undergo FGM, and thus they constitute a particular social group with a "well-founded fear of persecution." In the 1996 case *In Re Fauziya Kasinga v. U.S. Department of Justice*, Togolese asylum seeker Fauziya Kasinga (or Kassindja) was granted asylum on the grounds that if she was returned to Togo, she would be persecuted because she belonged to a "social group" composed of women who were from a tribe that ordinarily practiced female genital mutilation but who themselves rejected the practice. As Musalo, who litigated on behalf of Kasinga, explains in this volume, FGM claims initially "met resistance because they did not fit the existing paradigms" of persecution. Ultimately, the case helped set the stage for asylum claims about "social group" and "persecution" constituted through "cultural" practices and perceptions (Piot 2006, 503).

Asylum claims pertaining to witchcraft-based persecution operate according to similar logics. From the perspectives of the communities from which asylum seekers have fled, confirmed and potential practitioners of witchcraft and known and prospective victims of witchcraft are distinctly perceived as groups within society. Although the ability to practice witchcraft is an innate capacity fundamental to a witch's identity, the experience of being victimized by witchcraft and/or threats of it is likewise fundamental to the identity of a witch's target. Indeed, for a victim, the experience of being targeted by witchcraft emerges as the defining element in how the person sees himself or herself, and it is also the central experience through which others in the community come to identify the target of witchcraft (Ashforth 2000). Membership in the particular social group known as witches puts a person at grave risk of persecution, practiced through and because of the speech act of the witchcraft accusation. Belonging to the particular social group known as witchcraft targets indicates that the person has already experienced persecution or stands at serious risk of being persecuted through witchcraft methods and means.

## Assessing Social Worlds and Sources of Violence

The legal settings of the immigration court and the refugee board each constitute a "contact zone" or a "complex space between received knowledge and firsthand experience" (Lee 2010, 281). In that space, immigration authorities aim to assess asylum seekers' claims about the experience of communal cohabitation with witches in the context of their own legal expertise and evidence garnered from social science experts and other outside sources. The stories of witchcraft-based persecution that immigration authorities assess are narrated in asylum seekers' carefully crafted affidavits, which are underpinned by "compelling supporting materials" (Coffman 2007, 64). First, asylum seekers' attorneys work with claimants to help them articulate their experiences of personal distress as legally recognizable persecution. In turn, social scientists acting as expert witnesses respond in their own affidavits or in oral testimony to the asylum seekers' specific allegations about witchcraft and comment upon the more general sociopolitical and sociocultural environments from which the asylum seekers have fled; often, they translate aspects of the asylum seekers' narratives along linguistic, cultural, and disciplinary lines. Annotating, extrapolating, and contextualizing the asylum seekers' narratives, expert witnesses' testimony aims to assist immigration officers, judges, and board members who bear the double disability of having limited knowledge about the history of the asylum seekers' countries of origin and about the supernatural situations of these countries.

Often, such expertise is not available to the court or refugee tribunal, since most asylum cases are handled pro bono and limited budgets may preclude the enlistment of expert witnesses; in other instances, an expert with relevant knowledge cannot be located. Consequently, apprehending asylum seekers' witchcraft allegations becomes even more complex for immigration authorities. Whether or not expert witnesses contribute to or participate directly in the proceedings, immigration authorities also consider an amalgam of documentary evidence such as country of origin reports, responses to requests for information, and reports generated by nongovernmental organizations (NGOs)—some of which are supplied by the asylum seekers' attorneys and others of which are accessed by immigration authorities (Good 2003, 6).

Although focusing on witchcraft, these documents, which are recycled from case to case, typically attend to a singular definition of witchcraft and generally do not situate it within the deeper sociohistorical and legal history of the individual asylum seeker's country of origin.[5] This partial knowledge of witchcraft—especially when unmediated by expert witness testimony—risks producing significant misapprehensions, specifically about what witchcraft is or is not and what it does or does not do within a *particular* context in the country of origin. Further, operating in Western evidence-based legal systems that effectively legislated witchcraft out of existence more than two centuries ago (Niezen 2010), immigration authorities also have the complicated tasks of, on one hand, negotiating a standardized "culture of disbelief" (Good 2003, 3) that allegations about witchcraft only compound and, on the other, thinking "phenomenologically" in order to assess what kind of lifeworlds are constructed by profound, sincere convictions in the existence of witchcraft and witches (West 2007, 47).

Narrating how fear—which the UNHCR handbook for refugee status determination describes as "a state of mind and subjective condition"—has come to characterize and shape the asylum seeker's existence requires complicated discursive moves that bring to life the applicant's affective state while at the same time offering clear, discernible evidence about the objective conditions that have produced his or her fearfulness.[6] Despite expert testimony and resources directed to adducing the subtleties and lived experiences of witchcraft, the reshaping of highly personal, contingent affective stories of witchcraft-based persecution into legally usable narratives, structured according to legal protocols and frameworks, often results in a "massive reduction of vernaculars" (Scott 2011, 13) and a concomitant flattening of experience and context. In most instances, though they are of critical import, "witchcraft" and "witch" are condensed as taken-for-granted categories largely divorced from their local languages and meanings.

In the Mwakotbe, Fatoyinbo, and Ezomo cases, the terms *witchcraft* and *witch* appear as unexplained, uncritical producers of peril and persecution. For example, in *Mwakotbe v. Canada* (2006, 1), the word *witchcraft* appears sixteen times with no elaboration beyond the notation that the witchcraft practices engaged in by Mwakotbe's in-laws included the "ritualistic killing of relatives." In the Ezomo case, both witch and witchcraft are undefined even though the asylum seeker's allegation that he was in mortal danger due to his fellow townspeople's belief that he was a witch forms the core of his claim to refugee protection. Similarly, though *Fatoyinbo v. Canada* hinged on Fatoyinbo's claims that she had been accused of witchcraft, neither *witchcraft* nor *witch* is explained in the available documents. Accordingly, decisions in these cases suggest how the complexities of witchcraft can be subsumed through a neat recourse to easy terms.

In its original decision in Fatoyinbo's case, the IRB of Canada held that the witchcraft accusations of Fatoyinbo's son-in-law should be construed as a simple "vendetta" rather than persecution (*Fatoyinbo v. Canada* 2012, 2). Though the son-in-law's witchcraft accusations did, indeed, constitute a series of hostile acts, classing them as a vendetta overlooks how witchcraft—both accusation and practice—involves highly particular forms of life-threatening danger and produces exceptional types of terror. It occludes the ways in which witchcraft is socially saturating and thus how accusations of witchcraft have a power that other hostile speech acts and other kinds of threats do not. Within the social world that Fatoyinbo had inhabited, allegations about her witchcraft practice fundamentally remade her identity, transforming her from a mother, kinswoman, and neighbor into a serial killer in the eyes of her associates. Specifying the attitudes and actions with which the catchall term *witchcraft* is loaded in the understandings of Fatoyinbo's community would have made clear why it is so dangerous and fear inducing to be publicly called a witch.

Lack of clarity in terms was also central to the decision in Ezomo's case, which held that the asylum seeker was not eligible for protection because it was "objectively unreasonable" that he had not sought protection from authorities in Nigeria and that it was unlikely he would be subjected to torture upon removal to Nigeria ("Ezomo" v. Canada 2006, 8). Referring to a response to information request (RIR) on witchcraft in Nigeria generated by the Research Directorate of Citizenship and Immigration Canada (NGA100176.E 2005), the board acknowledged that "beliefs in witchcraft or 'juju' is [sic] widespread in Nigeria" ("Ezomo" v. Canada 2006, 4). However, despite this acknowledgment based on a widely used genre of "expert" knowledge, the decision falters on various grounds. Neither the RIR nor the decision clearly articulates what counts as witchcraft in the asylum seeker's particular context. The decision instead conflates witchcraft with "cult activity" and "traditional religious practice," referring to a case in which "over 30 priests were arrested on 4 August 2004 after 50 mutilated corpses and 20 skulls were found in the forests near the Okija shrines in Anambra State" as an example of how "the police have no reluctance in dealing with persons breaking the law under the guise of traditional religious practices" ("Ezomo" v. Canada 2006, 4–5).

In contrast, Ezomo had argued that members of his community believed he had "inherited witchcraft from his grandmother," thereby indicating that his neighbors believed he had an embodied capacity to perform witchcraft, a type of malevolent power most often countered by destroying the body of the witch ("Ezomo" v. Canada 2006, 4). His "well-founded fear of persecution" was rooted in a fear of becoming a victim of the sort of vigilante violence commonly directed against alleged witches. Although the decision again refers to the RIR to note that "those accused of killing witches have been 'arrested and prosecuted'" in Ezomo's home state of Edo, this evidence shows that the state is willing to deal with antiwitchcraft violence after the fact, not that the state offers protection to alleged witches ("Ezomo" v. Canada 2006, 4).

The available record in *Mwakotbe v. Canada* is more complete than that in Fatoyinbo's and Ezomo's cases, and it includes excerpts from Mwakotbe's affidavit. Her narrative weaves together affect, not only her own fear but the jealousy driving her relatives (an affective state well understood to be an engine of witchcraft), and an understanding of witchcraft that takes "gain" as a goal of witchcraft practice. Mwakotbe stated, "I discovered that in my husband's family belief in witchcraft and sorcery has been quite common, even when the late Mr. Lebi Mwakotbe [the applicant's husband's father] was still alive. During his life, it was not as rampant as after he passed away (in the late 1960s). A desire for wealth, power and fame have led many people from my husband's clan to become involved in killing people for wealth and power" (*Mwakotbe v. Canada* 2006, 6). In the original decision in *Mwakotbe v. Canada,* the immigration officer charged with assessing Mwakotbe's witchcraft allegations determined that although "there is widespread belief in witchcraft throughout Tanzania, which in some instances led to killing of suspected witches by those claiming to be their victims or aggrieved relatives of their victims," the harm feared in the Mwakotbe case was of a merely "criminal" character.

Importantly, the decision separated witchcraft and material gain, insisting that the relatives whom Mwakotbe claimed wished to do her harm were motivated only by a "search for wealth" (*Mwakotbe v. Canada* 2006, 3). Here, the immigration officer endeavored to mobilize knowledge about witchcraft in Tanzania, but in doing so, the officer arrived at a definitional understanding of witchcraft that, if not wholly inaccurate, is significantly incomplete. This understanding of witchcraft privileges the affective states of those "aggrieved" by the deaths of their family members who had been alleged to be witches, but it does not consider the witchcraft-inducing envy that Mwakotbe's afffinal relatives could likely have felt when confronted by prosperous kin. It also elides the ways in which the use of witchcraft and aspirations to material advancement, which have never been mutually exclusive, have only become increasingly interpenetrated since the 1980s (Smith 2008).

The affective state of envy and the disassociation of witchcraft and material gain are also significant in Ezomo's case, where the asylum seeker's success in using new farming techniques created "envy" in his community and "led to insinuations by his neighbours that he used witchcraft to enhance his farm's output" (*"Ezomo" v. Canada* 2006, 1–2). In both cases, the board failed to grasp how one of the central ways in which witchcraft operates is as part of what John and Jean Comaroff (1999, 279) have termed "occult economies," that is "the deployment, real or imagined, of magical means for material ends."

Geographic space emerged as a central concern in the *Fatoyinbo* and *Ezomo* cases. In its original decision in the *Fatoyinbo* case, the IRB also held that Lagos, a one-day journey from Fatoyinbo's hometown of Minna, offered her an internal flight alternative. In its 2012 review, the court concurred with the original decision, asserting that given its distance from Minna *and* the fact that Fatoyinbo's son-in-law had no history of conducting business there, Lagos did, indeed, provide a viable sanctuary where Fatoyinbo could live openly.[7] However, to readers familiar with the seriousness and scope of witchcraft accusations and the antiwitchcraft violence they consistently engender in Nigeria specifically and across the continent more generally, the notion that a distance coverable in a mere day's journey could provide a buffer against antiwitchcraft violence seems improbable; furthermore, the supposition that Fatoyinbo's son-in-law would apply himself to new business in Lagos—that of persecuting the witch lurking among his affinal relatives—appears entirely plausible (Bastian 2001).

In *"Ezomo"v. Canada,* the asylum seeker maintained that he had endeavored to escape persecution by hiding in Lagos but that the townspeople had hunted him there. Pointing importantly to the law-and-order environment in Nigeria, Ezomo explained that not only would the police fail to protect him from antiwitchcraft vigilantism, they would also join the townspeople in tracking and persecuting him. Although the board referred throughout its decision to the RIR and to other sources addressing how the police and the Nigerian legal system had dealt with the murders of alleged witches, it nonetheless found that "state protection . . . sufficient to help him ward off people intent on harming or killing him because of his suspected witchcraft exists in Nigeria" (*"Ezomo"v. Canada* 2006, 8).

In *Mwakotbe v. Canada,* the relationship of witchcraft to law and order in Tanzania was also at issue as the immigration officer in charge of the initial proceedings aimed to assess Mwakotbe's claims about the Tanzanian state's failure to provide protection from violence exercised through witchcraft. The officer found internal inconsistencies in Mwakotbe's narrative, noting that "the applicant stated the police will not protect her because they are corrupt, but she has approached them in the past, and the documents show that practicing witchcraft is a criminal offence and the police have been involved in investigating witchcraft related killings" (*Mwakotbe v. Canada* 2006, 3).

However, the analysis here constituted a semi-informed misreading of the legal landscape of Tanzania, similar to the misapprehension present in Ezomo's case. First, the "witchcraft-related killings" that Tanzanian police typically investigate belonged to the variety of violence that the original decision cast as being driven by witchcraft—the "killings of those suspected of practicing witchcraft" (Mesaki 2009). The police do *not* typically investigate the deaths of those believed to have been killed by having witchcraft exercised against them.

At the same time, in noting that "practicing witchcraft is a criminal offence," the decision assumed that the antiwitchcraft law is both useful and enforceable.[8] A report on antiwitchcraft legislation by HelpAge International, a prominent NGO operating in Tanzania, neatly summed up the legal situation vis-à-vis witchcraft, explaining, "The Witchcraft Act is seen to protect witches rather than to protect against the harm that witches are popularly believed to cause. As a result witnesses are unwilling to testify and name perpetrators of violence and police unwilling to enforce the law" (HelpAge 2011, 26). Further, it could reasonably be conjectured that Mwakotbe, having earlier failed to get assistance from the police, would be reluctant to seek protection from them again.

In its ultimate decision, which concurred with the original determination that Mwakotbe was not a refugee, the board accepted the original understandings of the threat posed—or not—by witchcraft. It went so far as to stipulate that since the sort of harm that Mwakotbe feared from her affines was purely mercenary and criminal in nature, the immigration officer need not have considered her claim that "wealthy, educated members of a family that practices witchcraft" constituted a particular social group subject to persecution (*Mwakotbe v. Canada* 2006, 3).

*Mhando v. Canada* differs from the cases addressed previously in that the asylum seekers wove together witchcraft and female genital mutilation as grounds for their well-founded fear of persecution. The initial decision in the case nonetheless exhibited many of the same trends in the constitution and use of "expertise" as present in the *Fantoyinbo, Ezomo,* and *Mwakotbe* cases. As in those cases, witchcraft figured in *Mhando v. Canada* as broadly undefined—a diffuse, widely dispersible variety of supernatural harm driven by a potent affective state: anger. In keeping with Peter Geschiere's (1997, 24) compelling contention that witchcraft can be readily understood as the "dark side of kinship," the couple feared they would be supernaturally harmed by witchcraft being perpetrated against them by elders from Mlowe's community due to the anger provoked among Mlowe's family and the community at large by the couple's refusal to submit Mhando to "the Mbena tribal custom of female circumcision, or female genital mutilation" (*Mhando v. Canada* 2005, 3).

In rejecting the couple's witchcraft allegations, the board focused on the spatiality of witchcraft, refusing to accept Mhando and Mlowe's contention that even though the elders' witchcraft was capable of menacing them throughout Tanzania and even across the entirety of the African continent, it could not follow them to Canada. Discounting documentary evidence presented about Tanzania and dismissing the couple's allegations about witchcraft as well as their claims about the risk of harm related to female genital mutilation, the board found that Mhando and Mlowe's fears of persecution in Tanzania were not well founded and that they were neither Convention refugees nor in need of protection.[9]

Like Mwakotbe and Fatoyinbo, Mhando and Mlowe requested a judicial review of this negative decision. The court responsible for weighing the couple's request for a judicial review focused on elucidating the lived realities of witchcraft in Tanzania, but it also looked closely at how the board had mediated the evidence presented by the asylum seekers. The court determined that rather than analyzing the preponderance of evidence about the place of witchcraft in Tanzanian society, the board had faltered in privileging its own legal expertise and substituting its own assumptions about the social world Mhando and Mlowe had inhabited. The court underscored that although texts presented by the claimants "discuss[ed] witchcraft as a belief system in Tanzania," the board's "conclusions were at odds with many [sic] of the documentary evidence" (*Mhando v. Canada* 2005, 5).

In its critique of the board, the court highlighted the 2002 US Department of State Country Reports on Human Rights Practices for Tanzania that had been presented in the original proceedings as support for Mhando and Mlowe's allegations about the place of witchcraft in contemporary Tanzania. The report noted, "The widespread belief in witchcraft in some instances led to the killing of alleged witches by their 'victims,' aggrieved relatives, or mobs. Government officials criticized these practices, and some arrests were made; however, most perpetrators of witch killing or mob justice eluded arrest and the Government did not take preventative measures during the year" (US Department of State 2002). Although the report spoke clearly to the level of violence perpetrated against alleged witches rather than to violence perpetrated by witchcraft, the court nonetheless read the findings broadly; it considered them as indicative of a generalized environment of violence surrounding witchcraft practices and beliefs in Tanzania and thus also as supporting Mhando and Mlowe's allegations that they would be at risk from witchcraft were they returned to their homeland. Finally, the court cited the overall failure of the board to consider "differences in cultural beliefs and practices between Canada and Tanzania" as a primary reason for granting Mhando and Mlowe a judicial review of their case (*Mhando v. Canada 2005,* 4).

WRITING ON THE conduct of occult-driven murder cases in Nigeria, David Pratten (2007, 21) remarks how "the exercise of power and the accumulation of knowledge were part of the same system." The decisions in *Fatoyinbo v. Canada, "Ezomo" v. Canada, Mwakotbe v. Canada,* and *Mhando v. Canada* illustrate clearly how knowledge about "objective conditions" in an asylum seeker's country of origin and the knowledge presented in his or her own testimony can be attenuated if not analyzed within deeply situated social, historical, and legal contexts. Indeed, as Bohmer and Shuman's chapter points out and as the experiences of Fatoyinbo, Ezomo, Mwakotbe, and Mhando and Mlowe underscore, often "an applicant's testimony is considered incredible because the official is inadequately informed."

Documentary evidence generated in immigration clearinghouses produces composite, recyclable texts about witchcraft that actually serve to produce significant gaps in immigration authorities' knowledge. At the same time, this genre of expertise effectively reduces the variables with which decision makers have to grapple, and it lends them a false sense of mastery over a complex issue and the even more complicated conditions in which it is situated. Testimony by expert witnesses speaks to these gaps in understanding, but the reception of experts' knowledge is broadly contingent upon immigration authorities' imaginings of their own expertise. The cases addressed here bear out the ways in which circumscribed knowledge is powerful as well.

## Notes

1. As the asylum seeker's name is redacted, I have selected "Adams Enofe Ezomo," following naming protocols and selecting names typical in the asylum seeker's home area. Sean Rehaag (2011, 83) notes that the IRB "redacts the decisions to remove identifying information . . . before publication." In the federal court, case reports have identifiers removed if the asylum seeker's counsel makes a successful confidentiality motion. I am grateful to David Matas for this information. See also Federal Court Rules, SOR/98–106, at 151, available at http://laws-lois.justice.gc.ca/eng/regulations /SOR-98–106/20060322/P1TT3xt3.html (accessed January 12, 2014).

2. A survey of legal databases including LexisNexis, Lexis-Nexis-UK, Quicklaw, Casetrack, Reflex, WorldLII, CanLII, and AustLII revealed thirty cases

from 2000 forward in which African asylum seekers cited witchcraft allegations as grounds for protection. Restrictions on reporting preclude a statistical analysis of witchcraft allegations leveled by African asylum seekers (Dauvergne 2012, 313–14). In 2009, the office of the UN High Commissioner for Human Rights noted that although there were "no reliable statistics on how many women and child 'witches' were killed annually," witchcraft-driven violence was a severe, widespread problem (Evans 2009).

3. Article A(1) of the 1951 convention explains that a refugee is any person who, "as a result of events occurring before 1 January 1951 and owing to well-founded fear of being persecuted for reasons of race, religion, nationality, membership of a particular social group or political opinion, is outside the country of his nationality and is unable or, owing to such fear, is unwilling to avail himself of the protection of that country; or who, not having a nationality and being outside the country of his former habitual residence as a result of such events, is unable or, owing to such fear, is unwilling to return to it" (United Nations 1951).

4. For instance, the IRPA also establishes refugee protection for "persons in need of protection," defined in the legislation as follows: "(1) A person in need of protection is a person in Canada whose removal to their countries of nationality or, if they do not have a country of nationality, their country of former habitual residence, would subject them personally (a) to a danger, believed on substantial grounds to exist, of torture within the meaning of Article 1 of the Convention Against Torture; or (b) to a risk of their life or to a risk of cruel and unusual treatment of punishment if (i) the person is unable or, because of that risk unwilling to avail himself of the protection of that country, (ii) the risk would be faced by the person in every part of that country and is not faced generally by other individuals in or from that country, (iii) the risk is not inherent or incidental to lawful sanctions, unless imposed in disregard of accepted international standards, and (iv) the risk is not caused by the inability of that country to provide adequate health or medical care" (Canada Department of Justice 2001, 62–63).

5. See Campbell's chapter in this volume on the consequences of the recycling and cherry picking of documentary expertise in British asylum courts.

6. The UNHCR's *Handbook and Guidelines on Procedures and Criteria for Determining Refugee Status* describes *fear* and *well-founded* as follows: "37. The phrase 'well-founded fear of being persecuted' is the key phrase of the definition. It reflects the views of its authors as to the main elements of refugee character. It replaces the earlier method of defining refugees by categories (i.e. persons of a certain origin not enjoying the protection of their country) by the general concept of 'fear' for a relevant motive. Since fear is subjective, the definition involves a subjective element in the person applying for recognition as a refugee. Determination of refugee status will therefore primarily require an evaluation of the applicant's statements rather than a judgement on the situation prevailing in his country of origin. 38. To the element of fear—a state of mind and a subjective condition—is added the qualification 'well-founded.' This implies that it is not only the frame of mind of the person concerned that determines his refugee status, but that this frame of mind must be supported by an objective

situation. The term 'well-founded fear' therefore contains a subjective and an objective element, and in determining whether well-founded fear exists, both elements must be taken into consideration" (UNHCR 2011a, 18).

7. Interestingly, a 2005 RIR produced by the Research Directorate of the Canadian Department of Citizenship and Immigration in response to the query on "whether there are safe areas or villages to which those accused of being witches can go" notes that "information on safe areas or villages to which those accused of being witches can go could not be found among the sources consulted by the research department." It is not possible to ascertain whether this document, based on Nigerian and international press reports about violence against alleged witches and on legal and ethnographic texts by Nigerian academics, was consulted by authorities assessing the *Fatoyinbo* case.

8. This assumption that the criminalization of witchcraft precludes the exercise of witchcraft offers an example of what Kristin Bergtora Sandvik (2010, 15) refers to as "magical legalism," that is, "the assumption that if an act or transaction is prohibited, then it effectively does not occur, or occurs only as an anomaly."

9. Although witchcraft-driven harm is less tangible and female genital mutilation has a more established history of being used in claiming culturally constituted persecution, the board lent nearly equal weight to Mhando and Mlowe's claims about witchcraft and FGM. It rejected both sets of claims, asserting that "ample opportunity" had existed before Mhando and Mlowe fled Tanzania for the elders to see female genital mutilation carried out forcibly on Mhando and to attack the couple with witchcraft. The board took the absence of violence against the couple in Tanzania to negate the potential for violence upon their return (*Mhando v. Canada* 2005, 3).

## References

Ashforth, Adam. 2000. *Madumo: A Man Bewitched.* Chicago: University of Chicago Press.

———. 2001. "On Living in a World with Witches: Everyday Epistemology and Spiritual Insecurity in a Modern African City (Soweto)." In *Magical Interpretations, Material Realities: Modernity, Witchcraft, and the Occult in Postcolonial Africa,* edited by Henrietta L. Moore and Todd Sanders, 206–25. London: Routledge.

———. 2005. *Witchcraft, Violence, and Democracy in South Africa.* Chicago: University of Chicago Press.

Bastian, Misty. 2001. "Vulture Men, Campus Cultists, and Teenaged Witches: Modern Magics in Nigerian Popular Media." In *Magical Interpretations, Material Realities: Modernity, Witchcraft, and the Occult in Postcolonial Africa,* edited by Henrietta L. Moore and Todd Sanders, 71–96. London: Routledge.

Canada Department of Justice. 2001. *Immigration and Refugee Protection Act* (S.C. 2001, c. 27).

Coffman, Jennifer E. 2007. "Producing FGM in U.S. Courts: Political Asylum in the Post-Kasinga Era." *Africa Today* 53 (4): 59–84.

Comaroff, John L., and Jean Comaroff. 1993. *Modernity and Its Malcontents: Ritual and Power in Postcolonial Africa.* Chicago: University of Chicago Press.

————. 1999. "Occult Economies and the Violence of Abstraction: Notes from the South African Postcolony." *American Ethnologist* 26 (2): 279–303.

Dauvergne, Catherine. 2012. "International Human Rights in Canadian Immigration Law: The Case of the Immigration and Refugee Board of Canada." *Indiana Journal of Global Legal Studies* 19 (1): 305–26.

Edwards, Alice. 2006. "Refugee Status Determination in Africa." *African Journal of International and Comparative Law* 14:204–233.

Evans, Robert. 2009. "Killing of Women, Child 'Witches' on Rise, U.N. Told." Accessed May 7, 2013. http://www.reuters.com/article/2009/09/23/us-religion-witchcraft-idUSTRE58M4Q820090923.

Evans-Pritchard, E. E. 1976. *Witchcraft, Oracles, and Magic among the Azande.* Oxford: Clarendon Press.

"Ezomo" v. Canada. 2006. Identified in the record as *XXXXX XXXXX XXXXX v. Canada* 2006.

Fatoyinbo v. Canada. 2012.

Geschiere, Peter. 1997. *The Modernity of Witchcraft: Politics and the Occult in Postcolonial Africa.* Charlottesville: University of Virginia Press.

————. 2008. "Witchcraft and the State: Cameroon and South Africa." *Past and Present,* supplement 3:313–35.

————. 2013. *Witchcraft, Intimacy, and Trust: Africa in Comparison.* Chicago: University of Chicago Press.

Good, Anthony. 2003. "Anthropologists as Experts: Asylum Appeals in British Courts." *Anthropology Today* 19 (5): 3–7.

HelpAge International. 2011. "Using the Law to Tackle Accusations of Witchcraft: HelpAge International's Position." Accessed October 10, 2012. http://a4id.org/sites/default/files/Using%20the%20law%20to%20tackle%20accusations%20of%20witchcraft-%20HelpAge%20International's%20position.pdf.

In re Fauziya Kasinga, 3278, United States Board of Immigration Appeals, June 13, 1996.

Lee, Christopher J. 2010. "Tricontinentalism in Question: The Cold War Politics of Alex La Guma and the African National Congress." In *Making a World after Empire: The Bandung Moment and Its Political Afterlives,* edited by Christopher J. Lee, 266–88. Athens: Ohio University Press.

Luongo, Katherine. 2011. *Witchcraft and Colonial Rule in Kenya.* Cambridge: Cambridge University Press.

McGhee, Derek. 2001. "Persecution and Social Group Status: Homosexual Refugees in the 1990s." *Journal of Refugee Studies* 14 (1): 20–41.

Mesaki, Simeon. 2009. "Witchcraft and the Law in Tanzania." *International Journal of Sociology and Anthropology* 1 (8): 132–38.

Mhando v. Canada. 2005.

Mwakotbe v. Canada. 2006.

Niehaus, Isak. 2001. *Witchcraft, Power, and Politics: Exploring the Occult in the South African Lowveld.* London: Pluto Press.

Niezen, Ronald. 2010. *Public Justice and the Anthropology of Law.* Cambridge: Cambridge University Press.

Allegations, Evidence, and Evaluation

Organization of African Unity (OAU). 1969. *Convention Governing the Specific Aspects of Refugee Problems in Africa.*

Piot, Charles. 2006. "Asylum and Culture: Comments on Khanna and Noll." *Texas International Law Journal* 41 (3): 503–7.

———. 2007. "Representing Africa in the Kasinga Asylum Case." In *Transcultural Bodies: Female Genital Cutting in Global Context,* edited by Ylva Hernlund and Bettina Shell Duncan, 157–66. New Brunswick, NJ: Rutgers University Press.

Pratten, David. 2007. *The Man-Leopard Murders: History and Society in Colonial Nigeria.* Bloomington: Indiana University Press.

Rehaag, Sean. 2011. "The Role of Counsel in Canada's Refugee Determination System: An Empirical Assessment." *Osgoode Hall Law Journal* 49:71–116.

Research Directorate, Citizenship and Immigration Canada. 2005. Response to Information Request. NGA100176.E.

Sandvik, Kristin Bergtora. 2010. "Blurring the Boundaries: Refugee Resettlement in Kampala – Between the Formal, the Informal, and the Illegal." *Political and Legal Anthropology Review* 34 (1): 11–32.

Scott, James C. 2010. *The Art of Not Being Governed: An Anarchist History of Upland South Asia.* New Haven, CT: Yale University Press.

Smith, James Howard. 2008. *Bewitching Development: Witchcraft and the Invention of Neoliberal Development in Kenya.* Chicago: University of Chicago Press.

United Nations. 1948. *Universal Declaration of Human Rights.*

———. 1951. *Convention Relating to the Status of Refugees.*

UNHCR. 2011a. *Handbook and Guidelines on Procedures and Criteria for Determining Refugee Status: Under the 1951 Convention and 1967 Protocol Relating to the Status of Refugees.* Accessed October 13, 2012. http://www.refworld.org/docid/4f33c8d92.html.

———. 2011b. *UNHCR Resettlement Handbook.* Accessed October 13, 2012. http://www.unhcr.org/4a2ccf4c6.html

US Department of State. 2002. US Department of State Country Reports on Human Rights Practices for Tanzania. Accessed October 10, 2012. http://www.state.gov/j/drl/rls/hrrpt/2002/18230.htm.

West, Harry G. 2005. *Kupilikula: Governance and the Invisible Realm in Mozambique.* Chicago: University of Chicago Press.

———. 2007. *Ethnographic Sorcery.* Chicago: University of Chicago Press.

# NINE

## Sexual Minorities among African Asylum Claimants

*Human Rights Regimes, Bureaucratic Knowledge,
and the Era of Sexual Rights Diplomacy*

Charlotte Walker-Said

CURRENT AMERICAN ASYLUM law has antecedents in the 1951 UN Convention Relating to the Status of Refugees (the Geneva convention), which contains the principle of nonrefoulement that obligates signatories not to forcibly return refugees and asylum seekers to countries of origin if doing so would pose a clear danger to their lives and freedom. Working with attorneys and immigration experts, I have utilized the US immigration laws of asylum and the protection process of "withholding of removal," as well as the UN Convention against Torture, to secure asylum for what I will call sexual minorities. In this chapter, the term *sexual minorities* is broadly conceived, referring to those Africans who face an exceptional level of violence as a result of their nonnormative sexual or conjugal status and also to those who, because of their sexual and conjugal roles, are vulnerable to cultural, social, and religious criticism. Foreign sexual minorities seeking to legally assimilate into American society face exceptional levels of scrutiny regarding their intimate practices.[1]

*Sexual minorities* has historically referred to individuals who identify themselves or are identified by others as gay, lesbian, or transgender. The International Lesbian and Gay Association and the International Gay and Lesbian Human Rights Commission, whose origins in the late 1970s led to the international defense of sexual minorities, termed nearly all sexual minorities *gays and lesbians,* which in essence transformed non-Western peoples from practitioners of same-sex contact, or sexual contact outside of locally acceptable parameters, into subjects who identify with *homosexual* or *gay* (Massad 2006, 162). During the 1980s and 1990s, the international human rights agenda became a constitutive site of sexual personhood, which sought to define, control, and assert particular notions of what became known as sexual orientation and gender identity (SOGI); in turn, SOGI informed the development of law concerning sexual rights (Phillips 2001; Roseman and Miller 2011). However, many activists and advocates of asylum seekers in the United States are currently working to include the delineation of rights and the assignment of status to any individual whose sexual behaviors deviate from locally accepted norms, including bisexuals; asexuals; those who deviate from local sexual or marital customs, among them the unmarried, polygamists, monogamists, and adulterers; those who marry outside of prescribed populations (mixed-race/ethnicity/clan spouses); childless women; widows; and other individuals whose sexual or reproductive behaviors or marital statuses have made them a target of violence, exclusion, or threats against their lives. Current asylum advocates and those who seek civil and political rights for individuals marginalized due to allegedly deviant sexual and reproductive behaviors struggle with such terms as *nonheteronormativity, LGBTTQQI, MSM, WSW,* and *queer.* These terms are seen not only as being weighted with their own localized meanings but also as carrying within them an explicitly American linguistic history that equates sexual identity with public identity, as well as a host of other hegemonic aspects of what might be described as culturalist rhetoric or what Joseph Massad (2007, 373) calls liberationist rhetoric.[2]

In working with those African individuals who have sought asylum in the United States due—in sum or in part—to sexual or reproductive "deviancy," asylum experts (i.e., lawyers, judges, and administrative adjudicators) struggle to incorporate the narratives, pleas, experiences, and identities of African sexual minorities into American legal conceptualizations of persecution. They also try to find a place for them within conceptualizations of sexual minorities as belonging to "a particular social group," which renders them suitable for asylum protections from the US government. The process by which African sexual minorities must make their sexuality "legible" to lawyers, adjudicators, and judges and, by extension, to the state of refuge reflects both the expansion and the restriction of sexual boundaries of local culture and international law, as they engage and compete with each other for dominance over individual identity and the place of the sexual self in the body politic. Asylum law seeks to make subjects legible in the process of claiming persecution and demanding safe haven, which often requires ascribing particular sexual and gender characteristics, behaviors, and practices to "inalienable rights" and their limit and prohibition to a "culture" that is portrayed as being antirights or antilaw.

Sexuality is as much about power as it is about the erotic, particularly in the realm of rights and law (Foucault 1978; Stoler 1995). But it also speaks to discourses of class, race, nation, gender, age, and status. Sexuality cannot be reduced to a single social relation. Instead, many different factors feed into the way different individuals and groups understand, interpret, and reinterpret their sexuality (Brown 1995; Lalor 2011). The mechanisms and avenues by which the sexual self, however, interfaces with the state of refuge create both opportunities and constraints for sexual minority asylum claimants, and they contribute to the construction of a particular kind of international human rights politics in the arena of sexual rights.

This chapter argues that asylum procedures for African sexual minority claimants reflect a growing hegemonic influence of American-led human rights politics together with a shift in US foreign policy in Africa. In its current state, the American asylum process for sexual minorities is largely shaped by US constitutional and statutory law relating to the rights of same-sex couples. This body of law has recently been greatly impacted by the 2013 Supreme Court ruling in *United States v. Windsor,* which guarantees US government recognition of same-sex marriages entered into in marriage equality states. This ruling, though largely hailed as a significant advancement for social justice, has been criticized by some in the LGBTQ (lesbian, gay, bisexual, transgender, queer) community as a push for "normativity," which does not further the cause of individual sexual rights and sexual liberation (Conrad 2010; Potter 2012; Redding 2013). Rather, the ruling may be viewed as culturally sanctioning specific configurations of (homo)sexual relationships but ignoring (and thus implicitly condemning) others.

Asylum claims based on persecution related to a lesbian, gay, bisexual, or transgender individual's sexual orientation are particularly difficult to file, argue, and win—even with substantial evidence of persecution and ill-treatment (Sridharan 2008). Yet cases have been won, albeit on problematic grounds and claims. Given US asylum precedent, the asylum process forces the claimant to reduce her or his sexuality to just one relationship—one of domination and subordination—understood in limited iterations, namely, gay, lesbian, or transgender. Particular notions and interpretations of sexual behavior and identity are privileged, essentialized, and isolated and are attached to this reified construction (Lalor 2011). Labels such as gay and lesbian are carelessly applied, and the complete content of sexual identity, behavior, and personal circumstance is forcibly removed from the asylum transcript or shoehorned into preexisting frameworks of immigration "exception." This is problematic for several reasons, which this chapter will delineate. These procedures mean that asylum hearings are a theatricalization of the power of the American refuge state: it compels representatives of the oppressed order to speak the language of sexual rights and confess in terms and experiences that reflect American "norms" of "nonnormative" sexual behavior with which the state can identify. Moreover, the procedure affirms the US government's juridical categories of sexuality, claiming sensitivity to the multiplicity of human identities but, in fact, only more firmly entrenching the juridical capacity to penalize sexuality. As the authors of the introduction to this volume state, "Each time an expert is engaged to produce a report to assist in the determination of a particular asylum or refugee claim, the archive of the contemporary African experience expands." However, the archive of African sexual experience in the asylum cases of sexual minorities is corrupted by narrative and testimonial practices that restrict experience and emphasize categories.

I do not deny the (sometimes unwittingly) complicit role of the African asylum claimant in constructing her or his sexual "identity" to run parallel to American sexual typologies. Nor do I deny his or her crucial function in forwarding the sexual rights agenda internationally and specifically in Africa by seeking asylum on grounds of the violation of sexual rights. In this chapter, I provide evidence that rights can be a technology of self-advancement. The manner in which African sexual minority asylum claimants (and sexual minorities in Africa) come to see their problems as human rights violations is a result of the intersections of law and culture—Western, non-Western, African, and postcolonial. The American export of human rights discourse, politics, activism, and even asylum law is changing rights consciousness at the grass roots, particularly in Africa where governance, justice, and law are continually negotiated between new regimes and old power networks. European law is perhaps even more influential in Africa, where much of the national criminal law has remained in force since its origins in colonial penal codes (Collingwood 1967). International human rights, however, have become part of individual legal consciousness throughout the world and can fulfill emancipatory potential, even though human rights is, in many ways, the latest iteration of Western law to be incorporated into local African jurisprudence and processes of cultural renovation (Merry 2006). Africans have been appropriating, repurposing, and manipulating facets of Western liberalism since precolonial times (Allman 1993; Walker 2010). And nowhere is this more evident now than in the complex arena of sexual rights asylum seeking.

The American immigration bureaucracy and the foreign policy apparatus, as well as the international mass media (although not necessarily in cooperation with one another), often reduce African sexual culture to two identity categories. The first is that of the rigidly heterosexual African, who has a voracious sexual capacity, is prone to rape and HIV transmission, and possesses strict gender identity ideologies and virulent bigotry toward gays and lesbians (Corey-Boulet 2012; Gettleman 2011; Lloyd-Davies 2011; McKaiser 2011; Mugisha 2011; Singh 2009; Sridharan 2008).[3] The second is the rigidly homosexual African, who is despised, marginalized, and hounded for threatening "timeless customs" and "cultural norms" of heterosexual marriage and reproduction, which African culture has upheld since time immemorial (Alexander 2006; "Gay Marriage in Africa" 2010; "Government Minister in Ghana" 2011; Pflanz 2011). If the international sexual rights agenda is intended to forward the cause of rights and respect for practitioners of nonnormative sexual and reproductive behaviors or marital statuses, it must confront the bureaucratic and propagandistic processes that create such "types" and work to replace them with better understandings of individuals and respect for the multiplicity of sexual orientations and gender identities.

Currently, mandates for African recipients of foreign assistance, capital investment, and military cooperation from the United States increasingly include conditions for the liberalization of African laws regulating intimacy. Although these conditions assume a liberal character, they include myopic stipulations concerning "sexual rights" and reflect a more and more aggressive American stance toward the renovation of African "sexual culture." These overtures are often rejected (or accepted with only a limited intent of implementation), citing "cultural rights" to guard and preserve national decency and respectability. As Charles Guébogo (2011), a Cameroonian gay rights activist, explained on France Culture, "As a result of globalization . . . Africans feel that they are losing the race. . . . Africa is poor, it is chaotic, it is badly governed, it is corrupt. The symbol of all the worst things in the world. . . . But politically Africans can say: 'ok, maybe we are not rich, maybe we don't know democracy. But at least we have our values. We have not become homosexuals, like you in the West. We have not lost our sense of social reproduction.'"

Complicating matters, evangelical Christian movements—frequently funded and promoted by American religious leaders—operate as a countervailing force to US human rights or foreign policy interventions, collaborating with African governments in rejecting directives aimed at liberalizing the African sociosexual landscape. American evangelicals work to preserve "traditions" of African heteronormativity and explicitly refute international sex and gender rights campaigns (Currier 2013; Gettleman 2010). This chapter argues that the asylum process for African sexual minorities is a microcosm of the transnational moral battle being waged between representatives of the international human rights agenda, American foreign policy leaders, evangelical missionaries, African clergy members, and African sexual minorities, as well as their families, communities, and governments.

In the following pages, I will discuss asylum cases and procedures of African sexual minorities, although their narratives do not (and did not) conform to American legal constructions of a sexual minority. In arguing for the inclusion of a multivalent understanding of sexual minority, I challenge preexisting frameworks created to guide asylum claims for those whose persecution is based on their identity as "a lesbian, gay, bisexual, or transgender (L.G.B.T.) individual" (UN High Commissioner for Refugees 2010). I also analyze the limitations of the American-led "sexual rights as human rights" agenda in Africa and the construction of cultural and sexual fallacies that fabricate a moral weak point against which US interests and agendas can be forwarded. Not only does the American sexual rights agenda problematically position US interests in Africa, it also fails to protect even those so-called sexual minorities that fall within its narrow scope; it is utterly unsuccessful at seeing the broad swath of challenges and violations that befall Africans whose sexual, marital, or reproductive behavior upsets local political, social, or religious standard practice. As Mindy Jane Roseman and Alice Miller (2011, 313–14) have argued, "The sexual rights project has been aimed at creating authoritative global standards, but so far . . . in forms sometimes insensible to other aspects of sexual rights."

### Offering to the Gaze: Asylum Narratives of Sexual Minorities

C. Y. Fouanta, a twenty-eight-year-old Cameroonian immigrant, began his story by telling his immigration attorneys about his father. Fouanta's father was a powerful Muslim Bamoun-Fulani *lamido* with ties to the Far North Region of Cameroon in the Chad basin.[4] His father and his father's associates—Fulani elders—managed an important trading business in Maroua, the provincial capital, and his uncles were part of the Muslim clerical hierarchy and oversaw the operation of mosques and pilgrimage organizations for the predominantly Muslim communities of the region. Fouanta enjoyed the benefits of his father's wealth and connections, until he engaged in a sexual liaison and married a Christian, non-Fulani woman without his family's approval. Fouanta was seeking asylum in the United States, he declared, because he feared that his father would execute him and his wife if he returned to Cameroon.

As part of the marriage, Fouanta had converted to Christianity. When his father and extended family learned of his conversion and marriage, they imprisoned him. While in prison, he was beaten and tortured by members of the local police force, and upon his release, he was expelled, along with his wife, from Maroua. Fouanta described his weeks in prison, the beatings and harassment by police, and the extrajudicial killings of those who marry outside the Fulani Muslim community; he emphasized that his rejection of community norms associated with being the son of a prominent lineage was the principal basis of his persecution.[5]

Fouanta's testimony centered largely on his father, whom he portrayed as a tyrannical figure wielding considerable power in the region. Fouanta's father had fifteen children (nine sons) from four different wives and considered his progeny essential to consolidating his power and controlling the extended family network of traders and clerics in northern Cameroon. Fouanta's marriage and conversion threatened to undermine his father's reputation and status as the lamido, as well as the reputations of all the members of his lineage in the Bamoun-Fulani community. His family's rigidly enforced expectations terrified Fouanta, and he expressed sincere anxiety about the prospect of returning to Cameroon with his wife, where, as noted, he believed they could face death.

After the initial meetings with Fouanta and his wife, a team of immigration attorneys engaged with his case. Since Cameroon had not been listed as a Muslim country in the original file, Fouanta's case had initially been assigned to attorneys without "experience in Muslim asylum."[6] Once the Islam dimension came to light, however, new lawyers joined the case. As Susan Musarat Akram (2000, 17) states, gender-related arguments in an Islamic context are "extremely useful categories" in assessing the claims of those fleeing repressive applications of Islamic law, and they have been incorporated in a number of countries' official guidelines to refugee and asylum adjudicators. In this vein, Fouanta's testimony was analyzed, deconstructed, and pitched on the basis of religious (Islamic) persecution of gender rights and freedom of conscience, rather than intergenerational transgression leading to persecution. Attorneys positioned Cameroonian Christian-Muslim relations as an impenetrable cultural and religious divide, where sexual engagement was viewed by Fouanta's Muslim community as forbidden. As the expert witness and historian, I was charged with illuminating the history of Christian-Muslim relations in northern Cameroon, with an emphasis on intercultural and interreligious violence, conflict, and bloodshed. The community's censure of the couple's sexual relationship was emphasized, with notes made to underscore the region's support of female genital cutting (FGC), codes of sexual purity as defined in local Islamic tradition, and illicit sexual activities that would endanger the lives of men and women who engaged in them.

Expert witnesses were questioned about the private and public influences determining "a Muslim Fulani Cameroonian's" sexual behavior, including the presence of Sufi orders, Islamic clubs and societies, and Islamic schools. Fouanta's accounts of his father's economic and political influence were clearly de-emphasized in order to highlight interreligious sexual taboos and crimes alluding to traditional beliefs in cultural purity and denial of independent sexual or martial agency. Instead of perceiving harm as persecution under the relevant international law standards, the only relevant issue became the source of persecution: Islam.

In a bizarre cooperative turn, Fouanta began relating the practice of female genital cutting in northern Cameroon among some Fulani Muslims, and he discussed that his wife's status as an uncircumcised Christian woman left her vulnerable to prejudice and attack. Knowing the asylum case law related to female genital cutting, the trial attorneys immediately shaped new tactics, aimed not only at explaining the Islamic customs of sexual repression that formed the illicit nature of the sexual affair but also detailing the traditions of FGC that marked the status of Christian women as social and sexual outcasts. These factors, it was argued, even constructed a threat to Fouanta's wife should she return to Cameroon, where she could face a forced FGC ritual in order to be socially accepted by his father's clan. Building on the case law on female genital cutting (*Adelaide Abankwah v. Immigration and Naturalization Service* 1999; Bashir 1996; *Matter of Kasinga* 1996; Harivandi 2010; see also Berger and Musalo, in this volume), the physical element was heavily emphasized in the asylum hearing.

The asylum process for C.Y. Fouanta can be seen as a process of signification, whereby immigration experts and the asylum claimant shaped the signifiers that completed the narrative to justify refuge. Islam, Christianity, and female genital mutilation powered the force of the asylum process for Fouanta, recasting an intergenerational conflict over economic, political, and social status into a larger, globally oriented narrative of Christian-Muslim division, criminal sexuality, and sexual sadism performed in the name of tradition and cultural continuity. Signifiers of sexual deviancy—of Africans and Muslims, in particular—weighed heavily in the asylum hearing. More than the threat of intergenerational strife and a lack of economic and social freedom, accounts of criminalized sexual activity, torture, beating, and imprisonment by Muslim elites together with the nefarious specter of FGC served to create what Miriam Ticktin (2011, 2–5) terms the "moral imperative" necessary for the existence of an "exceptional" human rights case to allow entry via asylum. Accounts of sexual transgression against Islamic law were particularly effective in the process of legal legitimization, in which Fouanta and his wife purposefully rejected Islamic law and sought the refuge of "secular" American law.

In Fouanta's case, the meaning of suffering was mediated by strictly Western social, political, and cultural contexts and by transnational regimes of rescue. The immigration process was managed by constructed sentiment—by the production of "others," as well as recognizable and sympathetic "victims," who could be imagined as either outside or inside the national community. Individual freedoms and individual responsibilities to the social in any national context were not interrogated. Rather,

Fouanta and his wife were presented as racialized, sexually violated bodies and victims of exoticized practices that themselves were evidence of cultural pathologies. Producing "expert" knowledge meant attending to the politics of compassion before lending expertise on the tensions inherent to sexual and marital choice in a particular cultural context.

In a separate case, a Cameroonian woman, Sabine M. K., and her son, Jonathan D. K., had arrived in the United States after suffering extreme violence at the hands of Cameroon's security police.[7] Jonathan, a twenty-three-year-old college student, had been caught protesting at the Université de Yaoundé I, one of the larger campuses of the Cameroonian capital's main university, and had been arrested and severely beaten and tortured in prison. Sabine, his forty-three-year-old mother, had also been imprisoned several times and severely beaten following her son's imprisonment, accused of supporting a "troublemaker" and, subsequently, for being an alleged thief and a fraud. Sabine and her son claimed that local police had routinely harassed them over the past year and that this abuse was known to the gendarmerie—the higher-level security forces in Cameroon—and was politically motivated.

The K. family was, by most measures, wealthy. Jonathan had traveled to Europe several times, and Sabine had been to the United States to visit family. As the asylum team convened to interview Sabine and Jonathan, it was revealed that Jonathan was known at the Université de Yaoundé as a "playboy" and a "homosexual," although he did not accept either of these labels. His mother believed that Jonathan had been targeted by the police during the student protests because of his sexual reputation and because he had a "rich girlfriend and many rich friends." Sabine also revealed that even though she was not legally divorced, she had been separated from her husband for many years and had numerous enemies among her former husband's friends. She blamed her husband's friends, family, and business associates for hounding her and her son and causing their imprisonment, abuse, and harassment.

Through the asylum process, the sexual orientation and sexual behaviors of Sabine and Jonathan became matters of greater juridical concern. Jonathan's conflicted testimony over the weeks of pretrial preparation revealed that he had a reputation for being a homosexual but that his homosexual activities were limited to "games" and "some secret exchanges." However, his testimony also showed that the abuse and allegations of homosexuality were due to his wealth and his sartorial ostentatiousness, which aroused jealousy among his classmates. Sabine, too, revealed that the police and her husband's affiliates accused her of being an adulteress, as she was not officially divorced and was living alone without her husband. Because adultery is technically illegal in Cameroon, she was vulnerable to arrest and charge, as well as police brutality.[8] Jonathan's identity was a larger and potentially explosive issue for the asylum court. The task was to determine whether Jonathan was "truly" a homosexual or bisexual; if he was simply perceived as a homosexual; or if, in the words of one asylum attorney, he "had homosexual tendencies and had experimented with homosexuality, but was not an open homosexual."[9]

Attorneys and immigration experts considered the asylum strategy amid evidence of the claimants' political activities and their (alleged) sexual behaviors as well as their role in shaping the claimants' status as social threats to Cameroonian society. The immigration attorneys understood that one's position as a supposed sexual minority could be powerful in the asylum process, but any such claim had to follow procedure. The immigration process had no space for poststructuralist concepts of the self as the location of multiple and potentially contradictory sexual subjectivities; it required the assertion of one singular subject position, preferably one with a typified sexuality, that would be easily understood on both American and African terms. For Jonathan, his encounter with immigration law affected the way he thought about himself, as he was forced to consider the relationship between his intimate world and American law. Many critical theorists argue that it is the law's hegemonic, ideological character that makes it more effective than violence. Austin Sarat and Thomas R. Kearns (2000, 6) aptly describe this process: "The focus on the production, interpretation, and consumption of legal meaning suggests that law is inseparable from the interests, goals, and understandings that deeply shape or comprise social life." Jonathan's experience could be read as a performance of what Michel Foucault (1978) and Judith Butler (1990) described as the production of the legal subject, where juridical power produces what it claims to represent. Jonathan's articulation of his sexual identity as an asylum claimant was forged in a legally regulated context, demonstrating the law's regulatory hegemony even in the most intimate of spheres.

Of particular interest to this case were the recent political developments in West Africa related to sexual rights and the gay rights movement. In what Jeff Haynes (2011) termed "the Second Liberation of

Africa" of the 1990s, demands for democratization and economic change caused many authoritarian regimes to engage more broadly with civil society and accept a greater multiplicity of voices in the public sphere. In Cameroon, the engagement of Christianity in the political sphere was propelled by antielite sentiments and confrontation with an unpopular government. Christian revivalist movements in rural and urban areas and even the long-established and highly popular Catholic Church harnessed mass frustration and rage against the elite cadres and the executive power to position themselves as defenders of the decency and simplicity of the disenfranchised masses. In doing so, these movements constructed sexual identity within the dichotomy of elitist and commoner, corrupt and decent, and foreign and local. In Cameroon, allegations of homosexuality became a means of attacking the elite while working within acceptable modes of discourse (Guébogo 2006; King 2007). Framings of the "colonial" and "imported" nature of homosexuality were paired with antigovernment sentiment. This led to the scapegoating of alternative sexual lifestyles and sexual minorities as "foreign elites" and "liberal elites" who adopted Western mentalities of greed, corruption, and deviance.

In 2005, Cameroonians were arrested on charges of homosexuality for the first time, and the archbishop of Yaoundé publicly condemned homosexuality in a holiday address. The following year, the Cameroon newspaper *L'Anecdote* published a list of fifty gay and lesbian Cameroonians, stating, "Men making love to other men . . . is filthy. It may be normal in the west, but in Africa and Cameroon in particular, it is unthinkable" (Meldrum 2006). Here, it is crucial to note that of the fifty "exposed" gay and lesbian Cameroonians, all were members of the upper or middle class and part of elite networks, and they included government ministers, athletes, clergymen, and prominent politicians. The newspapers publishing the list of "gay Cameroonians" sold out in a week: though circulation had been a few thousand per week in Cameroon before the list, over forty thousand copies were reported to have been photocopied across Yaoundé for distribution.

In Cameroon, Christianity has positioned itself as marginal and suppressed in contrast to its oppressors. Christian churches capitalize on the lack of democracy in a way that would be problematic for it should democracy ever be established. By defining Christians as victims of a hostile political elite, church leaders delineate "non-Christian" behavior—in this case, homosexual behavior—as bad in the process of "othering." This discourse dovetails with the continuance of the HIV/AIDS crisis and the worsening state of public health in Africa broadly (Dilger 2010; Murphy 1994). With the AIDS crisis, Christian rhetoric concerning cleansing, renewal, and purity has assumed new dimensions, and by extension, Christian communities construct representations of static African masculinities that are free of disease, that adhere to "pure" ideologies, and that are categorically compatible with "good" Christian norms. Local communitarian norms and traditionalist viewpoints also buttress various strains of Christianity to sanction narrow, heteronormative moral codes that place enormous pressure on women "to act with purity" (Hunter 2005).

Jonathan's and Sabine's experiences as individuals whose alleged sexual improprieties put them in the category of marginalized persons made their asylum case complex. However, their status as wealthy Cameroonians, with access to passports, visas, travel money, cars, and a firm financial foothold made them vulnerable to accusations of sexual deviance (homosexuality for Jonathan and adultery for Sabine) in the context of 2008–9 Cameroon. In the first decade of the 2000s, public sentiment surrounding wealth as a conditioner of behavior—namely, licentiousness, deviance, and corruption—circulated broadly and had popular appeal (Bainkong 2006; Dicklitch 2002; Efande 2010; Fombad 2004; Ignatowski 2006; Johnson-Hanks 2005; Nyamnjoh and Fokwang 2005; see also Terretta, in this volume).

This context places Jonathan's and Sabine's sexual conflicts in perspective and is essential to analyzing the interpretation of African sexual repression and the American and international human rights discourse concerning gay rights. Jonathan insisted throughout the asylum process that he was not a categorical homosexual and that his games and experiences with other young men at his university were not emblematic of his identity. He emphasized his girlfriend and their status as a couple at the university as a significant part of his identity, which, among other aspects, was the subject of jealousy among friends. His political protest at the university against rising tuition costs and the low standards of education was conducted as part of a large student crowd, but he was singled out for arrest and torture because of his clothes, his playboy reputation, and his friends' unwillingness to stand against the police with him, as they had for others.

Sabine, however, was open to arguing for Jonathan's status as a homosexual in Cameroonian society and his de facto vulnerability to violence.

She ardently described the deplorable social and political circumstances of Cameroonian gays, as well as the current tide of antigay public sentiment.[10] Immigration officials and attorneys demanded to know if Jonathan wished to go on the record as being gay, bisexual, transgender, or part of another legally defined sexual category. For Jonathan, the question of *identity* was far more important for the asylum process than the question of *behavior,* as is the case with other sexual minorities seeking asylum. For Sabine, though, identity was less foundational to the creation of an exceptional asylum plea, for the act of adultery is not criminalized within the United States. As Meredith Terretta (in this volume) states, "Through the channel of asylum, Cameroonians have refashioned migration into a process of débrouillardise, or improvisation." In the end, Jonathan negotiated a claim based on sexual identity, rather than behavior, yielding to Janet Reno's 1994 argument that one's status was the legal category in question, not one's behavior.

## Orientalist Narratives, Sexual Hegemonies, and Rights

The international gay rights movement has influenced the adjustment of US asylum law and immigration law to make exceptions for those seeking asylum based on their sexual orientation. Beginning in 1994, the number of LGBT asylum claims increased, and since then, international advocates for LGBT rights have pressured the United States not only to increase its asylum acceptances for victims of violence based on sexual orientation and gender identity but also to amplify calls for LGBT acceptance, tolerance, and decriminalization throughout the world ("Argentina Passes Gay Marriage Bill" 2010; Burke 2007; International Lesbian and Gay Association 2008; "Respect Gay Rights" 2012; Williams 2011). Historically, however, LGBT individuals have been subject to long-standing restrictions to entering the United States. Prohibitions on US entry against homosexuals were legally inscribed under the Immigration and Nationality Acts of 1917 and 1952, which placed homosexuals in the category of the "mentally or physically defective." This deviance ban was overturned only when Congress passed the Immigration Act of 1990 (Davis 2000).

Immigration and asylum law in the United States has been revised, but it still contains narrow language related to conditions for LGBT asylum. This situation reflects conflicted and ambivalent approaches to LGBT rights within the United States, as well as the continually shifting status of LGBT individuals (and those who do not fall explicitly under the terms included in LGBT or LGBTTQQI) as full citizens under American law. Under current US laws, personal sexual *identity* is not criminalized, but sexual *conduct* (in certain forms) still carries criminal penalties, not to mention social and political taboos. This difference is largely paralleled in the context of asylum, in which claims based on discrimination against sexual conduct are shaky (Sridharan 2008). In the 1994 decision in *Matter of Toboso-Alfonso,* which Attorney General Janet Reno declared to be precedent for LGBT asylum cases, the Board of Immigration Appeals (BIA) stated that the petitioner was not persecuted "in response to specific conduct on his part (e.g., for engaging in homosexual acts); [but] rather . . . simply from his status as a homosexual." In one of the asylum petitions to follow this precedent-setting case, the Eighth Circuit Court of Appeals denied the claim of Botswana citizen Mareko Molathwa in 2004, arguing, among other things, that "homosexual conduct is criminal in Botswana, as it is in some jurisdictions within the United States."

In the asylum process, American immigration bureaucracies clearly favor expression and evidence of what this chapter argues is a rigid sexuality and sexual orientation—firmly planted within a systematic, regulated, uncompromising set of behaviors and attitudes that is natural, or defined by its innate and unconditioned quality. For the immigration bureaucracy, evidence of rigid sexuality is required in order to guard against so-called deviance, which can include the widest range of sexual behaviors, practices, and leanings other than monogamous, exclusively homosexual practice. These "other" nonnormative sexual forms have less juridical appeal, as they indicate an unregulated, unfixed, and interpretive version of sexuality that arouses fears of perversion, licentiousness, and health crises (HIV/AIDS). Through the asylum process, one clearly perceives the emergence and sanctioning of queer subjectivity in American law and the conceptualization of queer sexualities as part of the international human rights agenda.

Conceptualizing queer sexualities and marginal sex status in Africa is a daunting task if one is wary of reproducing colonial typologies. Jasbir Puar claims that convivial relations exist between queer normativity movements and empire, nationalism, globalization, fundamentalism, secularism, and neoliberalism. I argue that queer normativity movements—sanctioned through law, political activism, and social policy—are concomitant with the rise of transnational human rights activism. What is clear is that the US simultaneously creates opportunities for

Sexual Minorities among African Asylum Claimants 217

forms of LGBTTQQI inclusion that require performances of American sexual exceptionalism vis-à-vis "perverse" improperly hetero and homo non-American sexualities, and also exports its vision of sexual inclusion as a mode of mediating new kinds of cultural conflicts alive in the Global South. As sex and gender struggles of individuals and groups—from female genital cutting traditions to headscarf restrictions to reproductive rights activism to legislation against homosexuality—continue to occupy greater political space in the Global South, the United States will seek to define its influence in these politics as liberalizing, emancipating, and nondiscriminatory. In truth, however, its stance will be conservative, molding new inflexible conventions and parochial standards that adhere to current articulations of American LGBT activism, legislative currents, and conventional wisdom, while claiming their basis in "universal" ideals of individual rights.

Human rights theory makes significant space for the multiplicity of sexual identities and behaviors that exist within the human condition, and it demands that they be respected and tolerated. However, the international gay rights and human rights agendas as they are currently practiced are too limited in their capacities to liberalize the social and political climate beyond visions of supposedly normative or sanctioned sexual minorities. Thus, the asylum processes of C. Y. Fouanta, Sabine M. K., and Jonathan D. K. are defined by blatant "othering" processes, accompanied by acceptance or resistance to new forms of subjectivity demanded by the requirements of the state of exception.

The danger in the asylum processes for the sexual minorities with whom I have worked was that alternative sexualities (or forms of non-normative sexualities according to both African and American frames of reference) were, as Sara Ahmed (2000) has argued, "colonized" through the regulatory function of law and reified to become a "known Other." Immigration experts and human rights professionals dominate the process and eventually speak on behalf of sexual minorities and impose their own monological view of what African or Muslim criminal sexuality is. American immigration bureaucracy becomes a regulatory power, defining queerness and privileging certain kinds of otherness that draw on sentimentality and form the image of the recognizable and sympathetic victim, which can be imagined as part of the national community.

In speaking about the laws against homosexuality in Cameroon, a Cameroonian woman interviewed on France Culture stated, "I cannot feel free because I live with the law. The law is always with me and I am never detached from it" (Guébogo 2011). In the same way as an oppressive law can "live with" its victim, a seemingly emancipatory law also inhabits its subject—holding the individual accountable to the law, even as he or she must live with its provisions.

## Final Thoughts

Human rights, like politics and ideology, speaks in universalisms. Notions of human freedoms and entitlements, such as life, conscience, speech, security, and education, are posited as universal values—shared, understood, and accepted by all (Chandler 2002; Glendon 2002; Ignatieff 2003). Gay rights, enveloped within the human rights agenda, similarly claim to speak to "natural" sexuality, akin to natural rights, which are universal and mutually recognizable. However, sexual identity and orientation are not necessarily transhistorical, mutually identifiable, and universal. The language of the "universality of sexual difference" in fact reflects American cultural specificities construed as universal experiences and identities. As scholars of human sexuality, we must recognize the enormous range of factors at work in the construction of sexual subjectivities, as well as the mutable and continually shifting terrains of sexual orientation and gender identity.

Asylum experts, translators, and consultants, along with attorneys and judges, work specifically within the construction of sex and gender categories, and by doing so, they demand that claimants occupy narratives, claims, and categories. Furthermore, asylum law professionals unwittingly encourage the self-construction and aspirations of other victim-subjects (as a mechanism to gain entry into the state), through their shaping of the victim-subject. They are unaware of or neglectful toward realities that "refuge" for the individual is similar to "home" in its problematic political marginalizations of sexual minorities. With widespread American resistance to gay marriage and gay adoption, together with the continuing marginalization of sexual minorities and resistance to the strengthening of hate-crime laws, the protection of the lives of sexual minorities offered asylum is precarious at best. Thus, we create problematic avenues for entry into the place of refuge and render the entry an ambivalent emancipation for the sexual minority. By constructing binaries of "free" and "unfree," "open identity" and "closed identity" in the United States and Africa, respectively, the sexual minority individual is made to assume that, even though his or her own constructed identity as a sexual minority in US courts includes elements of falseness, the new identity becomes "true," as it is the means for full inclusion in American life. Although the law may construct sexuality as an identifiable aspect of selfhood that can be defined and regulated, it cannot be allowed to offer us a blueprint for what a gay or lesbian or transgender person *is*. Asylum experts and immigration attorneys must seek opportunities where new narratives of sexuality can be told and integrated into the corpus of law in which the other becomes a rights-bearer (van Zyl 2005).

## Notes

1. This chapter refers to African asylum claimants for whom I have worked, testified, translated, or provided assistance in the asylum procedure in some way, as well as claimants' attorneys, family members, or consultants.

2. In this chapter, the term *deviant* will be used primarily to refer to those individuals who depart markedly from an accepted norm. It will not be used in the pejorative sense that colloquially refers to those whose social or sexual behavior is considered morally wrong or criminal. LGBTTQQI refers to lesbian, gay, bisexual, transgender, two-spirited, queer, questioning, and intersex. MSM refers to men who have sex with men. WSW refers to women who have sex with women.

3. Marc Epprecht has documented the construction of the African sexualities blind spot by the medical and scientific communities in the 1980s, during the early years of HIV/AIDS research, where even *Lancet* and *Science* data reports did not investigate homosexual intercourse as a mode of disease transmission in Africa.

4. Names have been altered to protect the identities of clients. A *lamido* (pl. *lamibé*) is a traditional ruler with spiritual and political influence. Bamoun-Fulani is an ethnoregional and transethnic identity. Fouanta had family in both western Cameroon (the Bamoun region) and northern Cameroon (the Fulani region). Members of his own particular community *considered* themselves Fulani-Bamoun, as his father had a mixed heritage. There are almost no texts that explicitly delve into the identity politics of the Bamoun-Fulani, but it is clear that this community possesses its own localized codes and practices, which can be interpreted along different lines, drawing from a range of oral histories that help understand broadly how it governs itself and disciplines community members.

5. Charlotte Walker-Said, Expert Testimony for C.Y. Fouanta and Family, October 18, 2010.

6. Charlotte Walker-Said, Notes from C.Y. Fouanta Case, September 23, 2010.

7. Names have been altered to protect the identities of clients.

8. The Cameroon Penal Code, sec. 361, states: "Any married woman having sexual intercourse with a man other than her husband shall be punished with imprisonment for two to six months and with fine of from twenty-five thousand to one hundred thousand francs" (Yotnda 1975).

9. Charlotte Walker-Said, Notes from K. Family Asylum Case, December 9, 2009.

10. Charlotte Walker-Said, Notes from K. Family Asylum Case, December 14, 2009.

## References

*Adelaide Abankwah v. Immigration and Naturalization Service*. 1999. 185 F.3d 18 (2d Cir.).

Ahmed, Sara. 2000. *Strange Encounters: Embodied Others in Post-coloniality*. New York: Routledge.

Akram, Susan Musarat. 2000. "Orientalism Revisited in Asylum and Refugee Claims." *International Journal of Refugee Law* 12 (1): 7–40.

Alexander, Mary. 2006. "South Africa Legalizes Gay Marriage." December 1. Accessed August 12, 2011. http://www.southafrica.info/services/rights/same-sex-marriage.htm#.VAKjNEgwLog.

Allman, Jean. 1993. *The Quills of the Porcupine: Asante Nationalism in an Emergent Ghana*. Madison: University of Wisconsin Press.

"Argentina Passes Gay Marriage Bill." 2010. *Advocate*, July 15.

Bainkong, Godlove. 2006. "Football Stars Stand Accused of Bribery." *Cameroon Tribune*, June 25.

Bashir, Layli Miller. 1996. "Female Genital Mutilation in the United States: An Examination of Criminal and Asylum Law." *American University Journal of Gender, Social Policy and Law* 4 (2): 415–54.

Brown, Wendy. 1995. *States of Injury: Power and Freedom in Late Modernity*. Princeton, NJ: Princeton University Press.

Burke, Hilary. 2007. "Uruguay OKs Gay Unions in Latin America First." *Reuters*, December 18.

Butler, Judith. 1990. *Gender Trouble: Feminism and the Subversion of Identity*. New York: Routledge.

Chandler, David. 2002. *From Kosovo to Kabul: Human Rights and International Intervention*. New York: Pluto Press.

Collingwood, J. J. R. 1967. *Criminal Law of East and Central Africa*. London: Sweet and Maxwell.

Conrad, Ryan. 2010. *Against Equality: Queer Critiques of Gay Marriage*. San Francisco: Against Equality Press.

Corey-Boulet, Robbie. 2012. "The Obama Administration's Bold but Risky Plan to Make Africa Gay-Friendly." *Atlantic*, March 7.

Currier, Ashley. 2013. *Out in Africa: LGBT Organizing in Namibia and South Africa*. Minneapolis: University of Minnesota Press.

Davis, Tracy J. 1999. "Opening the Doors of Immigration: Sexual Orientation and Asylum in the United States." *Human Rights Brief* 6: 3–13.

Dicklitch, Susan. 2002. "Failed Democratic Transition in Cameroon: A Human Rights Explanation." *Human Rights Quarterly* 24 (1): 152–76.

Dilger, Hansjorg. 2010. *Morality, Hope, and Grief: Anthropologies of AIDS in Africa*. New York: Berghahn Books.

Efande, Peter. 2010 "Funeral Service of a Businessman Assassinated by Unknown Assailants." *Cameroon Tribune,* April 7.

Epprecht, Marc. 2006. *Heterosexual Africa? The History of an Idea from the Age of Exploration to the Age of AIDS.* Athens: Ohio University Press.

Fombad, Charles Manga. 2004. "Cameroon's Emergency Powers: A Recipe for (Un)Constitutional Dictatorship?" *Journal of African Law* 48 (1): 62–81.

Foucault, Michel. 1978. *History of Sexuality,* vol. 1. New York: Vintage.

"Gay Marriage in Africa: Gay Marriage Is Wrong." 2010. *Economist,* May 20.

Gettleman, Jeffrey. 2010. "Americans' Role Seen in Uganda Anti-gay Push." *New York Times,* January 3.

———. 2011. "Ugandan Who Spoke Up for Gays Is Beaten to Death." *New York Times,* January 27.

Glendon, Mary Ann. 2002. *A World Made New: Eleanor Roosevelt and the Universal Declaration of Human Rights.* New York: Random House.

"A Government Minister in Ghana Calls for Gays and Lesbians to Be Rounded Up and Arrested." 2011. Free Speech Radio News (Pacifica Radio Network), August 12. Accessed January 30, 2014. http://fsrn.org/audio/a-government-minister -ghana-calls-gays-and-lesbians-be-rouned-and-arrested/8856.

Guébogo, Charles. 2006. *La question homosexuelle en Afrique: Le cas du Cameroun.* Paris: L'Harmattan.

Guébogo, Charles, and Louis-Georges Tin. 2011. "Droits et perceptions des personnes homosexuelles dans le monde 3/4—Vers une dépénalisation universelle de l'homosexualité?" *France Culture: Cultures Monde,* July 6. Accessed September 2011. http://www.franceculture.fr/player/reecouter?play=4279527.

Harivandi, Zsaleh E. 2010. "Invisible and Involuntary: Female Genital Mutilation as a Basis for Asylum." *Cornell Law Review* 95:599–626.

Haynes, Jeffrey. 2011. *Religion, Politics, and International Relations: Selected Essays.* New York: Routledge.

Hunter, Mark. 2005. "Cultural Politics and Masculinities: Multiple-Partners in Historical Perspective in KwaZulu-Natal." *Culture, Health, and Security* 7 (4): 389–403.

Ignatieff, Michael. 2003. *Human Rights as Politics and Idolatry.* Princeton, NJ: Princeton University Press.

Ignatowski, Clare. 2006. *Journey of Song: Public Life and Morality in Cameroon.* Bloomington: Indiana University Press.

International Lesbian and Gay Association (ILGA). 2008. "Mexico City Extends Official Rights to Transgender Individuals." www.igla.org, accessed August 29, 2010.

Johnson-Hanks, Jennifer. 2005. "When the Future Decides: Uncertainty and Intentional Action in Contemporary Cameroon." *Current Anthropology* 46 (3): 363–85.

King, Micah. 2007. "Homosexuality in Cameroon's Public Sphere: Rejecting Homosexuality as Protest against the Other." BA thesis, Department of Anthropology, Washington University, St. Louis.

Lalor, Kay. 2011. "Constituting Sexuality: Rights, Politics, and Power in the Gay Rights Movement." *International Journal of Human Rights* 15 (5): 687–88.

Lloyd-Davies, Fiona. 2011. "Why Eastern DR Congo Is "Rape Capital of the World." CNN, November 25.

Massad, Joseph. 2007. *Desiring Arabs*. Chicago: University of Chicago Press.

*Matter of Kasinga*. 1996. 21 I. & N. 357 Board of Immigration Appeals.

McKaiser, Eusebius. 2011. "Gay Rights, Homophobic Wrongs in South Africa." *New York Times,* November 9.

Meldrum, Andrew. 2006. "Fifty Public Figures Named in Gay Witchhunt by Cameroon's Papers." *Guardian*, February 5.

Merry, Sally Engle. 2006. *Human Rights and Gender Violence: Translating International Law into Local Justice*. Chicago: University of Chicago Press.

Mugisha, Frank. 2011. "Gay and Vilified in Uganda." *New York Times,* December 22.

Murphy, Timothy. 1994. *Ethics in an Epidemic: AIDS, Morality, and Culture*. Berkeley: University of California Press.

Nyamnjoh, Francis B., and Jude Fokwang. 2005. "Entertaining Repression: Music and Politics in Postcolonial Cameroon." *African Affairs* 104 (415): 251–74.

Pflanz, Mike. 2011. "Africa Reacts to Obama's Pro-Gay Rights Foreign Policy." *Christian Science Monitor*, December 9.

Phillips, Oliver. 2001. "Constituting the Global Gay: Issues of Individual Subjectivity and Sexuality in Southern Africa." In *Law and Sexuality in the Legal Arena*, edited by Carl Stychin and Didi Herman, 17–34. Minneapolis: University of Minnesota Press.

Potter, Claire. 2012. "On Beyond Windsor: The Future of an Activist Queer Theory." *Jacobin: A Magazine of Culture and Polemic* 11 (September): 21–25.

Puar, Jasbir. 2007. *Terrorist Assemblages: Homonationalism in Queer Times*. Durham, NC: Duke University Press.

Redding, Jeffrey A. 2013. "Querying Windsor, Querying Equality." *Villanova Law Review* 59:9–16.

"Respect Gay Rights, UN's Ban Tells African Leaders." 2012. *Nyasa Times,* January 29.

Roseman, Mindy Jane, and Alice M. Miller. 2011. "Normalizing and Its Discontents: Establishing Sexual Rights in International Law." *Harvard Journal of Law and Gender* 34 (2): 313–76.

Sarat, Austin, and Thomas R. Kearns. 2000. "The Cultural Lives of Law." In *Law in the Domains of Culture*, edited by Austin Sarat and Thomas R. Kearns, 1–20. Ann Arbor: University of Michigan Press.

Singh, Vijai. 2009. "Confronting Rape on Zimbabwe's Border." *New York Times,* March 7.

Sridharan, Swetha. 2008. "The Difficulties of US Asylum Claims Based on Sexual Orientation." Migration Information Source, US Council on Foreign Relations, October.

Stoler, Ann Laura. 1995. *Race and the Education of Desire: Foucault's History of Sexuality and the Colonial Order of Things*. Durham, NC: Duke University Press.

Ticktin, Miriam. 2011. *Casualties of Care: Immigration and the Politics of Humanitiarianism in France*. Berkeley: University of California Press.

UN High Commissioner for Refugees. 2010. "The Protection of Lesbian, Gay, Bisexual, Transgender, and Intersex Asylum Seekers and Refugees." Discussion paper, UNHCR Roundtable on Asylum Seekers and Refugees Seeking Protection on Account of Their Sexual Orientation and Gender Identity, Geneva, Switzerland, September 30–October 1.

van Zyl, Mikki. 2005. "Shaping Sexualities—Per(Trans)forming) Queer." In *Performing Queer: Shaping Sexualities, 1994–2004,* edited by Mikki van Zyl and Melissa Steyn, 19–38. New York: Kwela Books.

Walker, Charlotte. 2010. "The Trafficking and Slavery of Women and Girls: The Criminalization of Marriage, Tradition, and Gender Norms in French Colonial Cameroon, 1914–1945." In *Sex Trafficking, Human Rights, and Social Justice*, edited by Tiantian Zheng, 150–69. New York: Routledge.

Williams, Steve. 2011. "Mozambique Gay Rights Group Wants Explicit Sexual Protections." Care2MakeADifference, March 2. Accessed April 13, 2011. http://www.care2.com/causes/mozambic-gay-rights-advocates-push-for-constitutional-amendment.html.

Yotnda, Maurice Knouendjin. 1975. *Le Cameroun à la recherche de son droit de la famille.* Paris: Librairie Générale de Droit et de Jurisprudence.

# TEN

# The "Asylum-Advocacy Nexus" in Anthropological Perspective

*Agency, Activism, and the Construction of
Eritrean Political Identities*

Tricia Redeker Hepner

IN ASYLUM AND refugee determination cases, expert witnesses—often anthropologists and other academics—are frequently called upon to provide contextual analysis that supports the "nexus" of a claim. Since the US Supreme Court decided *INS v. Elias-Zacarias* in 1992, immigration courts have been charged with interpreting this nexus, or the interface between past or future persecution and one of the five protected grounds for asylum status (race, political opinion, nationality, membership in a particular social group, and religion). Through providing analyses of country conditions, often based on research findings and firsthand experience, such "experts" help lawyers and courts to understand the relationship between past or possible future persecution on the basis of the protected grounds and to make determinations accordingly (Mahmood 1996; Good 2004, 2007).

Having moved beyond its more narrow legal usage, the concept of the nexus has recently been expanded by social scientists as a way to analyze the linkages among motivations for migration and the constraints and opportunities associated with migration policies and discourses. Stephen Castles and Nicolas Van Hear (2005; see also Betts 2009) refer to a "migration-asylum nexus," or a dynamic political economy of forced migration in which the distinctions between so-called economic and forced (e.g., political) migration are blurred. Within this migration-asylum nexus, conflict and human rights abuses, North-South inequalities, development dynamics, diasporic or transnational networks, and international and national migration policies together form a shifting complex that structures and contextualizes the movements and claims of refugees and asylum seekers.

The chapters in this book have critically examined distinct but overlapping facets of the asylum process, from the prehistory of African refugee status determination ( Joanna T. Tague), the historical development of asylum law and its subjects (Karen Musalo), and the cross-cultural construction of credibility and fraudulence (Iris Berger, Meredith Terretta, Katherine Luongo); to problems of documentation, language, and narration (Carol Bohmer and Amy Shuman, E. Ann McDougall) and tensions between imposed legal categories and the welter of subjectivities and motivations at work among asylum seekers and adjudicators alike (John Campbell, Charlotte Walker-Said). Together, the chapters demonstrate how African asylum embodies dense and tangled histories, economic inequities, cultural and political nuances, and changing legal norms internationally and domestically.

As an overdetermined phenomenon, asylum is deeper and richer than it appears on the surface. It is also more than the sum of its parts. A reality sui generis, asylum is a complex system simultaneously constituted by human action and yet external to it, exercising objective constraints on agency through proscriptive norms and rules. As such, it is especially amenable to social scientific analysis. In this chapter, I view asylum as a sociopolitical process in which academic expertise, legal advocacy, human rights or political activism, and the asylum seekers' own strategic objectives interface. Drawing on political and legal anthropological approaches and ethnographic fieldwork with Eritrean asylum seekers in Ethiopia, the United States, and Europe, I explore how asylum becomes a site of convergence among intimately related dynamics that are irreducible to either legal procedures or political-economic contexts governing migration. In particular, I build on Castles' and Van Hear's (2005) "migration-asylum nexus" to suggest that the concept of an "asylum-advocacy nexus" helps us think about how asylum procedures constitute a political economy of knowledge and identity that is coproduced by experts, advocates (both lawyers and activists), and refugees themselves.[1]

For the expert, analyzing and contextualizing asylum claims can enrich one's academic knowledge and research (or activist) agenda, whereas the migration-asylum process can shape and give expression to refugees' changing consciousness and political-legal subjectivities. Within legal proceedings, moreover, expert analysis may not only tangibly assist asylum seekers in making successful claims but also produce (through precedent, case law, and so forth) a codification or essentialization of knowledge about countries of origin and legitimate versus illegitimate claims. For example, expert testimony that demonstrates how political repression is operationalized through militarized development and labor schemes (as in Eritrea) can challenge the distinctions between political and economic migration inherent in refugee policy and law. Directing one's expertise and argumentative capacities to such specific tasks may push the expert to think through research findings and contexts more rigorously. After repeatedly arguing in expert reports that political repression, forced labor, and economic deprivation are inherent to indefinite military conscription in Eritrea, for instance, I finally published a peer-reviewed article addressing the issue of "development-forced displacement" more rigorously (Hepner and Tecle 2013). I also articulated my argument at the request of Israeli refugee activists in a short, direct statement entitled "Open Letter to Israel: Eritreans Are Not Economic Refugees" (Hepner 2012a) and later in a full expert report submitted to the Israeli court. And after writing countless expert reports about religious persecution in Eritrea, I finally published an article on that as well (Hepner 2014). Indeed, the present volume is itself a testament to the richness of asylum as a field of critical inquiry for scholars across disciplines.

If expert witness work has informed and motivated my research agenda, at least in some cases it also informs and motivates asylum seekers' identities and agency. For some asylum seekers, crafting the narrative with an attorney, reading the expert report and other country conditions information, and giving testimony might encourage new reflections and even inspire political action. Asylum seekers in Germany elaborated how the telling of their stories of persecution helped them gain a sense of empowerment and mastery over abuse, generated new forms of solidarity among them, and awakened them to conscientious objection as a political option (Hepner 2013). One young man detained first in Eritrea and later in Texas by Immigration and Customs Enforcement (ICE) became very active with the nongovernmental organization

(NGO) DetentionWatch after receiving asylum in the United States. Still others were motivated to join chapters of Amnesty International or newly emergent Eritrean human and refugee rights organizations, a phenomenon I also charted in my research (Hepner 2013).[2] Some reported that they came to view their own experiences as human rights abuses as a result of having to frame them in those terms. And more than a few noted that even when they found asylum procedures frustrating or confusing, they were deeply appreciative of a system that operated according to the "rule of law."

Hence, asylum procedures embody and reflect the ways that political-economic and legal forces interface with the academic production of knowledge about refugees and their countries of origin. And at least for some asylum seekers, the process also enables refugees to critically reflect and act upon their individual and collective identities and interests.[3] This interface is what I call the asylum-advocacy nexus.

In this chapter, I focus on and problematize three dynamics associated with the asylum-advocacy nexus. First, I critically examine how the role of anthropologists and other researchers as experts in asylum and refugee claims may represent a form of "critically-engaged activist research" (Speed 2006) in which research findings, on-the-ground experience, and other specialized knowledge can become a powerful—if sometimes problematic—tool for supporting members of a research population. Second, I examine the experience of seeking asylum itself as a form of agency and consciousness-raising, in which refugees and asylum seekers exercise a measure of choice and control, make critical decisions, and for some reflect on their experiences in terms of concepts such as rights. Finally, I show how asylum procedures become sites for the formation and contestation of transnational political identities and social power, as refugees contend with ongoing efforts by political actors from their home country and within the diaspora to intervene in their asylum claims and control changing political and legal identities and behaviors. As refugees exercise agency and mobilize movements on the basis of their changing identities and concepts of rights, they often do so with the aid of both lawyers and expert witnesses. These individuals simultaneously work on their specific cases, act as purveyors and packagers of information that may precipitate shifts in refugees' consciousness and action, and critique and sometimes help to transform the laws and policies that structure the political economy of migration generally.

## The Expert as Critically Engaged Activist

In recent years, asylum studies has emerged as a distinct field in the social sciences and humanities. Insofar as academic interest reflects empirical trends in the world, we might suspect that rising numbers of asylum applications worldwide are responsible for this visibility. Yet according to the UN High Commissioner for Refugees (UNHCR 2011), numbers of asylum applications lodged in the industrialized North in 2010 were at their lowest in a decade. The need for academic expertise in the context of legal proceedings becomes more vital to refugee protection than ever before as restrictions and obstacles in northern asylum policy and procedure increase—including greater border controls and technologies of surveillance (for instance, Frontex); "externalization" and securitization measures that diminish eligibility and further prevent refugee movements; application of domestic policies on terrorism that adversely affect refugees from conflict regions; and virtual extension of state jurisdictions to prevent asylum seekers from reaching northern shores and borders in the first place. Consequently, much recent scholarship in this burgeoning field of asylum studies has focused on the problems facing asylum seekers amid these new restrictions and the capriciousness of asylum procedures generally (Bohmer and Shuman 2008; Coutin 2000; Good 2007; HRF 2009; Huysmans 2006; Hyndman and Mountz 2008; Mountz 2010; Price 2009; Ramji-Nogales, Schoenholtz, and Schrag 2009; Tazreiter 2004). Additionally, the role of expert witnesses in supporting refugee and asylum claims has also received some attention (Good 2004, 2007; Mahmood 1996).

Despite a drop in asylum applications in the first decade of the twenty-first century, some countries have been overrepresented in total numbers of refugees and asylum seekers worldwide. Since 2001, the Horn of Africa nation of Eritrea has consistently ranked among the top ten refugee-generating countries due to political repression, forced and indefinite military conscription, systematic and egregious human rights violations (such as widespread arbitrary detention without charge and use of torture), and economic deprivation (especially within the military and National Service). The United States experienced a 166 percent increase in asylum applications filed by Eritreans between 2005 and 2010, and more Eritreans applied for asylum in 2009 than Iraqis or Somalis (UNHCR Statistical Database). Many European countries also witnessed dramatic upturns in first-time Eritrean applications between

2005 and 2010. Thus, despite increasingly restrictive migration policies in the North, the overrepresentation of Eritreans has boosted the demand among lawyers and advocacy organizations for expert reports and testimony by anthropologists and other researchers.

Scholars with expertise on Eritrea are few in number; hence, those willing to participate tend to accumulate much experience over a short period of time.[4] For some, such as myself, a convergence of scholarship and activism takes place, as fieldwork among Eritrean refugees opens up spaces wherein asylum and refugee procedures, the experiences of refugee "research subjects" themselves, and our shared knowledge of sending and host country conditions may move seamlessly between analytical problems to legal strategies to ethical imperatives and back again. That is, as fieldworkers engage with refugees directly and learn firsthand of the dilemmas they face within the migration-asylum nexus, they are often called upon by refugees and their families, by lawyers, and by their own convictions to put their expertise and knowledge to work. Packaging information in ways that are consistent with the requirements of legal proceedings can thus expose or aggravate tensions among the analytical, strategic, and ethical imperatives of the researcher. This, in turn, may become a fruitful area for critical theoretical and methodological reflection on the praxis of "engaged anthropology."

The concept of engaged anthropology was prompted by scholar-activists such as Paul Farmer (Farmer and Gastineau 2002), Carole Nagengast and Carlos Velez-Ibañez (2004), Nancy Scheper-Hughes (1995), Shannon Speed (2006), Catherine Besteman (2010), and others whose positionalities variously reflect and embody the view that it is not enough to study suffering—we must endeavor to do something about it.[5] Farmer and Nicole Gastineau (2002) propose a "pragmatic solidarity," in which our skills and resources can help alleviate suffering while remaining consistent with broader goals of justice and human rights. Noting that cultural relativism does not entail moral relativism, Scheper-Hughes (1995), following Martin Buber, admonishes anthropologists working with populations mired in conflict and violence to reject "suspending the ethical" and to defend the rights of exploited populations in the practice of a "militant anthropology." More recently, anthropologists of human rights have further elaborated and problematized the ways scholars may engage in forms of activism that align with the struggles and needs of the people among whom they work. In her critical analysis of indigenous rights struggles in Mexico, Speed (2006, 70) proposes that "critically-engaged activist research provides an important approach to addressing the practical and ethical dilemmas of research and knowledge production." Moreover, by reflecting on the process of putting cultural analysis to work in the service of "shared political goals" with research subjects, the inevitable "tensions and contradictions" that arise can become a source of new theoretical and methodological insights (Speed 2006, 71).

Anthropologists who serve as expert witnesses enact one possible form of critically engaged activist research. That is, by drawing upon our research findings, in-country experiences, and firsthand engagement with refugees and asylum seekers, we are positioned to collaborate with attorneys, NGOs, and refugees themselves. In this way, we also contribute to reshaping the structural power imbalance that has long troubled feminist fieldworkers (e.g., Wolf 1996); these fieldworkers have argued against the notion of an objective, distanced researcher in favor of a "situated" one (Haraway 1988) who actively uses her training, skills, and connections to resources and institutions to intervene on behalf of research subjects in need of assistance. This process—in which the researcher rejects exploitation as the basis for career advancement and academic prestige in favor of a more reciprocal relationship with research populations—can thus become fertile ground for further analytical insights as well as a site of cotheorization with research populations on the problems they face and strategies for amelioration. This has certainly been the case in my own work with Eritrean communities in Africa, Europe, and the United States, who regularly request my interventions and advocacy in both overseas matters and domestic asylum claims; members of their activist community engage with me and my analyses of Eritrea and its diasporas to inform their own strategies and positions. These engagements, in turn, shape, hone, and sharpen my research questions and analysis.

Yet the role of the researcher as expert witness or activist is not without problems. As Catherine Besteman (2010) notes regarding her work on Somalia and with Somali Bantu refugees in Maine, "collaborative anthropology" can be a highly frustrating endeavor insofar as researchers face constraints and obstacles similar to those confronting migrants themselves. Discussing her efforts to inform US policy makers on Somali culture, politics, and society, she notes how anthropological knowledge is often too nuanced to impact the policies and laws that embody and operationalize larger state agendas (in the Somali case, the American imperative to counter "terrorism"). Additionally, the goals of activism and the time-sensitive and time-intensive nature of responding to communities' needs can preclude the luxury of developing the theoretical and methodological insights that such processes might ideally generate (Besteman 2010). Balancing the work of anthropological reflection (and meeting the demands and criteria for success in university employment) with activism may become unsustainable in the long run, she adds.

Even more troubling is the way in which our intimate knowledge of the social and political contexts from which refugees and asylum seekers come may be at cross-purposes with the intent of asylum itself and the legal procedures involved. Cynthia Mahmood (1996), writing about the "tangled web" surrounding militant Sikh separatists seeking refugee protection or asylum, points out that asylum laws and procedures set critical limits on whether and how researchers can be advocates. An intimate knowledge of the conflicts that generate forced migration and of the political biographies of individual people enmeshed in them can place researchers in a difficult spot. In situations where research participants are also (or have been) armed militants engaged in violently overthrowing a government, she asks, "how can one live up to a responsibility to the people one studies in these cases without becoming a partisan to their causes?" (Mahmood 1996, 496). With respect to clauses that exclude from refugee status those who have engaged in nonstate armed movements or who may be implicated in human rights violations or persecution by virtue of the very dynamics that made them refugees, she observes that "[Sikh separatists] have to understand why I can not know some things, why I in fact do not want to know some things, and furthermore recognize that my burden as a law-abiding U.S. citizen might put me on the other side of some critical issues at some point" (Mahmood 1996, 496). In effect, the depth of our knowledge and the bonds of trust that enable it (and on which research participants base expectations of our assistance) can render us ineligible or at least very problematic as expert witnesses.

I recently encountered such a situation with a young Eritrean man in Ethiopia, who spent hours explaining to me why he was involved in an ethnic resistance movement and how he was attempting to organize other Eritrean refugees to overthrow the government in an armed struggle. Some months later, having fled to Djibouti, he requested my help in presenting his case to the UNHCR. My intimate knowledge of his involvement in advocating the armed overthrow of the Eritrean government made it impossible for me to assist him, and I found myself explaining to him why the UNHCR, the United States, and other governments may, in fact, view him as a terrorist and therefore deem him ineligible for refugee status or asylum. For someone who saw himself as struggling for freedom against a ruthless dictatorship, this was understandably difficult to accept. And though my knowledge of the context of his claim may have made it possible for me to package it convincingly (for, in many ways, I believe his claim to refugee protection was valid), doing so would have been at cross-purposes with refugee law and possibly would have entailed perjury on my part. That it would have also entailed essentializing and reducing the complexity of Eritrean ethnic identities and grievances is perhaps less serious on the face of it, but this, too, raises concerns in the realm of anthropological knowledge.

On this point, Shannon Speed (2006) acknowledges how the process of making effective human rights claims sometimes requires a "strategic essentialization" of the identities, histories, and cultures of research populations who must effectively "package" the latter to conform to the requirements of relevant laws and policies. Speed's research findings and knowledge of Mexican Tzeltal communities complicated the notion of "authentic" indigenousness, but mounting an effective human rights claim vis-à-vis the Mexican state required her and her research participants to coproduce a very different picture of timeless, unchanging Indian identity. Such strategic essentialization, especially when produced by anthropologists whose disciplinary imperatives and commitments to relativism otherwise aim for de-essentialization, can be uncomfortable at best and inimical at worst to longer-term goals of producing accurate analyses of fluid and dynamic sociocultural and political contexts. Hence, academics who serve as expert witnesses risk finding that the knowledge they produce for adjudicators may contribute to the *reification* of populations, identities, and cultures rather than the more nuanced and multidimensional portraits we otherwise strive to produce (and which are ostensibly useful in our expert reports for asylum and refugee cases). How this political economy of knowledge may then reciprocally inform refugees' and asylum seekers' self-understandings becomes another, related dimension of the asylum-advocacy nexus.

The "Asylum-Advocacy Nexus" in Anthropological Perspective

Eritrean refugees and asylum seekers, like those from other countries, are not simply passive victims or objects of the larger structural, legal, and policy-related constraints that give rise to displacement and shape the quest for safe haven. Numerous studies have documented the ways that refugees and asylum seekers make active choices and seek to exercise control over their fates, often in the face of considerable indifference and seemingly insurmountable odds (e.g., Agier 2007; Sandvik 2011; Turner 2009; Verdirame and Harrell Bond 2005). Arguably, asylum seeking itself is a form of agency, insofar as it represents an individualized attempt at securing a "durable solution" otherwise not forthcoming in other refugee contexts. When neither formal resettlement nor integration—let alone repatriation—appear to be on the horizon, refugees may choose to move across multiple spaces and undertake extremely risky journeys. The opportunity to individually present one's case to the domestic courts of a preferred country stands out as possibly the only solution for those who would otherwise languish in camps and cities. In this sense, at least some asylum seekers have skipped over the interminable and indeterminate workings of the "refugee regime" to take their fates into their own hands. In so doing, they embody an insistence on the recognition of their rights as individual persons and expose the inability of the refugee regime to adequately fulfill its mandates (Hepner 2011).

Although my research with Eritreans does not indicate a clear or causal relationship between seeking asylum and articulating a specific political or rights-based consciousness, almost all Eritrean asylum seekers describe making an active decision at some point to pursue their own "durable solution." And at least some indicate that the process of becoming and being a refugee has shaped their understanding of what it means to struggle for legal recognition and rights (Hepner 2009b). This refugee process encompasses the reasons they fled from Eritrea, the various experiences of seeking protection in camps or cities, and/or the journey to a country where they believe their chances of securing permanent protection are more promising. The problems and challenges encountered along the way inevitably shape political and legal subjectivities. These range from brutal exploitation by traffickers (see van Reisen, Estefanos, and Rijken 2012), the callous treatment meted out by migration authorities (including the UNHCR), and confinement in detention centers and asylum houses to the bureaucratic surrealism of rendering social suffering and trauma meaningful, "credible," and sufficiently individualized in asylum interviews and hearings. Some people reflect on these experiences more than others, of course, and not all possess the education or critical thinking skills to move beyond the biographical narrative description painstakingly elicited by lawyers and other advocates. A few, however, not only reflect critically on the refugee experience but also become activists on their own and others' behalf. And still others demonstrate how shifting subjectivities prompt them to theorize and strategize new sociopolitical possibilities for Eritrea and its diasporas.

Among the hundreds of thousands of Eritreans who have sought refuge and asylum since 2001, my ethnographic work has identified how differentiated layers of activists have emerged and coalesced into various organized efforts to represent their interests and concerns as forced migrants from an authoritarian regime (see Hepner 2012b). These refugee activists have advanced strategies to address and transform the conditions in Eritrea that create refugees; they have organized within camps and urban centers to confront immediate conditions and the possibilities for durable solutions; and they have exposed the violence and exploitation inherent in perilous extralegal migration routes (precipitated in many ways by the failures of legal migration establishments). In demanding attention and action from governments, NGOs, the UNHCR, and regional governance and human rights bodies such as the European Union and European Court of Human Rights, Eritreans are active subjects responding to specific political and legal dilemmas.

The activism observable among Eritrean refugees and asylum seekers highlights their agency and in some cases explicitly reveals how the refugee or asylum process can be a transformative one in terms of political consciousness and the articulation of more complex political and legal subject positions. But the ethnographic evidence also suggests an instrumental and strategic dimension to this. At least some asylum seekers in the United States and Europe describe how they joined political opposition movements or became refugee activists in order to enhance their own chances of securing asylum. In Ethiopia, Eritrean refugees often accused one another of making alliances with Ethiopian government and refugee agencies or becoming vocal and active in the camps, in order to strengthen the substance of their claims and to become eligible for "rewards" through the refugee system (including resettlement). Kristin Bergtora Sandvik (2011) has examined how such strategies were deployed by Congolese and other refugees in Uganda, where politically contentious, strategizing refugees tended to receive the most attention and secure the best opportunities but "good" refugees languished in obscurity. The thematizing of refugee or asylum stories, in which people coach one another on what authorities want or need to hear, is also a major dynamic in which refugees may claim a set of experiences or political opinions that are not, in fact, their own because these are believed to "work" (Harmon-Gross 2009). And in several cases, asylum seekers described to me how lawyers suggested they become visibly active in political movements in the diaspora, including having their photographs taken at demonstrations and published online, in order to strengthen their claims. Some lawyers I spoke with confirmed that this was not uncommon in the counseling process.

These data suggest several crucial issues at work here. First, there is no *necessary* connection between refugee/asylum experiences and genuine, critical political consciousness or activism, although for some there does appear to be a strong correlation—even a productive tension—in which the refugee process is a radicalizing one. Second, when researchers serving as expert witnesses evaluate and contextualize a particular claim, they are in some sense participating in a performance in which the facts may be less representative of the individual's experience and more reflective of how the collective circumstances facing a national population interface with the specific requirements of asylum policy and law. How we contribute our knowledge to support a claim can therefore have several related but quite disparate implications. We may possibly contribute to transformative consciousness and even activism among refugees as we help reflect on the larger context in which their lives have unfolded, typically couching these in terms of a rights discourse. We may participate (unknowingly?) in the "falsification" of specific claims in order to highlight the more general context in which any given claim might be meaningful. And we engage in a strategic essentialization of the collective political, cultural, and social context in order to demonstrate the validity of the specific claim. In short, the lines between refugee agency and political-legal strategy are blurry at best and hopelessly entangled at worst. Researchers as expert witnesses and/or activists are heavily implicated, whether we like it or not. Although our contributions may lead to an ossification of a more dynamic, fluid, and ambivalent reality when encoded as authoritative knowledge in the strategic service of law, they also help achieve tangible solutions for people in desperate, vulnerable situations, at least some of whom are struggling to challenge and transform the conditions that precipitated their suffering. The picture becomes yet more complex when we situate all of this in a transnational context that accounts for the ongoing influence of the sending state in the lives and political-legal dilemmas facing refugees, asylum seekers, and expert witnesses.

## Asylum and Transnational Political Pressures

Long before the advent of rapid communications technologies and other trappings of globalization, migrants and diaspora communities maintained linkages with their sending states and societies (Glick Schiller 1999) and were important players in political struggles ranging from decolonization to revolution. Eritreans are among the best contemporary examples of this. As I have argued elsewhere, the Eritrean nation-state and the thirty-year war of independence that created it was a thoroughly transnational process to which refugees and exiles made essential political and economic contributions (Hepner 2009a). This enabled the historical development of a transnational social field in which the government has maintained a considerable institutional and ideological presence, such that we can characterize Eritrea today as exemplifying forms of transnational governance and transnational civil society (Hepner 2003, 2005, 2008, 2009a, 2009b). Also of considerable import are organized political opposition movements, "civic societies" (autonomous, nonaligned voluntary organizations), and human and refugee rights initiatives that challenge the Eritrean government's legitimacy and authoritarian power. Not surprisingly, among those active in these organizations are refugees and asylees of different "vintages" (Koehn 1991) who fled Eritrea at various periods of crippling political and economic conditions.

Eritrea's transnational realities continue to shape the refugee process in both dramatic and subtle ways. Whether migration leads people to neighboring countries such as Ethiopia and Sudan or to distant locations such as the United States and Europe, refugees and asylum seekers find that they remain embedded in—and are often "recaptured" politically, financially, or even physically by—the transnational reach of the Eritrean state (see Hepner 2009a; Hepner and Tecle 2013). The Eritrean state, moreover, remains cognizant of the need to maintain acquiescence, if not genuine consent or support, among refugees and asylum seekers, on whom it relies for ongoing economic infusions through the 2 percent diaspora tax, remittances, and other financial transactions. There is also considerable pressure on recent refugees and asylum seekers wherever they go, from refugee camps to urban centers in the Global North, to either remain silent on matters of politics—to not join the opposition or initiatives based on human rights, for example—or to become visible participants in these same organizations. Many earlier refugees who are active with opposition organizations admonish recent arrivals to demonstrate their political critique of the conditions and government from which they fled. There is an expectation among members of opposition groups, especially veterans of the independence war, that new refugees and asylum seekers should automatically articulate a political critique because they have fled from a militarized, authoritarian regime.

This presumed causal link between the refugee process and a critical political consciousness, as I noted earlier, is more complicated than it appears. My research suggests that the majority of recent refugees or asylum seekers from Eritrea do not become politically active in the diaspora, and some even appear to support the regime after migrating by contributing finances or attending regime-sanctioned events. Several factors help explain this, many of them related to the transnational realities that structure Eritrean life at home and in the diaspora. First, most recent refugees and asylum seekers from Eritrea have lived much of their lives in the postindependence dispensation in which militarization is the common denominator shaping social life. The militarization of education (Müller 2009; Riggan 2009), long-term conscription, and emphasis on strict obedience and conformity have produced a generation of young people whose critical thinking skills and political imaginations are thwarted by the constant threat of violent repression. Second, those who leave Eritrea illegally, as most refugees and asylum seekers do, are painfully aware that repercussions on their families will follow: authorities in Eritrea routinely fine the parents of absconders 50,000 nakfa (about USD 4,775 at the time of writing) and often imprison them for periods of time.[6] The Eritrean government also pressures refugees and asylees to sign a document of regret known as *te'asa*. The te'asa is essentially a formal written apology to the government of Eritrea for "betraying" the nation by becoming a refugee and a pledge to remain quiet on matters of politics. As a result of these coercive measures, many asylum seekers and refugees eschew any association with opposition movements or human rights initiatives and even participate in social events sponsored by the government itself as strategies of protection for themselves and their loved ones in Eritrea. These people are then criticized by members of the opposition and sometimes accused of being "fake" refugees or asylees. The issue is even more contentious if asylum seekers have followed the advice of attorneys and joined an opposition party for matters of strategic legal expediency.

The government's use of the te'asa and punishments meted out on loved ones in Eritrea are examples of transnational leverage exerted by the state on refugees and asylees. Evidence gathered in Germany suggests that the Eritrean transnational government has pressured asylum seekers not only to sign the te'asa but also to pay additional fines and sign other documents, such as a recent petition condemning UN Security Council resolutions to block arms shipments to Eritrea due to its alleged backing of Somali militants. In cases where refugees have traveled using a *nom du migration,* Eritrean authorities may issue the passport in the false name, while retaining the migrant's real name on his or her Eritrean national identity card. Should the person become active in opposition movements or otherwise get out of line, Eritrean authorities can threaten to expose to German authorities the false passport identification. Beyond these forms of asylum-specific coercion, the Eritrean government uses *seleyti* (spies) to help keep track of who is where in order to demand the payment of the annual 2 percent income tax on all diaspora residents. Clearly, asylum seekers are in the most vulnerable position should they refuse to pay.

The situation demonstrates that transnational political pressures exert considerable force on Eritrean refugees and asylum seekers, and neither the specific decisions they make and strategies they pursue nor their political identities and behaviors can be understood apart from this reality. That some Eritreans do develop a critical consciousness, voice clearly dissident political opinions, and muster the courage to become activists in the diaspora is a minority trend. These nuances can produce considerable difficulty with respect to the convention definition of a refugee insofar as it presumes that political and economic factors, on one side, and sending and receiving countries, on the other, are *separate and distinct.* For instance, Israel has witnessed a dramatic influx of Eritrean asylum seekers in recent years, many of whom are involved in a highly visible, rights-based movement responding to the country's poor refugee status determination procedures and detention practices (see Yaron, Hashimshony-Yaffe, and Campbell 2013). Together with Israeli human and refugee rights activists, Eritreans have pushed back against these policies and reactionary public discourses that refer to them as "infiltrators," economic migrants, and military deserters. The Eritrean government, for its part, has promoted the view of Eritreans as ineligible for asylum by similarly referring to them as deserters and economic migrants (see Hepner 2012a).

In late 2013, I was asked by colleagues in Tel Aviv to write an expert report for the Minister of the Interior clarifying how flight from compulsory military service may represent a dissident political opinion and is invariably construed as such by Eritrean authorities. In particular, I had to address the confounding fact that many Eritrean asylum seekers were unable to express to Israeli authorities a clearly "dissident" political opinion that was unmuddled by economic factors—for example, "I left because I could not provide food for my family" or "I wanted opportunities to work or go to school but was forced to be a soldier." I took considerable pains to explain in my report how political and economic repression is endemic in forced military conscription, which may last for many years despite Eritrea's own legal maximum of eighteen months. For instance, I had interviewed encamped Eritrean refugees in northern Ethiopia who described being beaten, tortured, and accused of dissidence for getting caught earning extra pay (by fixing cars or the like) while conscripted. Moreover, students must complete the senior year of high school at the military training facility, and the University of Asmara no longer exists; colleges are geographically scattered technical outposts under military control. Harsh punishment is exacted on conscripts for even minor offenses that suggest a dissident political opinion (such as asking for more food because it implies a critique of the government for not feeding soldiers well).

To even mention politics, let alone express an opinion, can result in detention, beatings, hard labor, and torture. For those safely abroad, furthermore, finding and using one's political voice can bring punishment on family left behind. It is therefore unsurprising that young people raised in Eritrea today would have difficulty expressing the kind of political opinions that adjudicators in more liberal societies expect; neither the objective conditions in Eritrea nor the subjective experience of militarization enables the separation of political and economic realities from freedom of conscience and expression. Moreover, Eritrea is not just constituted geographically; the government and its repressive capacities are deterritorialized and transnational. What requires more explanation is how so many Eritrean refugees, albeit a minority, do find a political voice and the courage to organize.

Academic researchers who serve as expert witnesses possess nuanced knowledge not only of sending country conditions but also, ideally, of diasporic and transnational realities that impinge on migrants' ability to make effective refugee and asylum claims, as well as their changing consciousness and identities. This can certainly enhance the ability of the expert to assess an asylum claim and comment on the larger context, yet it also contributes to some of the dilemmas noted earlier. If an asylum claim is based on a person's political activism in the diaspora, how can the experts be certain that this activism is the genuine expression of a political opinion and not simply a strategic move? The answer is that we cannot. And conversely, how can we use our nuanced understandings to press the limitations of the convention definition of a refugee, which, as Meredith Terretta points out (in this volume), unrealistically separates the political from the economic and views the sending country as geographically contained rather than transnationally constructed?

We experts may therefore find ourselves discussing contextual scenarios that may or may not have anything to do with the authenticity of an individual claim and, in the process, participating in the reification of a more complex lived reality that is at odds with our actual knowledge and findings outside the asylum context. Alternatively, we may find that our nuanced understandings and argumentative abilities push convention definitions—and perhaps even asylum case law—to fit more effectively with these complex realities.

Our knowledge of the exigencies faced by refugees who exist uneasily in transnational spaces and must contend with political pressures of the sending state also makes us enormously useful as collaborating partners with our research community. That is, when researchers and refugees together generate information and cotheorize the dilemmas faced in countries of origin and in the various locations through which migrants move and where they settle, we can develop richer analyses; moreover, we can also help with devising legal strategies to combat corruption within refugee regimes and transnational interference by states and other political actors. If we are successful in these endeavors—and certainly when our knowledge aids in rulings that establish precedent—we are actively engaged in shaping the political and legal constraints that impinge on refugees. And thus, a key part of the asylum-advocacy nexus is how it forms a coherent, if troubled, circle of praxis, in which advocacy or activism enriches research and knowledge; aids refugees in tangible ways; contributes to their changing political and legal subjectivities; and participates in shaping the policies, laws, and practices that structure the refugee experience itself.

## Conclusion: Fertile or Fraught?

Is the asylum-advocacy nexus a site where researchers' commitments to accurate, critical, and nuanced knowledge of sending countries and diaspora communities is hopelessly compromised by a range of dynamics endemic to the legal and policy procedures and the larger political-economic contexts in which refugee migration and asylum seeking occurs? Or is the asylum-advocacy nexus a fertile arena where new analytical insights, forms of collaboration with research communities, and strategies for activism and the transformation of policies, laws, and practices may take place? I would suggest it is all of these things. To return to Speed's formulation, anthropologists, by virtue of their disciplinary training, are critically engaged in nuanced, complex cultural analysis. When their knowledge is put to work for strategic and activist or advocacy-oriented goals, spaces may open up—including problematic dilemmas—that provide additional opportunities for theory building and political, legal, and cultural critique. As Speed (2006, 71) puts it, although cultural analysis and activism "are distinct and often are carried out separately . . . the two can be productively practiced together, as part of one undertaking. This does not mean that the multiple tensions and contradictions that exist between them cease to exist, but, instead, that these are productive tensions that we might strive to benefit from analytically, rather than seeking to avoid."

The choice thus does not seem to be between acting or not acting, for, as Scheper-Hughes (1995), Farmer and Gastineau (2002), and others have argued, the very privilege afforded to those who amass considerable knowledge about a particular place, population, or set of issues entails a responsibility to engage on behalf of vulnerable or exploited people. My analysis has suggested that our very research and knowledge complicate the easy categorization or support of refugees and asylum seekers who themselves act strategically within the context of policies, legal procedures, and the politics of their own communities. But I nonetheless embrace the view that scholars can and should put their expertise to work on behalf of research populations to counter the "epistemology of ignorance" endemic to the courts (Bohmer and Shuman 2007 and in this volume; Campbell, this volume) and enduring violations experienced abroad. The key, however, is to remain critical and highly aware of the various implications of doing so, to adjust one's methods and strategies accordingly, and to draw upon all that is fraught in the asylum-advocacy nexus to enhance its fertility in the service of knowledge and social justice.

## Notes

1. I tend to use *refugee* and *asylum seeker* more or less interchangeably throughout this chapter. My research among Eritreans includes those who are recognized refugees by UNHCR as well as those seeking asylum under various domestic legal systems. I use *refugee process* to refer to the conditions of flight and/or encampment and *asylum process* to refer to the domestic legal procedures in specific countries.

2. Clearly, not all asylum applicants read expert reports or possess an understanding and awareness of the legal process deciding their fates. However, as Tague's chapter (in this volume) illustrates, refugees and asylum seekers are internally diverse according to class and educational level, and those who "make it" to North America and Europe are often more privileged than those who stay behind. My research has involved interviewing successful asylum applicants about their subjective experiences with the asylum process itself. Many of the Eritrean asylees I have worked with as an anthropologist and expert witness are well-educated men and women (among them trained lawyers) who take considerable interest in the content of their asylum case files and actively engage with the process. A few have gone on to become asylum lawyers or counselors.

3. The Eritrean government construes applying for asylum as an act of political dissidence at best and treason at worst. Two asylum seekers deported to Eritrea from Germany described how they were detained, beaten, interrogated, tortured, and explicitly called traitors for having fled military conscription and sought asylum in Germany. Their experience is typical and well documented by the German NGO Connection e.V. (2010).

4. I have provided written and/or oral testimony in an estimated 275 to 300 asylum cases since 2004. The vast majority of these have been pro bono cases in the United States.

5. Related "anthropologies" include public, collaborative, strategic, and (perhaps more generally and less activist or political in connotation) applied anthropology.

6. Anthony Good (2007, 60) describes a similar phenomenon among Tamils vis-à-vis the Liberation Tigers of Tamil Eelam, or LTTE.

## References

Agier, Michel. 2007. *On the Margins of the World: The Refugee Experience Today*. Cambridge: Polity Press.

Besteman, Catherine. 2010. "In and Out of the Academy: Policy and the Case for a Strategic Anthropology." *Human Organization* 69 (4): 407–17.

Betts, Alexander. 2009. *Forced Migration and Global Politics*. Malden, MA: Wiley-Blackwell.

Bohmer, Carol, and Amy Shuman. 2007. "Producing Epistemologies of Ignorance in the Political Asylum Application Process." *Identities* 14 (5): 603–29.

———. 2008. *Rejecting Refugees: Political Asylum in the 21st Century*. London: Routledge.

Castles, Stephen, and Nicolas Van Hear. 2005. "The Migration-Asylum Nexus: Definition and Significance." Oxford University, COMPASS, January 27. Accessed June 12, 2009. http://www.compas.ox.ac.uk/.

Connection e.V. 2010. *Eritrea—Desertion and Asylum*. Offenbach, Germany: Connection e.V.

Coutin, Susan Bibler. 2000. *Legalizing Moves: Salvadoran Immigrants' Struggle for U.S. Residency*. Ann Arbor: University of Michigan Press.

Farmer, Paul, and Nicole Gastineau. 2002. "Rethinking Health and Human Rights: Time for a Paradigm Shift." *Journal of Law, Medicine, and Ethics* 30:655–66.

Glick Schiller, Nina. 1999. "Transmigrants and Nation-States: Something Old and Something New in the U.S. Immigrant Experience." In *The Handbook of International Migration: The American Experience*, edited by Charles Hirschman, Philip Kasinitz, and Josh DeWind, 94–119. New York: Russell Sage Foundation.

Good, Anthony. 2004. "'Undoubtedly an Expert'? Anthropologists in British Asylum Courts." *Journal of the Royal Anthropological Institute* 10 (1): 113–33.

———. 2007. *Anthropology and Expertise in the Asylum Courts*. Abingdon, UK: Routledge-Cavendish.

Haraway, Donna. 1988. "Situated Knowledges: The Science Question in Feminism and the Privilege of Partial Perspective." *Feminist Studies* 14 (3): 575–99.

Harmon-Gross, Elizabeth C. 2009. "Seeking Resettlement and Navigating Transnational Politics: The Intersection of Policies, Human Rights, and Individuals in Shimelba Refugee Camp." MA thesis, Department of Anthropology, University of Tennessee.

Hepner, Tricia Redeker. 2003. "Religion, Nationalism, and Transnational Civil Society in the Eritrean Diaspora." *Identities: Global Studies in Culture and Power* 10 (3): 269–93.

———. 2005. "Transnational Tegadelti: Eritreans for Liberation in North America and the Eritrean People's Liberation Front." *Eritrean Studies Review* 4 (2): 37–83.

———. 2008. "Transnational Governance and the Centralization of State Power in Eritrea and Exile." *Ethnic and Racial Studies* 31 (3): 476–502.

———. 2009a. *Soldiers, Martyrs, Traitors and Exiles: Political Conflict in Eritrea and the Diaspora*. Philadelphia: University of Pennsylvania Press.

———. 2009b. "Seeking Asylum in a Transnational Social Field: Struggles for Autonomy and Human Rights." In *Biopolitics, Militarism and Development: Eritrea in the 21st Century*, edited by David O'Kane and Tricia Redeker Hepner, 115–33. New York: Berghahn Books.

———. 2011. "Human Tsunamis: Refugees and the Failure of Forced Migration Policy." *Counterpunch*, April 26.

————. 2012a. "Open Letter to Israel: Eritreans Are Not Economic Refugees." *Maariv,* June 6. [Published in Hebrew; English document on file with author].

————. 2012b. "Militarization, Generational Conflict and the Eritrean Refugee Crisis." In *African Childhoods: Education, Peacebuilding, Development and the Youngest Continent,* edited by Marisa O. Ensor, 109–26. New York: Palgrave Macmillan.

————. 2013. "Emergent Eritrean Human Rights Movements: Politics, Law and Culture in Transnational Perspective." In *Worlds of Human Rights: Ambiguities of Rights Claiming in Africa,* edited by William Derman, Anne Hellum, and Kristin Bergtora Sandvik, 277–302. Leiden: Brill.

————. 2014. "Religion, Repression and Human Rights in Eritrea and the Diaspora." *Journal of Religion in Africa* 44:151–88.

Hepner, Tricia Redeker, and Samia Tecle. 2013. "New Refugees, Development-Forced Displacement, and Transnational Governance in Eritrea and Exile." *Urban Anthropology and Studies of Cultural Systems and World Economic Development* 42 (3-4): 377–410.

Human Rights First (HRF). 2009. *Denial and Delay: The Impact of the Immigration Law's "Terrorism Bars" on Asylum Seekers and Refugees in the United States.* http://www .humanrightsfirst.info/pdf/RPP-DenialandDelay-FULL-111009-web.pdf.

Huysmans, Jef. 2006. *The Politics of Insecurity: Fear, Migration, and Asylum in the EU.* London: Routledge.

Hyndman, Jennifer, and Allison Mountz. 2008. "Another Brick in the Wall? Neorefoulement and the Externalisation of Asylum in Europe & Australia." *Government and Opposition* 43 (2): 249–69.

Koehn, Peter. 1991. *Refugees from Revolution: U.S. Policy and Third-World Migration.* Boulder, CO: Westview Press.

Mahmood, Cynthia. 1996. "Asylum, Violence, and the Limits of Advocacy." *Human Organization* 55 (4): 493–97.

Mountz, Allison. 2010. *Seeking Asylum: Human Smuggling and Bureaucracy at the Border.* Minneapolis: University of Minnesota Press.

Müller, Tanja. 2009. "Human Resource Development and the State: Higher Education in Postrevolutionary Eritrea." In *Biopolitics, Militarism and Development: Eritrea in the Twenty-First Century,* edited by David O'Kane and Tricia Redeker Hepner, 53–71. New York: Berghahn Books.

Nagengast, Carole, and Carlos M. Velez-Ibañez, eds. 2004. *Human Rights: The Scholar as Activist.* Oklahoma City: Society for Applied Anthropology.

Price, Matthew E. 2009. *Rethinking Asylum: History, Purpose and Limits.* Cambridge: Cambridge University Press.

Ramji-Nogales, Jaya, Andrew I. Schoenholtz, and Philip G. Schrag. 2009. *Refugee Roulette: Disparities in Asylum Adjudication and Proposals for Reform.* New York: NYU Press.

Riggan, Jennifer. 2009. "Avoiding Wastage by Making Soldiers: Technologies of the State and the Imagination of the Educated Nation." In *Biopolitics, Militarism and Development: Eritrea in the Twenty-First Century,* edited by David O'Kane and Tricia Redeker Hepner, 72–91. New York: Berghahn Books.

Sandvik, Kristin Bergtora. 2011. "Blurring Boundaries: Refugee Resettlement in Kampala—Between the Formal, the Informal, and the Illegal." *PoLAR: Political and Legal Anthropology Review* 34 (1): 11–32.

Scheper-Hughes, Nancy. 1995. "The Primacy of the Ethical: Propositions for a Militant Anthropology." *Current Anthropology* 36 (3): 409–40.

Speed, Shannon. 2006. "At the Crossroads of Human Rights and Anthropology: Towards a Critically-Engaged Activist Research." *American Anthropologist* 108 (1): 66–76.

Tazreiter, Claudia. 2004. *Asylum Seekers and the State: The Politics of Protection in a Security-Conscious World*. Aldershot, UK: Ashgate.

Turner, Simon. 2009. *Politics of Innocence: Hutu Identity, Conflict, and Camp Life*. New York: Berghahn Books.

United Nations High Commissioner for Refugees. 2011. *UNHCR Global Trends 2001: A Year of Crises*. Accessed 23 August 2012.

van Reisen, Mirjam, Meron Estefanos, and Conny Rijken. 2012. *Human Trafficking in the Sinai: Refugees between Life and Death*. Brussels: Tilburg University and European External Policy Advisors.

Verdirame, Guglielmo, and Barbara Harrell-Bond. 2005. *Rights in Exile: Janus-Faced Humanitarianism*. New York: Berghahn Books.

Wolf, Diane, ed. 1996. *Feminist Dilemmas in Fieldwork*. Boulder, CO: Westview Press.

Yaron Hadas, Nurit Hashimshony-Yaffe, and John Campbell. 2013. "'Infiltrators' or Refugees? An Analysis of Israel's Policies towards African Asylum Seekers." *International Migration* 51 (4): 144–57.

# AFTERWORD

Fallou Ngom

THE BOOK BRINGS together a unique group of scholars working on various aspects of African asylum cases in developed countries, an emerging field at the crossroads of African studies, anthropology, history, human rights, immigration and international law, and linguistics. Although many of the cases examined in the book are from the United States (with a few from the United Kingdom, the Netherlands, Switzerland, South Africa, Israel, and Canada), the central issues addressed mirror those in asylum cases in Germany, Sweden, Belgium, Australia, and New Zealand.

Despite the localized procedural differences in the adjudication of African asylum cases, the primary preoccupation across Western governments is to discern genuine asylum seekers who deserve assistance from the fraudulent ones, the so-called economic asylum seekers who attempt to misuse the system. The task is not easy, as both genuine and bogus asylum seekers generally arrive in the host countries with no reliable forms of identification to validate their claims, as Meredith Terretta discusses in her chapter.

The chapters of the book provide an excellent overview and in-depth analysis of a range of procedural, political, ethical, and cultural challenges inherently involved in the serious process of identifying legitimate African asylum cases. The volume is the first collective work of its kind to bring together a diverse group of specialists from disciplines that generally stand apart. The authors include lawyers, historians, and anthropologists with firsthand experience in this new interdisciplinary field, a field that also increasingly calls for the expertise of professional linguists who serve as experts in the initial phases of the asylum application and as contra-experts in appeal cases.

Naturally, a groundbreaking book of this kind cannot realistically do justice to all aspects of asylum applications that African claimants file in developed countries beyond the United States. Although Carol Bohmer and Amy Shuman briefly examine the flaws found in some practices of Language Analysis for the Determination of Origin (LADO), also known as Language Analysis, the invitation to offer an afterword presents me with an opportunity to bring linguistic analysis to the table. LADO is an important procedure in the validations and invalidations of the asylum claims in Australia, Belgium, Germany, the Netherlands, Sweden, Switzerland, and New Zealand, as John Campbell (2013), Diana Eades (2005, 2009), Eades and Jacques Arends (2004), Eades et al. (2003), Helen Fraser (2011), Noé Mahop Kam (2015), Tim McNamara and Carsten Roever (2006), Peter Patrick (2011, 2012), Maaike Verrips (2010, 2011), Karen Zawaa, Maaike Verrips, and Pieter Muysken (2010), and others demonstrate.

Language analysis has not yet become a significant part of North American asylum adjudication systems. However, with its recurrent use in several Western countries and the growing number of European private companies that specialize in providing language analyses to immigration agencies seeking to expand their businesses outside of Europe, it is only a matter of time before the practice reaches the United States and Canada.

As the chapters herein demonstrate, asylum has become a highly charged political issue across developed countries, raising a host of difficult ethical issues and political questions ranging from the responsibilities that the world's richest countries have to refugees arriving at their borders to whether nations are justified in implementing measures to prevent the influx of economic migrants if those measures also block entry for refugees (Gibney 2004). Though many people apply for asylum for genuine reasons, some undoubtedly use the asylum procedure to immigrate to developed countries in search of better opportunities by claiming that they are eligible for asylum.

LADO is performed in cases where the applicant's claimed place of origin is doubted by authorities in the Western countries listed earlier. The practice is grounded in the belief that one's speech necessarily contains typical features of one's country of origin. Thus, asylum applicants are interviewed and recorded, and their speech is subsequently analyzed in order to determine whether their linguistic features (phonological, lexical, morphological, and so on) are consistent with the patterns typically found in the speech communities from where they claim to come. The results of the language analysis are used for two main purposes. They are used to validate or invalidate the applicant's claim and to determine the country to which the applicant should be deported in case the asylum application is denied.

This use of language to identify the origin of people is neither restricted to African asylum applicants nor new in human history. As Michael Erard (2003) notes, because the number of asylum seekers increased in the 1990s as the Soviet Union fell and war erupted in the Balkans and throughout West Africa, the Swedish Migration Board pioneered a modern version of the Bible's "shibboleth test" for authenticating the claims of some asylum seekers. Erard historicizes the use of LADO. In the book of Judges 12:6 of the Hebrew Bible, the pronunciation of the word *shibboleth* (meaning "floodwater"), he notes, was used to distinguish members of the Ephraim group, whose dialect lacked a *sh* sound, from the Gilead tribe, whose dialect did include the sound. The inhabitants of Gilead tried to identify their enemies among the hordes fleeing a key battle and designed the test to expose foes, who could not pronounce the *sh* in the word, and expel them from the land of Ephraim. Anyone who wanted to escape by crossing the Jordan River had to say *shibboleth*.

According to the book of Judges, forty-two thousand men of Ephraim perished for want of the correct sibilant. Similar tests have also been used in Nigeria and Sri Lanka. During the Nigerian civil war in the late 1960s, government soldiers stationed at roadblocks made travelers say *tóró* (the Yoruba word meaning "three pence") in order to cull Igbo "rebels" from the general public; those who said *tóló* were arrested and sometimes assaulted. Additionally, during fierce rioting by the Sinhalese majority population against the Tamils in Sri Lanka in 1983, the police stopped civilians and asked them to say the Sinhalese word for bucket, *baldiya*. Tamils were killed for saying *paldiya* (Erard 2003).

Nowadays, a more elaborate shibboleth test is used to regulate national borders and to determine the origin of asylum seekers whose only form of identification may be their bodies, as many refugees avoid carrying documents for legitimate reasons. If they belong to a persecuted group back home, they might not have been able to get identification cards; they may have fled their homes too quickly to collect their requisite papers; or they may have discarded their documents for their protection or on the advice of smugglers (Erard 2003). Similarly, allegedly bogus asylum seekers often fail to present travel documents in an attempt to hide their national origin.

The difficulties in reliably identifying genuine asylum seekers have led many developed nations to resort to LADO, the twenty-first century's shibboleth test. The practice is one of the latest developments in the broader field of linguistics. It falls within the subfield of so-called forensic linguistics, an emerging area that studies the use of linguistic evidence in legal contexts. As Eades (2005, 504) correctly observes, though linguists have dealt with a number of aspects of criminal and civil cases for the past two decades, the most recent legal area in which linguists are becoming involved is the use of language analysis in the investigation of nationality claims made by asylum seekers.

However, LADO has faced serious criticism and challenges from the outset. Very often, there is extremely limited research conducted on applicants' speech communities and languages, and experts specializing in the given languages are difficult to find. As a result, some governments have resorted to using native speakers with limited or no training in linguistics to conduct these serious language analyses.

Because many of the native speakers who served as experts lacked the necessary academic training, their analyses and final conclusions were often determined to be scientifically unfounded by numerous linguists who reviewed their reports during the appeal phases in which they participated as contraexperts.

Although the linguists did not dispute the assumption that people's spontaneous speech contains features of their speech communities, they strongly disputed several aspects of the processes involved in this form of linguistic identification, including the qualification of the government experts, the nature of the data they analyzed, their methods of analysis, and the simplistic assumptions about language that pervaded their reports (Eades 2005). The concerns of the linguists largely stemmed from the fact that many of the experts who performed the language analyses had no verifiable linguistic training, as their reports demonstrated. The most important requirement that qualified them to be experts was that they were native speakers of the languages in question, born and raised in the countries where the applicants claimed to come from. The situation led Eades (2005, 512) to note that language analysis was not valid or reliable because it was based on "folk views" about the relationship between language, nationality, and ethnicity rather than on sound linguistic principles; furthermore, she asserted that although people often believe that they can determine a speaker's place of origin from his or her use of particular words or pronunciation, such judgments are not always validated by linguistic research.

Additionally, some immigration lawyers complained about the lack of uniform standards for evaluating the language analyses, and they argued that the governments in question should not heavily rely on them as evidence because the procedure was flawed. To highlight the flaws embedded in the procedure, Erard (2003) emphasized the Australian government's disagreement with Eqvator and Sprakab (two Swedish companies that conduct language analysis in asylum cases) for failing to use the International Phonetic Alphabet, the standard phonetic alphabet used by linguists. The Scottish court has also recently issued a critical assessment of the works of Sprakab (BAILII Databases 2013).

The reliability of these language analyses was also challenged by a group of Australian linguists. Their investigation found that these two companies contradicted the applicants' claims in 48 of 58 cases, but when those 48 applicants appealed, 35 of them were granted asylum. According to Erard (2003), this finding led an Australian judge to note in one case that "there is no indication of the qualification or experience of the person who provided the linguistic analysis." Because many analysts lacked the proper linguistic training, they justified their assessments with nothing more than an explanation that "they stem from the country in question and know how they speak there" (Bobda, Wolf, and Peter 1999, 301).

The problems in the use of LADO are particularly serious in cases of asylum applicants who speak less studied African languages that have several dialects, such as Fula. Fula (also referred to as Fulani, Fulfulde, Peul, Pular, or Pulaar) is one of the most widely distributed West Atlantic languages of the Niger Congo phylum in West Africa. The language has over twenty dialects and is spoken in more than fifteen countries by over 15 million people. Despite its wide distribution in West Africa, the features of its numerous dialects, their interactions, and the specific communities where each variety is typically spoken remain largely unstudied.

Consequently, it is quite easy for untrained native speakers (even when supervised by qualified linguists with limited or no experience in the region) to conclude mistakenly that Fula speakers from Guinea-Bissau, Sierra Leone, or Liberia (three countries that experienced civil wars in the 1990s) are not from where they claim but rather are from Senegal (among the more stable democracies in West Africa) and vice versa. In the cases involving Fula speakers, the presence of a few French loanwords in the applicants' speech was regularly treated as definite evidence that they came from the French-speaking countries of Senegal or Guinea Conakry, regardless of whether the words were parallel loans (words used across Fula varieties) or unilateral loans (words borrowed by a particular variety). The government experts also did not account for the significance and crucial differences between the applicants' fully incorporated loanwords (which have been in their language for so long that native speakers do not know their foreign origins) and partially and nonincorporated loanwords (which have retained part or all of their foreign features). Yet each of these patterns conveys important information about the level of education and the socialization history of the applicants. The misunderstanding of these linguistic patterns resulted in incorrect conclusions, leading to the likely denial of genuine asylum cases.

In some instances, certain Fula words commonly used in rural varieties in the speech of applicants were also taken as evidence against their claims simply because the government's native speaker expert hailed from an urban area and thus spoke the urban variety, which uses French or English loanwords in lieu of the applicants' rural Fula words. The process of new loanwords replacing their local synonyms is referred to as native synonym displacement. Although this phenomenon is a common process in language contact situations and has been documented in sociolinguistic scholarship (Duran-Deska and Duran 1994), it is often not taken into account in the reports on Fula cases conducted by the native speakers who serve as "experts." Because many of them come from urban areas and lack basic academic training in linguistics, their conclusions were anything but credible. Nonetheless, their reports were determinant in the approval, denial, and subsequent deportation of Fula asylum applicants.

Beyond that, some analysts regularly downplayed or simply ignored the complex evidence they could not account for with sound linguistic arguments, and they tended to emphasize features that might appear to be easy to explain. For example, the presence of a few French loanwords in Fula applicants' speech was often overemphasized as proof that the applicants originated from a French-speaking country, regardless of their understanding and pronunciation of the words in question or whether the words resulted from the influence of the interpreters. In many instances,

French loanwords initially used by the interpreter in the recording, and subsequently repeated by the applicants, were used against the applicants as evidence of their origin from a French-speaking country. But, in fact, the use of such words only demonstrated a well-known linguistic accommodation phenomenon—the natural repetition of linguistic features of one's interlocutor to reduce social distance.

These problems largely resulted from the prevailing assumption in some immigration agencies that being a native speaker of a language is a sufficient credential to serve as an expert, coupled with the popular belief that people from one country all speak the same way. Though this view is popular, it is based on a myth about the homogeneity of speech communities, one that has long been refuted in linguistic scholarship (Eades 2005, 511). Linguists unanimously appreciate the knowledge of native speakers, but extensive peer-reviewed linguistic research has demonstrated unequivocally that being a native speaker alone does not necessarily make an individual an expert in his or her language (Eades 2005, 522). Even if native speakers have intuitive knowledge of their native tongues, they are unable to account for the array of dialectal, sociolectal, idiolectal, genderlectal, and theolectal variations in their languages in a reliable scientific manner.

The challenges in the language analyses are compounded by the limited number of linguists specializing in the applicants' languages and the resulting limited research on variations and speech communities. Some linguists object to the practice of governments heavily relying on native speakers with questionable linguistic expertise as "experts" authorized to conduct such intricate language analyses, given the serious consequences for some of the world's most vulnerable individuals. They deem such language analyses to be ethically and scientifically indefensible because the conclusions of the putative experts have allegedly resulted in the erroneous denial of asylum applications submitted by people who genuinely deserved assistance; in some cases, this has triggered their wrongful deportation to countries where they have never even resided.

Many reports by government Fula experts demonstrate that the interpreters and interviewers who elicited the data used in the language analyses, as well as the experts who performed the analyses, needed to be trained in sociolinguistic research and methods of triggering and analyzing spontaneous speech. They require such training in order to overcome the grave reliability and objectivity challenges in the reports they produced. They also need to be aware of the artificial nature of political borders, the past and present population movements, and the centuries-old ethnic and linguistic ties between the Fula people that transcend political borders in West Africa (Ngom 2008).

Many of these recommendations were included in a document produced in 2004 by a group of concerned linguists, entitled "Guidelines for the Use of Language Analysis in Relation to Questions of National Origin in Refugee Cases" (broadly referred to as the *Guidelines*) (Eades 2005, 520–26). Eades provides a more detailed discussion on the concerns about the language analyses performed by government experts, which is beyond the scope of this afterword. The *Guidelines* were partly designed to assist immigration agencies in assessing the general validity of language analyses and offering them suggestions for best practice. The effort to raise awareness on the challenges in LADO endures, as evidenced by the recent creation of the Language and Asylum Research Group based at the University of Essex, whose primary goal is to foster scholarly inquiry on best practices in LADO.

Although some governments and private companies have yet to fully implement the recommendations contained within the *Guidelines,* others have significantly improved their language analysis methods by hiring analysts with postgraduate degrees; still others have implemented more rigorous supervision of their untrained native speaker experts. Some significant progress has been made since the first publication of the *Guidelines* in 2004, but there is still room for improvement to ensure (1) that the interviews with asylum applicants are conducted in ways that capture spontaneous speech, and (2) that both the linguistic and cultural data collected are analyzed based on up-to-date factual knowledge and peer-reviewed research on the region in question.

One area that needs particular attention entails devising customized interview models that elicit the asylum seekers' actual knowledge, especially gendered and taboo knowledge. Eliciting and assessing this kind of knowledge remains a concern that has yet to be addressed. For instance, young Fula women who claim to come from remote rural areas of Sierra Leone at the northern border with Guinea were often asked to describe and to talk about the people on the banknotes used in the country. For anyone familiar with the lives of women in the Fula cattle camps called *wuro* in the northern hinterlands of Sierra Leone, where these individuals claimed to come from, such questions were clearly inappropriate to test local knowledge. Such Fula women would typically be uneducated, and their knowledge base would be confined to the localized culture (pertaining to food, wedding rituals, songs, and so forth), as well as the local fauna and flora of their communities; hence, their interviews should be customized to target these areas.

Additionally, in the case of young Mandinka speakers of Senegambia (including Guinea-Bissau), asylum applicants claiming to have fled Guinea-Bissau during the 1999 civil war may be silent when asked questions about their circumcision rituals. Though silence is, indeed, what is expected of a young Mandinka man in such circumstances, that very silence may be misconstrued as evidence that the applicant lacks the knowledge of his claimed area of origin. Mandinka young men are taught not to divulge ritual secrets of circumcision to women and the uncircumcised people they call *soloma*. A response of silence is thus evidence of local cultural knowledge, certainly not the lack of it.

Many linguists share the goal of ensuring fairness and reliability in asylum cases for some of the world's most vulnerable individuals. The authors of this important book reveal a new promising area of fruitful disciplinary cross-fertilization. If pursued, the cross-pollination will engender insights that will be valuable to immigrant officials, lawyers, and scholars concerned with both the misuse of the asylum system and the need to assist those whose claims are credible.

### References

BAILII Databases. 2013. "*M.A.B.N. and Anor v The Advocate General for Scotland Representing the Secretary of State for the Home Department and Anor,*" ScotCS CSIH_68 (July 12, 2013). Accessed January 28, 2013. http://www.bailii.org /scot/cases/ScotCS/2013/2013CSIH68.html.

Bobda, Augustin S., H. G. Wolf, and L. Peter. 1999. "Identifying Regional and National Origin of English-Speaking Africans Seeking Asylum in Germany." *Forensic Linguistics* 6 (2): 300–319.

Campbell, John. 2013. "Language Analysis in the United Kingdom's Refugee Status Determination System: Seeing through Policy Claims about 'Expert Knowledge.'" *Ethnic and Racial Studies* 36 (4): 670–90.

Duran-Deska, A., and P. Duran. 1994. "La forme sonore des emprunts: Les mots anglais en polonais et en français." *Travaux: Cercle linguistique d'Aix-en-Provence* 12:79–105.

Eades, Diana. 2005. "Applied Linguistics and Language Analysis in Asylum Seeker Cases." *Applied Linguistics* 26 (4): 503–26.

———. 2009. "Testing the Claims of Asylum Seekers: The Role of Language Analysis." *Language Assessment Quarterly* 6:30–40.

Eades, Diana, and Jacques Arends, eds. 2004. "Language Analysis and Determination of Nationality." *International Journal of Speech, Language and the Law* 11 (2): 179–266.

Eades, D., H. Fraser, J. Siegel, T. McNamara, and B. Baker. 2003. "Linguistic Identification in the Determination of Nationality: A Preliminary Report." *Language Policy* 2 (2):179–99.

Erard, Michael. 2003. "Immigration by Shibboleth: Should a Refugee Be Judged by What He Says or How He Says It?" *Legal Affairs: The Magazine at the Intersection of Law and Life.* Accessed April 2, 2013. http://www.legalaffairs.org/issues /November-December-2003/story_erad_novdec03.msp.

Fraser, Helen. 2011. "The Role of Linguists and Native Speakers in Language Analysis for the Determination of Speaker Origin: A Response to Tina Cambier-Langeveld." *International Journal of Speech, Language and the Law* 18 (1): 121–30.

Gibney, Matthew J. 2004. *The Ethics and Politics of Asylum: Liberal Democracy and Response to Refugees.* New York: Cambridge University Press.

Kam, Noé Mahop. 2015. "Recovering the Sociological Identity of Asylum Seekers: Language Analysis for Determining National Origin in the European Union." In *Adjudicating Refugee and Asylum Status: The Role of Witness, Expertise, and Testimony,* edited by Benjamin N. Lawrance and Galya Ruffer, 54–83. Cambridge: Cambridge University Press.

McNamara, Tim, and Carsten Roever. 2006. *Language Testing: The Social Dimension.* Oxford: Blackwell Publishing.

Ngom, Fallou. 2008. "Forensic Language Analysis in Asylum Applications of African Refugees: Challenges and Promises." In *Migrations and Creative Expressions in Africa and the Diaspora,* edited by Toyin Falola and Niyi Afolabi, 219–37. Durham, NC: Carolina Academic Press.

Patrick, Peter L. 2011. "Key Problems in Language Analysis for the Determination of Origin." Plenary address to the International Association of Forensic Linguistics Tenth Biennial Conference at Aston University. Accessed January 28, 2014. http:// privatewww.essex.ac.uk/~patrickp/papers/IAFL10plenary_July2011.pdf.

———. 2012. "Language Analysis for Determination of Origin: Objective Evidence for Refugee Status Determination." In *The Oxford Handbook of Language and Law,* edited by Peter M. Tiersma and Lawrence M. Solan, 533–46. Oxford: Oxford University Press.

Verrips, Maaike. 2010. "Language Analysis and Contra-expertise in the Dutch Asylum Procedure." *International Journal of Speech, Language and the Law* 17 (2): 279–94.

———. 2011. "LADO and the Pressure to Draw Strong Conclusions: A Response to Tina Cambier-Langeveld." *International Journal of Speech, Language and the Law* 18 (1): 131–43.

Zawaa, Karin, Maaike Verrips, and Pieter Muysken, eds. 2010. *Language and Origin: The Role of Language in European Asylum Procedures—A Linguistic and Legal Survey.* Nijmegen, the Netherlands: Wolf Legal Publishers.

# About the Authors

**CAROL BOHMER** is Visiting Associate Professor at the Department of Government at Dartmouth College and a visiting lecturer at the Department of War Studies at King's College London. She has published a number of books and articles on issues relating to asylum, gender, public policy, and law. In her most recent book, *Rejecting Refugees: Political Asylum in the 21st Century* (with Amy Shuman, 2007), she investigates the asylum procedure in the United States and United Kingdom and asks whether the current practices of states reflect the moral and legal obligations to genuine refugees. http://www.dartmouth.edu/~govt/faculty/bohmer.html

**IRIS BERGER**, Vincent O'Leary Professor of History at the University at Albany, State University of New York, joined the Albany faculty in 1981. She has published numerous books and articles on both precolonial and colonial African history and on African women's history. Her most recent book, *South Africa in World History,* was published in 2009. Berger was director of the Women's Studies Program from 1981 to 1984, director of the Institute for Research on Women from 1991 to 1995, and chair of the Department of History from 2001 to 2007. Her administrative expertise has been an important factor in the honors she has received, such as the President's Award for Excellence in Academic Service, the Bread and Roses Award for Excellence in Service on Behalf of Gender Equity, and the Distinguished Africanist Award from the New York African Studies Association. She has received research fellowships from the National Endowment for the Humanities, the Social Science Research Council (SSRC), and the Rockefeller Foundation and has served as vice president for research of the American Historical Association and as president of the African Studies Association. She has been an editorial board member for four major journals and an editor of the *Journal of African History.* In addition, she was a member of the Board of Directors of the SSRC and a delegate to the American Council of Learned Societies. http://www.albany.edu/history/faculty/iris_berger.shtml

**JOHN CAMPBELL** is Reader in the Anthropology of Africa and Law in the Department of Anthropology and Sociology at the School of Oriental and African Studies (SOAS) in London. His has published papers on many aspects of development in Africa. Campbell joined SOAS in 2001, and his interests focus on development and refugees. Between January 2007 and January 2009, he undertook research funded by an ESRC Grant entitled "Refugees and the Law: An Ethnography of the British Asylum System," which followed refugees from Eritrea and Ethiopia who were seeking asylum in the United Kingdom. In April 2009, he convened a conference at SOAS to look at how European nations and the United States handle and assess asylum applications. (Papers from this conference can be found at www.nomadit.co.uk/refuge/.) He has recently published a book about statelessness in the Horn of Africa. http://www.soas.ac.uk /staff/staff30720.php

**BENJAMIN N. LAWRANCE** is the Hon. Barber B. Conable, Jr. Endowed Chair in International Studies at the Rochester Institute of Technology. He is a graduate of Stanford University and University College London, and his research interests include comparative and contemporary slavery and trafficking, citizenship, human rights, and asylum and refugee law. He has authored ten books, most recently *Amistad's Orphans: An Atlantic Story of Children, Slavery, and Smuggling* (2014); *Adjudicating Refugee and Asylum Status: The Role of Witness, Expertise, and Testimony* (with Galya Ruffer, 2015); and *Trafficking in Slavery's Wake* (with Richard L. Roberts, 2012). Lawrance is a legal consultant on the contemporary political, social, and cultural climate in West Africa. He has served as an expert witness for over 280 asylum claims of West Africans in fifteen countries. Lawrance is the recipient of several national and international awards, including a fellowship from the National Endowment for the Humanities and fellowships at Yale, Harvard, the University of Notre Dame, and the Rotary Foundation. He was also awarded an inaugural University of California President's Fellowship in the Humanities. http://www.lawrance.org

**KATHERINE LUONGO** is Associate Professor of History at Northeastern University. She studies legal systems in colonial and contemporary Africa and global legal regimes. She is particularly interested in the intersections of the supernatural, law, and politics in Africa and in the interactions of African witchcraft and forced migration. Her ethnography of Kamba witchcraft, *Witchcraft and Colonial Rule in Kenya, 1900–1955,* was a finalist for the inaugural Bethwell Ogot Prize for the Best Book on East African History. Luongo has also published on diverse topics, including the Mau Mau rebellion, the Kenya National Archives, witchcraft as a form of domestic violence, and the legal genealogies of key concepts such as "malice aforethought" and "provocation." Her current research project examines how African asylum seekers appearing in immigration courts in North America and Europe and before UNCHR protection officers across the globe have mobilized witchcraft beliefs as a basis for asylum claims. http://www.northeastern.edu/history/faculty/katherine-a-luongo/

**E. ANN MCDOUGALL** is Professor of African History in the Department of History and Classics at the University of Alberta. McDougall joined the University of Alberta in 1986, having received her PhD from the University of Birmingham, United Kingdom, as well as a BA and an MA from the University of Toronto. She is the author of numerous journal articles and book chapters on Mauritanian history and culture. McDougall was awarded an SSHRC research grant to look more closely at the *hratîn* comparatively (between southern Morocco and Mauritania) over time and with respect to their contemporary political position. This often marginalized class of cultivators, workers, and (in Mauritania) former slaves constitutes in each country a politically significant contingent of voters. http://www.historyandclassics.ualberta.ca/en/People/Faculty /McDougallEAnn.aspx

**KAREN MUSALO** is Professor of Law at the University of California, Hastings College of the Law, in San Francisco. She is lead coauthor of *Refugee Law and Policy: An International and Comparative Approach* (4th edition) and has written numerous articles on refugee law issues, with a focus on gender asylum, as well as religious persecution and conscientious objection as bases for refugee status. Musalo has contributed to the evolving jurisprudence of asylum law not only through her scholarship but also through her litigation of landmark cases. She was lead attorney in *Matter of Kasinga* (fear of female genital mutilation as a basis for asylum), which continues to be cited as authority in gender asylum cases by tribunals around the world. Her recent litigation victories include *Matter of R-A-, Matter of L-R-,* and *Matter of A-R-C-G-,* cases establishing that women fleeing domestic violence may qualify for refugee protection. Musalo is recognized for her innovative work on refugee issues. She was the first attorney to partner with psychologists in her representation of traumatized asylum seekers, and she edited the first handbook for practitioners on cross-cultural issues and the impact of culture on credibility in the asylum context. Her current work examines the linkage between human rights violations and migration, with a focus on child migration, as well as the phenomenon of femicides in Guatemala, El Salvador, and Honduras and its relation to requests for refugee protection by women from these countries. She is the founding director of the Center for Gender and Refugee Studies, which is internationally known for its research and legal advocacy and for its program of expert consultation to attorneys around the world. http://www.uchastings.edu/academics/faculty/facultybios/musalo/index.php

**FALLOU NGOM** is Associate Professor of Linguistic Anthropology and Director of the African Language Program at Boston University. His current research interests include the interactions between African languages and non-African languages, the Africanization of Islam, and Ajami literatures—records of West African languages written in Arabic script. He hopes to help train the first generation of American scholars to have direct access to the wealth of knowledge still buried in West African Ajami literatures and the historical, cultural, and religious heritage that has found expression in this manner. Another area of Ngom's work is language analysis in asylum cases, a subfield of the new field of forensic linguistics. His work in this area addresses the intricacies of using knowledge of varied West African languages and dialects to evaluate the claims of migrants applying for asylum and determine if the person is actually from the country that he or she claims. His work has appeared in the *International Journal of the Sociology of Language,* the *Journal of Multilingual and Multicultural Development, Language Variation and Change,* and the *African Studies Review,* among others. http://www.bu.edu/anthrop/people/faculty/f-ngom/

**TRICIA REDEKER HEPNER** is Associate Professor of Anthropology at the University of Tennessee, Knoxville, and Director of the Disasters, Displacement, and Human Rights (DDHR) program, which fosters collaboration among cultural, archeological, and biological/forensic anthropologists as well as multidisciplinary approaches to the study of natural and anthropogenic disasters, conflict and violence, and historical and contemporary processes of displacement and development. Her research has addressed refugee and asylum migration, transnationalism, political conflict, peacebuilding, and human rights discourse and activism in the Horn of Africa and its diasporas. She is also engaged in research on transitional justice and the problem of the missing and anonymous dead in northern Uganda. She is the author of *Soldiers, Martyrs, Traitors, and Exiles: Political Conflict in Eritrea and the Diaspora* (2009), coeditor (with David O'Kane) of *Biopolitics, Militarism and Development: Eritrea in the Twenty-First Century* (2009), coeditor (with Kenneth Omeje) of *Conflict and Peacebuilding in the African Great Lakes Region* (2013), and author of numerous journal articles and book chapters. She is also cofounder and associate coeditor of the *African Conflict and Peacebuilding Review*. http://web.utk.edu/~anthrop/faculty/hepner.html

**AMY SHUMAN** is Professor of English at Ohio State University and Director of Disability Studies. She is the author of articles on conversational narrative, literacy, political, food customs, feminist theory, and critical theory, as well as the books *Storytelling Rights: The Uses of Oral and Written Texts by Urban Adolescents*; *Other People's Stories: Entitlement Claims and the Critique of Empathy*; and (with Carol Bohmer) *Rejecting Refugees: Political Asylum in the 21st Century*. She was a Guggenheim Fellow, a fellow at the Hebrew University Institute for Advanced Studies in Jerusalem, and the recipient of the Ohio State University College of Humanities Exemplary Faculty Award, 2007. http://english.osu.edu/people/shuman

**JOANNA T. TAGUE** is Assistant Professor of History at Denison University. She teaches survey courses on precolonial Africa and Africa after 1800, as well as upper-level courses on women and gender in African history, comparative African liberation movements, rebellion and resistance in South Africa, and nineteenth- and twentieth-century East Africa. Her research explores the relationship between refugee settlement, international humanitarianism, rural development, and decolonization in Portugal's former African colonies. She is currently working on a manuscript that is tentatively entitled "A War to Build the Nation: Mozambican Refugees, Rural Development, and State Sovereignty in Tanzania, 1964–1975." Her research has been supported by Fulbright-Hays and the National History

Center of the American Historical Association. http://www.denison
.edu/academics/departments/history/dr_joanna_tague.html

**MEREDITH TERRETTA** is Associate Professor of History at the University of Ottawa. She teaches history and specializes in themes of African nationalisms, decolonization, independence-era political processes, and human rights. Her research has been supported by the American Council of Learned Societies; the Centre for Research in the Arts, Social Sciences and Humanities at Cambridge University; the Social Sciences and Humanities Research Council of Canada; the Andrew W. Mellon Foundation and the Society for the Humanities at Cornell University; and the Fulbright IIE. Her articles have appeared in such publications as the *Journal of African History*, the *Human Rights Quarterly* and the *Journal of World History*. Her book entitled *Nation of Outlaws, State of Violence: Nationalism, Grassfields Tradition, and State Building in Cameroon* was published by Ohio University Press, New African Histories series, in 2013. http://www.history
.uottawa.ca/faculty/terretta.html

**CHARLOTTE WALKER-SAID** is Assistant Professor in the Department of Africana Studies at John Jay College of Criminal Justice, City University of New York. Walker-Said is an African historian by training. She is completing a book manuscript on Christianity, human rights, and family law in French colonial Cameroon. Her research focuses on three broad issues: the relationships of Africans to legal and moral (secular and religious) codes communicated in the colonial process; the construction of gender and family models based on the integration of local and international ideologies; and the articulation of human rights claims as part of social, cultural, and sexual struggles of the modern age. She was previously a postdoctoral fellow in the Human Rights Program at the University of Chicago and the Lentz Fellow in Human Rights at Webster University. She is the editor, with John Kelly, of *Corporate Social Responsibility? Human Rights in the New Global Economy*, which will be published by the University of Chicago Press in 2015. http://www.cwalkersaid.com

# Index

election fraud in, 61–62; fraudulent
  asylum claims from, 59–60, 62–64,
  68–70; human rights abuses in, 20;
  incest in, 91; US embassy in, 61, 63
Cameroonian Peoples' Democratic
  Movement (CPDM), 65
Canada: asylum claims related to witchcraft
  in, 183; as asylum host nation, 1, 25, 247
*Canas-Segovia vs. I.N.S.,* 85
Center for Gender and Refugee Studies, 92,
  96n15
Central African Republic (CAR), asylum
  seekers from, 164–66, 176, 178
Central America, incest in, 96n15
child marriage, 170, 176
children: abuse of, 91, 92–93, 96n14,
  96n16; fleeing incest, 91–92, 96n15;
  persecution of, 91, 94, 96nn14–15
China: asylum seekers from, 18, 61; birth
  registrations in, 153; persecution of
  dissidents by, 87
Chissano, Joaquim, 47
Citizenship and Immigration Services (CIS),
  95n6
civil disobedience, 67, 71n1, 71n12
Coffman, Jennifer, 174–75
Cold War end, 8, 54n2, 95n4
collaboration: among African studies
  scholars, 5, 15; with attorneys, 94, 142,
  231; with experts, 77, 83, 94; with
  NGOs, 231; with relief agencies, 52;
  with research communities, 242; with
  the state, 43, 53, 62
Colombia, asylum seekers from, 61
colonialism, 41
Comaroff, Jean, 194
Comaroff, John, 194
Committee against Slavery in Mauritania and
  the Sudan (CASMAS), 124
communication: barriers to, 76;
  intercultural, 143–44, 156–57, 158
Community Refugee Immigration Services
  (Ohio), 142
Conable Conference Plenary Session,
  31nn6–7
Conference on the African Refugee Problem,
  51
confidentiality, 4, 198n1
Congo. *See* Democratic Republic of Congo
  (DRC)
conscientious objection, 85, 227
conscription, forcible, 78–79, 229. *See also*
  military service, compulsory

consent, 4
Convention against Torture (CAT), 82, 95n5,
  203
Convention Governing the Specific Aspects
  of Refugee Problems (OAU), 187
convention refugees, 187. *See also* asylum
  seekers
corruption, 20, 150, 214, 215, 241; in
  Cameroon, 64–70
Corruption Perceptions Index (CPI), 60
Côte d'Ivoire, refugees from, 4
Cotton, Samuel, 124, 133
country conditions experts, 169
"country guidance" (CG) cases, 103–4, 110,
  113
country reports, 7, 13, 135, 197
Court of Appeals (COA; United Kingdom),
  104, 107–8, 111
credibility: and demeanor, 80; legal basis of,
  4; of refugees, 16, 27–28, 77–84, 144,
  154
critical consciousness, 228, 236–37
cultural dissonance, 19
cultural idioms, 9–11
cultural practices, 21, 189–90
cultural relativism, 169, 230
cultural rights, vs. sexual rights, 208
cultural silences, 144, 158–60
culture: and affect, 188–90; and
  belonging, 188–90; and cross-cultural
  misunderstandings, 80
Curtin, James P., 80, 95n9

Dah Abeid, Biram ould, 139n23
*débrouillardise,* 66–67, 70, 216
decolonization, 8, 31n5, 53, 237
decontextualization, 26, 31n9
Democratic Republic of Congo (DRC):
  asylum seekers from, 4, 20, 39, 164;
  civil war in, 62
deportation, withholding of, 82, 95n5, 203
Derrida, Jacques, 18–19
detention centers, 234
DetentionWatch, 228
Diallo, Amadou, 18
Diallo, Nafissatou, 27, 163
disciplinarity, and expertise, 29
*Discipline and Punish* (Foucault), 146
disclosure, 4
discovery, 4
displacement: criteria for, 187–88;
  development-forced, 227. *See also*
  migration

Immigration and Refugee Board (IRB; Canada), 182, 183, 190, 192
Immigration and Refugee Protection Act (IRPA; Canada), 188; guidelines for refugee protection, 199n4
immigration law, 104, 216. *See also* law
incest: in child asylum claims, 91–92, 96nn15–16; expert testimony about, 97n18
infanticide, 168
infibulation, 167, 180n2. *See also* female genital cutting (FGC)
*In re Fauziya Kasinga v. U. S. Department of Justice*, 168, 189
*In re H*, 88
*In re V-T-S-*, 88
INS. *See* Immigration and Naturalization Service (INS); US Citizenship and Immigration Services (USCIS)
*I.N.S. v. Elias-Zacarias*, 85–6, 93, 225
internally displaced persons (IDPs), 55n3. *See also* asylum seekers; refugees
international development professionals, 10, 11
International Gay and Lesbian Human Rights Commission, 203
International League of the Rights of Man, 31n5
International Lesbian and Gay Association, 203
International Organization of Migration, 109, 118n14
International Phonetic Alphabet, 251
international refugee law, 40
Internet, influence of, 8
Iraheta, Berta Lidia, 80–81
Iraq, asylum seekers from, 4, 18, 229
Islamic law. *See* Sharia law
Israel: asylum seekers in, 4, 247; Eritrean asylum seekers in, 239–40
Istanbul protocol, 12
Italy, documentation of asylum claims in, 148

Joffe, George, 133, 134, 138n16
juridical proof, 6, 25, 26–27

Kambona, Oscar, 49
Karl, Terry, 80, 86–87
Kasinga (Kassindja), Fauziya, 18, 30n2, 78, 79, 88, 166–68, 172, 173, 174, 179n1, 189
Kawawa, Rashidi, 49
Kearns, Thomas R., 213
Kenya: asylum seekers from, 19, 39; incest in, 91; witchcraft in, 4
knowledge: academic, 10; about Africa, 254; anthropological, 231; circumscribed, 198;

gendered and taboo, 254–55; production of, 2–3, 5, 227; of refugees, 254
Koso-Thomas, Olayinka, 167
Kratz, Corrine, 172–73

language: Fula, 251–54; linguistic barriers, 19; Mandinka, 255; as proof of identity, 151, 154
language analysis: difficulties inherent in, 250–52; purpose of, 248–49
Language Analysis for the Determination of Origin (LADO), 247–48, 250, 251, 254
Language and Asylum Research Group, 254
Latour, Bruno, 103, 104
law: in asylum determination, 2; customary, 4; humanitarian, 17; immigration, 104, 216; international refugee, 40; intersection with African social and political life, 3. *See also* asylum legislation and law; attorneys
lawyers. *See* attorneys
legal decisions: *Canas-Segovia vs. I.N.S.*, 85; *"Ezomo" v. Canada*, 193, 195, 196, 198; *Fatoyinbo v. Canada*, 182, 188, 192, 194, 196, 198; *In re Fauziya Kasinga v. U. S. Department of Justice*, 168, 189; *In re H*, 88; *In re V-T-S-*, 88; *I.N.S. vs. Elias-Zacarias*, 85–86, 93, 225; *M.A. (Ethiopia) [2009] E.W.C.A. Civ. 289*, 113–14; *M.A.B.N. and K.A.S.Y. v. Adv. Gen. for Scotland*, 151; *Matter of Acosta*, 88; *Matter of C-A-*, 89; *Matter of Fuentes*, 88; *Matter of Kasinga*, 87, 88, 90; *Matter of R-A-*, 88, 89; *Matter of Toboso-Alfonso*, 87, 88, 217; *Mhando v. Canada*, 188, 196–97; *Mwakotbe v. Canada*, 188, 192, 193–96; *Mwakotbe v. Tanzania*, 183, 195; *Niang v. Gonzales*, 170; *Osorio v. I.N.S.*, 86, 87; *R.B. [Somalia] v. S.S.H.D.*, 151; *Ramirez-Rivas v. I.N.S.*, 87; *United States v. Windsor*, 205; *Valdiviezo-Galdamez v. Attorney General*, 89; *Zhou v. Gonzalez*, 87
legal counsel. *See* attorneys
legal scholarship, 169
legal studies, 29
Lemon, Nancy, 97n17, 97n19
lesbian individuals, 203–6, 214, 216–17, 220
LGBT rights and activism, 208, 216–17, 218
LGBTQ community, 205
LGBTTQQI rights and inclusion, 217, 218, 220n2
Liberation Tigers of Tamil Eelam (LTTE), 243n6
Liberia, asylum seekers from, 251

National Immigrant Justice Center, 31n6
Ndi, John Fru, 61
Neldner, Brian, 49
Netherlands, as asylum host nation, 1, 247
*Niang v. Gonzales*, 170
Nicoll, Alison, 168
Nigeria: civil war in, 249; claims of
    witchcraft in, 182–83, 193–95, 198,
    200n7
nongovernmental organizations (NGOs),
    42, 148, 191, 196, 227–8, 235;
    collaboration with, 231
nonheteronormativity, 204, 217
nonrefoulement, 24, 76, 154, 188, 203
norms: asylum, 64; cultural, 79, 80; legal,
    17, 90, 91; patriarchal, 92; political, 26;
    religious, 91; social, 26, 78, 80, 90, 21
North America: African refugees in, 40;
    asylum cases in, 19; migration policies
    in, 4. *See also* Canada; United States
Nyerere, Julius, 51, 55n4

Obermeyer, Carla M., 170–71
Organization for African Unity (OAU),
    187–88
*Osorio v. I.N.S.*, 86, 87
Osuna, Juan, 31n7
Overseas Refugee Program (ORP), 76–77,
    95n4

Palange, Antonio, 47
passports, forged, 22, 153–54
peacekeeping, 43
peer review, 5, 227, 253–54
perjury, 27, 233
persecution: "on account of," 85; acts of,
    114–15; claims of, 11; effects of, 82;
    fear of, 3, 7, 18, 24, 86, 199n6; gender-
    specific, 94, 168–69, 189; and the
    motivation of persecutors, 86, 93; need
    to prove, 84; past and possible future,
    225; political, 7, 10, 87; reasons for,
    26; religious, 85, 210; due to sexual
    orientation, 94, 205–6; due to status as
    a child, 94; subordination of women as,
    167; threat of, 64. *See also* social groups
physicians. *See* medical professionals
Piot, Charles, 172–73
politics: political opinion, 84; and sexual
    rights, 206; transnational political
    pressures, 237–42
polygraph tests, 81
Portugal, in Mozambique, 45

Posnansky, Merrick, 79
postconflict resolution, 43
post-traumatic stress disorder (PTSD), 81, 83
power imbalances, 143, 231
Practice Directions, 103
Practice Rules, 103
Pratten, David, 198
precedent, role of, 4
prostitution, coerced, 168
psychological evaluations, 13, 82, 83
psychological trauma, 80
psychologists, 12–13
Puar, Jasbir, 217
public health, in Africa, 215

queer normativity movements, 217

racism, 128, 133, 139n23
*Ramirez-Rivas v. I.N.S.*, 87
rape, 80, 123, 128, 155, 158, 163, 168, 170,
    173, 207
*R.B. [Somalia] v. S.S.H.D.*, 151
REAL ID Act (US), 26, 83
recognizability, 26, 31n8, 31n11
Refugee Act (1980), 75–77, 87
Refugee and Human Rights Clinic (UC
    Hastings), 92
Refugee/Asylee Relative Petition, 165
refugee roulette, 141
refugees: as activists, 235–37; Bantu, 231;
    and the burden of proof, 75; criteria for,
    187–88; definition of, 40; determination
    of status of, 1, 187–88; economic/
    political, 19, 64, 67, 226; group vs.
    individual experience, 54; labeled as
    problems, 43; legitimate vs. illegitimate,
    65; political engagement of, 237–41;
    political pressures on, 348–41, 243n3;
    potential contributions of, 44; status
    appeals with expert reports, 2; US
    Congress definition of, 18, 75, 84. *See
    also* asylum seekers; refugee settlements
refugee settlements: camp model vs.
    settlement model, 52; in camps, 238;
    management of, 42; in Tanzania, 48–54
Reno, Janet, 216, 217
reproductive rights activism, 218
research and researchers: by critically
    engaged activists, 228; informed by
    expert witness work, 227; with legal
    subjects, 4; situated, 231
response to information request (RIR), 193,
    200n7

"restriction on removal," 95n5
Roseman, Mindy Jane, 209
rural development, 43, 44–45, 48–54
Rutamba Refugee Settlement (Tanzania) 49, 52, 55n6
Rwanda: ethnicity and genocide in, 152; refugees from, 39; self-identification in, 22

Sandvik, Kristin Bergtora, 200n8, 235
Sarat, Austin, 213
Scheper-Hughes, Nancy, 230, 242
scholars. *See* academics
scholarship: engaged, 15, 166, 186, 229–30; feminist, 170, 171; legal, 166, 169, 170; linguistic, 253; sociolinguistic, 252
scopolamine, 81
Scotland, language analysis in, 251
Scott, Michael, 31n5
Secretary of State for the Home Office (SSHD), 103, 108, 109, 111, 116
Senegal: as asylum host country, 123; asylum seekers from, 252; war with Mauritania, 123, 125, 127
Senegambia, 255
Setareh, Daliah, 166–67
sexual abuse. *See* abuse, sexual
sexual assault, 168; *See also* abuse, sexual; rape; violence
sexual deviance, 215
sexual minorities: as asylum seekers, 6, 10, 21, 23; defined, 203–4; marginalization of, 219–20
sexual orientation and gender identity (SOGI), 21, 87, 204; persecution due to, 94
sexual rights, 204, 206; in Africa, 207–8, 209; and asylum law, 206–7; as human rights, 206, 208
sexuality: and asylum law, 205; nonnormative, 217
Sharia law, 131, 139n23, 211
shibboleth tests, 249–50
Shweder, Richard, 170–72, 178
Sierra Leone: asylum seekers from, 4, 251; identity documentation in, 22
Sikh separatists, 232
*Silent Terror*, 124
slavery: in Mauritania, 4, 20, 122–24, 128, 133, 139n23; sexual, 170; slave traders, 124
social groups: and accusations of witchcraft, 182, 184, 188–90, 196; difficulty in

determining, 18, 22–23; experts' knowledge of, 9; as reason for persecution, 26, 75, 84, 225; sexual minorities as, 204; women objecting to FGC as, 87–94, 166, 168–69, 172, 174, 175, 196
social justice, 2, 205, 243
social scientists, as expert witnesses, 190
social visibility, 89–91, 94
Somalia: asylum seekers from, 19, 151, 229; identity in, 22, 152–53; refugees from, 4, 231
sorcery, 185–86. *See also* witchcraft
SOS Slaves, 124
South Africa: asylum seekers in, 4, 19, 247; refugees from, 39
Southern Rhodesia, refugees from, 39
South Korea, as asylum host nation, 1
Soviet bloc collapse, 8
Speed, Shannon, 230, 231, 233, 242
Sprakab, 151, 154, 251
Sri Lanka, 249
statelessness, 4, 24, 116
sterilization, forced, 170
Stern, Amy, 167
Strauss-Kahn, Dominique, 27, 158, 163
Sudan: asylum seekers from, 4, 19, 39; witchcraft in, 185
surveillance technologies, 229
Swedish Migration Board, 249
Switzerland, asylum seekers in, 247

Tamils, 243n6, 249
Tanganyikan Christian Refugee Service (TCRS), 42, 52, 54; and refugees in Tanzania, 45, 48, 49, 50–51, 53
Tanzania: claims of witchcraft in, 183, 195–97; history of, 54n1; as host nation, 45–54; liberation groups in, 39; Mozambican refugees in, 39, 41, 44–45, 49–51; refugees from, 4; rural development in, 43, 44–45, 48–54
technology, transnational, 8
terrorism, 229, 232
Ticktin, Miriam, 211
Togo: asylum seekers from, 18, 78, 166; female genital cutting in, 79, 169, 172, 180n9, 189
torture: documentation of, 12–13; in Eritrea, 229; reports of, 132; UN convention against, 82, 95n5, 203
transgender individuals, 203–6, 216–17, 220
translation, of case by experts, 10